WHAT THE GROWN-UPS WERE DOING

'Hanson's family is Jewish and the truth and laughter surrounding the
Jewishness of her life is what lifts this account to a level of its own . . .
This is a memoir that catches the flavour of the times as felt from within . . .
A tender tale of a young Jewish girl growing into an understanding of her
noisy, quarrelsome and passionately alive family' – *Observer*

'She writes fluently and delightfully about suburban life in the Fifties as
it were yesterday . . . Beneath the surface, many of the families who
seemed averagely dull and conformist were in fact averaging dull and
conformist. Some weren't, as *What the Grown-ups Were Doing*
eloquently and hilariously reveals. Often, it transpires, what the grown-
ups were doing were each other' –*Sunday Telegraph*

'Michele Hanson grew up an 'oddball tomboy disappointment' in a Jewish
family in Ruislip in the 1950s – a suburban, Metroland idyll of neat lawns,
bridge parties and Martini socials. Yet this shopfront of respectability
masked a multitude of anxieties and suspected salacious goings-on . . .
there's already quite a bit of buzz around Michele Hanson's funny,
touching memoir that immerses the reader into 1950s society in an
exploration of her Jewishness' – *Stylist*

'With a twist of wit, Hanson good-naturedly tells it like it awkwardly was
in Fifties suburbia for a tentative but tomboyish teenager' – *SAGA magazine*

'In this briskly enjoyable portrait of 1950s suburban Jewish
childhood, Hanson's mother is a screamer, her father a sulker, and
their daughter perpetually ashamed . . . On the whole, Hanson plays it
for laughs, but a seam of darkness runs through the book: Hitler is
still   se is

Other books by Michele Hanson

Living With Mother – Right to the Very End
Age of Dissent
Treasure: The Trials of a Teenage Terror
What Treasure Did Next

WHAT THE GROWN-UPS WERE DOING

AN ODYSSEY THROUGH 1950S SUBURBIA

MICHELE HANSON

SIMON &
SCHUSTER

London · New York · Sydney · Toronto · New Delhi

A CBS COMPANY

First published in Great Britain by Simon & Schuster UK Ltd, 2012
This paperback edition published by Simon & Schuster UK Ltd, 2013
A CBS COMPANY

1 3 5 7 9 10 8 6 4 2

Simon & Schuster UK Ltd
1st Floor
222 Gray's Inn Road
London WC1X 8HB

www.simonandschuster.co.uk

Simon & Schuster Australia,
Sydney
Simon & Schuster India,
New Delhi

A CIP catalogue record for this book is available from the British Library

ISBN: 978-0-85720-489-9
ISBN: 978-0-85720-490-5 (ebook)

Typeset in Bembo by M Rules
Printed and bound by CPI Group (UK) Ltd, Croydon, CR0 4YY

For my mother and father

CONTENTS

1: THE TROUBLE WITH CHRISTIANS

My mother is driving me home from my friend Linda Bates's house, where I have been to play after school. She would like to know what I had to eat. This is important to her. So I tell her. I have no choice. I explain that the Bateses were having cauliflower cheese for supper, but I couldn't have any, because there wasn't enough. Seemed reasonable to me. There were four Bateses: Linda, her brother, her mother and her father, and the cauliflower only divided into four. By the time my mother had arrived it was nearly 6.30 p.m., the golden, sizzling, lovely-smelling cauliflower cheese was on the table, and the Bateses were sitting ready to eat and waiting for me to go.

It was in the car that I made my big mistake. I asked my mother for cauliflower cheese.

'Why don't we ever have it?'

She laughed loudly and harshly. She hadn't seemed cross when she arrived. Now suddenly she was in a temper, shouting on and on about the Bateses and their dinner.

'That's what they had? That was it? For their dinner? One cauliflower cheese?'

One other good thing about the Bateses – they never shouted. It was always quiet at their house and they talked politely and not very much. But my mother liked to talk loudly to everyone, about everything: strangers in shops, Ruth Kingsley the hairdresser, Bernard the assistant hairdresser, Miss Hilary the vet, Mister Clanfield the chicken farmer, Horace the coalman, Gracie, June and Elsie, the lady bridge players. Yakety, yakety, yakety. Within two or three days she had told them all and my father and my aunties and uncles about the Bateses' cauliflower cheese, in a mocking way, as if it were a terrible thing that they had one cauliflower cheese between four of them. A disgrace. She didn't call that a proper dinner. And what annoyed her even more, she informed the neighbourhood, was that I now wanted her to cook some. What a *chutzpah*!

'The Bateses have cauliflower cheese, so now *she* wants it. My cooking isn't good enough. She doesn't want a proper meal. She wants cauliflower cheese.'

How could I have known this would happen? I only saw something that looked tasty, asked for it to be cooked at home and there was uproar. Whatever I told my mother was a bit of a risk really because you could never quite tell whether or why there would be an uproar, but there often was. Then it would spread out and grow bigger, and when family members and Jewish acquaintances came near, my mother could really let rip, because they understood her outrage. They felt the same. They also knew that this was how the worst *goyim*[1] behaved. The *goyim* were not generous. Only *goyim* would tell a 9-year-old child that there wasn't enough food for them, and that they should sit there, watching and hungry, while others ate. Because that's what would have happened, had my mother not turned up in time. But luckily she did, and as soon as she heard about the cauliflower cheese, she started questioning:

'Did they give you a snack at least? A drink? A biscuit?'

'Yes.'

'Yes what?'

'Cake and orange juice.'

'What cake? *Drek*[2] from a shop, wasn't it? I'll bet she doesn't bother to cook her own cakes.'

Mrs Bates had sinned in a number of ways. I could see that. Everything was her fault, because she was the mother and in charge of food, and she had not done what a proper mother should do. Firstly and most importantly, she had offered me no dinner. Secondly, what she had given me had been *drek*. And furthermore, the Bateses probably ate spam and margarine, and cooked in pig-fat lard, because that was what *goyim* did. I knew because my mother had always told me so, and worse still, they rarely washed their bottoms.

It had to be true, if my mother said so. Why would she lie? She was very hot on truth.

[1] Christians. *Goy* – singular, *goyim* – plural.
[2] Rubbish.

'I don't care what you do,' she often said, 'as long as you tell me the truth.'

The worse thing on earth, said Mummy, was to tell a lie. Unforgivable. She knew from experience. Her younger sister, my Auntie Celia, was a frightful liar. Since she was a little child, she told fibs, told tales and made Mummy's life a misery. And the terrible thing was that people believed Celia, because she was such a good fibber. She would look up at people with her little freck-led moonface, her pretty blonde hair and her blue eyes wide open and staring right at them, and fib. And they believed her. But Mummy could never lie. She just couldn't do it. Her face would have given her away. And things did happen which proved that she always told the truth. They didn't happen all that often, but enough to prove that Christians could not, on the whole, be trusted to look after children properly.

This was the trouble with talking to my mother about friends, I realized. They need only make one tiny mistake in my mother's book and that was it. Mummy disliked them forever. She did not take prisoners. Throughout my life, friends have made mistakes: one combed her hair in the lounge, another had smelly feet, another married a German – American really, but he had a German name and ancestors – and for her, that was the end. Nothing they could ever do would put things right, so when I described my friends' houses and what they ate or did, I had to be very careful not to release any information that she might think was bad. I tried my best to keep the bad things a secret, but you could never be quite sure what they were. Something not at all bad to me could be a terrible thing to my mother.

I was pretty sure that Doctors and Nurses would not go down well, so I never told her about it. Cauliflower cheese was the best thing at Linda's house. She had no dog, no mice, no big garden, and all she wanted to play was Doctors and Nurses. I thought it was horrid. Vets, yes. Doctors and Nurses, no. Was I peculiar not to want to play? All over Ruislip, children seemed to be playing Doctors and Nurses. Paula Cattermole, whose house was down by the woods, and who had television before anybody else, had been playing it last week in a tent in her front garden, with her sister and the two boys from next door.

It was almost the end of our summer holidays and still lovely and warm for playing outdoors. We often played out in our gardens, which in Ruislip were enormous. Ours had a terrace, a long, rectangular lawn, easily big enough for playing Jokari,[3] surrounded by flower beds and ending, half-way down, in a wooden trellis covered in roses, which divided the lawn section from the rest of the garden, which was even longer, wilder, and full of fruit trees: plums, greengages, pears, apples and a vegetable section all down

---

[3] Game comprising a ball on a long elastic attached to a heavy box, which one could bat away and it came zinging back. Suitable for playing alone or with a friend.

the left-hand side. It was a heavenly place to play. Also, half-way down, hidden behind the garage and surrounded by blackberries, was a small shed. My shed really, in which I kept my mice, some little chairs and a table, and some candles, and where I could take my friends to play a decent distance away from my mother. Right at the very end of the garden was a greenhouse and, beyond a criss-cross wire fence, the field, with nothing particular in it, just tufty grass, making a huge play extension for us and the dog. Further on, there was the road down the hill to Paula's house and, beyond that, the woods and lido. Endless places to play, but Paula chose to play Doctors and Nurses in the front garden, just feet away from the front door, her mother, and any passers-by in the street.

'If you want to come in,' she said bossily, 'you must take off your shoes and socks.'

But I didn't want to go into the tent. It didn't look very nice, what they were doing in there. I could see somebody's bottom and what was Paula doing with those handfuls of long grass? And even worse, a grown-up could have entered with barely a moment's notice. What danger. I knew in my heart that any grown-up, particularly my mother, would not be pleased about this game. But that wasn't why I disapproved. On my own behalf, I did not fancy it. I knew that if there was one thing one should not play with, it was a bottom.

So I wouldn't take my shoes and socks off, which saved me from going in, and that way I escaped and ran home.

I was nine so I could run all the way back myself, up Paula's road, which ran parallel to the edge of the woods, then turn right and straight up Windmill Hill to the roundabout at the top, then left to my house, or through the field and into our side gate.

But there was no getting away from Doctors and Nurses. I got to Linda's house and she wanted to play it too on the upstairs landing before supper. What a silly place to choose. Again, very dangerous. If Linda's big brother or anyone had come up the stairs, which were just a straight flight up and then a small curve round at the top, they would have seen everything. Linda wasn't even properly round the corner where she would have been hidden by the filled-in banisters, just on the top stair doing funny things to herself. Who wanted to look at that? Not me, and after the cauliflower cheese, the game might have started up all over again, so in a way it was a good job my mother came and took me away.

A month or so after the cauliflower cheese business, the Andrews next door made another Christian mistake. The Andrews were Christian Scientists, but I was still friends with the children, Mary and Peter. I had to be extra careful when talking about the Andrews, not to stoke my mother up, because Christian Scientists were a particularly bad sort of Christian – a kind of extra strong version, so bad that my mother almost shuddered when she spoke of them. My mother felt sorry for the children and so

Mary and Peter often came to play at our house and stayed for tea. Children couldn't help it if their parents were raving mad, said my mother.

But although I did not share my mother's horror of Christian Scientists, we did share strong feelings about Binkie, the Andrews' cat. It had taken to taunting our dog, a young, handsome, red-brown, affectionate and benign Boxer called Lusty.

Everyone can like a Boxer. Men admire them because they have huge slathering jaws and rippling muscles, women love them because they are affectionate and hang about looking at you fondly, but they were rare in Ruislip in the fifties. They were robust, squash-faced, expressive and exotic-looking dogs and my mother was keen on anything startling or out of the ordinary.

As far as we knew, Lusty and his mother Gaddy (short for Gadabout of Woodfree who lived down the road at my friend Kathy's house) were the only Boxers around. Nothing annoyed them except cats, particularly the Andrews' cat. Lusty would press his nose against the wire dividing fence and Binkie would scratch it spitefully. When you are an only child, a dog becomes your friend. Intensely. It will love you and play with you and go for a walkie with you when everyone else will not, or is too busy, or has their own problems. So you become very close to this dog, and you do not like to see its face punctured with little bleeding claw-holes made by the cat next door. And there was nothing one could do to stop this problem. You cannot stop a dog from pressing its nose against a fence if a cat is on the other side, and you cannot stop the cat from scratching it, which was very upsetting. So this cat had been the only really hateful member of the Andrews family, until Mrs Andrews' big mistake.

One day, when Mummy was unusually late home, I couldn't get in after school, so I went next door to the Andrews. That's what I'd been told to do, if something like this should happen. The Andrews children would come to our house for tea, so I should go to their house. I went and knocked. They were having their tea in the kitchen, said Mrs Andrews, so I could wait in the dining room.

The dining room was chilly, wood-panelled and filled with a long dark brown wooden dining table and dining chairs with bobbly legs. The French windows looked out on to a long, neat lawn with straight borders, like ours but duller: no fruit trees, no vegetable section, and by now rather bleak. Most of the border flowers had died, leaves were falling off and it was already starting to get a little dark. I kept my school mac on. What could I do in the Andrews' dining room? Nothing much, and there was nothing to eat. But luckily I had a pink sugar mouse in my pocket that I'd bought in the sweet shop next to the station on my way home, a special treat because rationing rather limited my choices (my other favourite was chocolate limes) so I ate the mouse, standing up. Then my mother came home and collected me. She had guessed where I would be – the Andrews' house, where she had assumed, wrongly, that I would be looked after.

My mother did not come into the Andrews' house. She'd been up to town, come home in the car with my father, the traffic had been *geferlekh,*[4] which is why she was late, and looking smart in her ocelot coat. She was concerned, naturally, about my tea. What had I eaten at the Andrews'? To my mother it was vitally important that a child should eat when it entered a house, especially if it had been at school all day and perhaps not eaten enough. It must be given a snack at once, perhaps a nice sandwich and a piece of cake, to sustain it for an hour or so, by which time she would have cooked it a proper dinner. A child must never feel hungry. So what did the Andrews give me?

I told her. She was outraged again. This was a hundred times worse than the Bateses' cauliflower cheese. Her worst fears about Christians were being reinforced. She had been a blackout warden in the war, she had thrown rotten potatoes at the fascists in Cable Street, and now, barely six years later, the Blackshirts were still out and about for all she knew, and I needed protecting at all times. Naturally it did not take much to churn up her terrors and the Andrews had done it again. She had left me unattended for one brief hour and in that time, someone had treated me badly.

[4] Terrible. The 'kh' is pronounced gutterally, as if clearing your throat.

'How could they do that to a child? I've never heard anything like it!' She repeated this incredulous story, as if forcing herself to believe it.

'They had their tea and they didn't give you any? They left you by yourself in the lounge, while they ate? You had to eat a sugar mouse? In a cold room? Bloody disgusting!'

The mouse story became a legend, together with the cauliflower cheese story. They were episodes of such horror, examples of such grotesque meanness, that throughout my life, my mother would dredge them up, like the *Iliad* and the *Odyssey*, which we were doing at school. They were that important – food stories which must never be forgotten, basics of Christian culture, a mark of this religion's inferiority, the sort of thing that would never, ever happen in a Jewish home.

And the Andrews weren't even poor. The street was full of detached houses, in one of the swankier areas of Ruislip, where every house was different – some the same style as ours, painted white, double-fronted, four big bedrooms, mock-Tudor, pointy roofs decorated by black-and-white beams. Other houses were red brick, like the Andrews', or even wider, some as big as castles, with turrets, and all with lovely front gardens, properly tended, probably by garden-ers, and huge back gardens, with smartly mowed lawns and lush herbaceous borders, and perhaps even an orchard like ours. The Andrews didn't have an excuse to be mean, unlike the Bateses, who were poorer, and lived in a semi-detached house, pebble-dashed, with only a hint of Tudor – perhaps a couple of beams in the one small top pointy bit.

Now compare and contrast. In our house, food was busting from every cupboard: snacks, fruit, puddings, sandwiches, cakes and extra portions were always available. No shop-bought or tinned *drek*. Mummy cooked everything herself, and any visiting child would be fed at once. My mother also kept a close eye on the progress of my food. I must stuff it in and make sure it came out properly. My mother checked up on all this. Had I eaten enough dinner? Had I had a *kak*[5] the next morning? Had I washed my *tokhes*?[6] Had I washed my hands? This all made my mother very anxious. She needed to know the answers as things were happening. She couldn't wait, and sometimes called out her questions from outside the lavatory door. What sort of a *kak* was it? Was it too hard? Would I like prunes?

Yes, yes, yes, yes, all right, no, no. I answered without really thinking of the content because in my immediate world, lurking at the back of everybody's life were the bowels.

Auntie Celia was also concerned with the same process. Much more concerned. She could easily be trapped in her home by the vagaries of her bowels. They could even prevent her from getting to the hairdresser. My mother had explained this one day when we were hanging about waiting and waiting for Auntie to come shopping with us. We

[5] Bowel movement.
[6] Bottom.

were waiting because she could not go out until she'd washed her *tokhes* and she could not wash her *tokhes* until she had had a *kak,* and she could not *kak* unless she'd eaten her prunes the preceding night. But although she tried so hard to regulate her bowels, she could never really count on the whole process running smoothly, so she lived on a knife-edge. Sometimes she scarcely dared make any arrangements. She didn't worry that people were annoyed that they could never get a straight answer out of her about when or where or if she could meet them at any particular time. She couldn't hurry just because Mummy and I had been waiting for half an hour, bored and annoyed. She couldn't help it. The *kak* dictated her movements. It ran her life for her.

In our house, like Auntie Celia's, the bowels had great power. They could set the mood for the day. All possible medicaments were available should anything go wrong with them. In the bathroom beneath the spare toilet roll, under its hat-shaped, purple and black crocheted cover – my mother liked strong colours – was a hidden tube of Preparation H, for haemorrhoids.

I barely noticed all this worry. It was just a part of everyday goings-on. I did not question it, I knew no different. I did not mention it to my friends. Why would I? They probably had things they didn't mention. We didn't discuss our parents all that much. We had more interesting things to talk about.

*

It was no wonder, really, that my mother was always worried about my welfare, especially when she was not around to keep an eye on things. She had started her worrying in the war, understandably, forever throwing herself over my cot in air raids, and rushing me down into shelters or the underground stations. Worse still, I was a sick child, covered in eczema. People approached my pram, loomed over to admire a dinky baby, but what did they see? A red face covered in scabs and weeping sores. Naturally they recoiled in horror. And where were my scabby little hands? Both tied down in tiny white cotton mittens to stop me ripping at my face.

Another difficulty about eczema babies is that their wee stings. My mother could not leave me in a wet nappy, not for one second, or I would start to sting and scream. So what with the air-raids, the bombs, the eczema and my father off patrolling with the river police (he had a heart defect caused by rheumatic fever in his youth and was not allowed to join up) my mother learned to worry tremendously. And the main source of her worry was me. I wasn't quite sure why. Nothing really dangerous had happened so far that I could remember, but there were other things that my mother could not forget.

She had often told me about this busy-body woman who came along one day and started chatting to her at the front gate. After a couple of minutes, Mummy heard me screaming from indoors.

'I must go,' she said. 'Michele's screaming.'

'Oh you mustn't go whenever they scream,' said Busy-body. 'You'll make a rod for your own back. She'll stop in a minute.'

But I didn't, and in the two extra minutes that my mother was delayed by this woman, I had managed to escape the mittens and tear my face to ribbons. There was blood everywhere. All over the pillow.

'That's the last time I'll listen to that bloody *yakhne*[7],' my mother told my father, and everyone else.

Which is perhaps why it was always torment for my mother to have to leave me unsupervised, or in someone else's charge, whether there was reason to worry or not. Because you never know what's going to happen to your child when you're not about. Look what can happen when you are about, and you know what you're doing and you know what your child is probably doing, and then along comes some clever dick and tells you you're wrong and making a fuss about nothing, and your child ends up scratched to buggery. And if that can happen when you're only yards and seconds from your child, imagine what can happen if you're miles away. Just look what happened to me at the Andrews'.

Luckily, my mother did not make blanket judgements. She knew that there were Christians and there were Christians. Not all Christians were like the Bateses and

[7] Gas-bag; loud-mouthed woman.

the Andrews. Some families were perfectly all right – generous, honest, suppliers of good-quality dinners and knew how to look after a child. She approved of these families. They could almost have been Jewish. I played with their children and visited their homes and often stayed the night. All my best friends were Christians. Kathy, Jacqueline and Pamela were Christian. I hadn't spotted any spam or margarine in their homes. They were all nice and clean. My mother even played bridge with Kathy's mother, Gracie. And on occasions, in my opinion, the Christian food was better than my mother's food. It was different: the cauliflower cheese at Linda's, for a start, the gravies and custards at Jacqueline's, and Pamela's own improvisations.

Pamela made her own snacks because her mother was often not around. It was our last summer holiday together before I started my new school, before we all went in different directions. One sunny day Pamela made this new snack she'd invented, with tomatoes and Heinz salad cream. She chopped the tomatoes up into tiny pieces, then she mixed them with the salad cream and she and I ate the mixture sitting at the kitchen table looking out of the bay window into the wide green garden.

We could see Pamela's father Albert out there, attending to his bantams in their run on the right-hand side of the garden, or outside his shed, where he had a large flat bench, upon which he built complex wooden hutches for Pamela's pet mice, with wooden apparatus: runs, wheels, tunnels, climbing frames, stairs, balconies and bedrooms. Fun palaces for mice. No child ever had such magnificent mice homes. Kathy and I only had plain hutches from the pet shop, so I was a bit jealous. My father couldn't do things like that. He probably wouldn't have wanted to, because he never did handiwork, or mended things round the house, and anyway he was at work all day until late, but Albert was an old man, looking more like a grandfather, who was retired with time to build hutches. Day after day, he was out in the garden, sawing and hammering, because he loved Pamela.

Meanwhile, Pamela's mother was upstairs. She was often upstairs and when she did come downstairs the morning we were eating the tomato snack, she was wearing a pale silky green dressing gown and had lipstick on, bright red, in the late morning. Why? Where was she going? Where had she been? Lipstick was for going out dancing, which is when my mother wore it – bright red, with turquoise eye shadow and an evening dress, to the Orchard Hotel, to have dinner and dance – but Mrs Saunders had her lipstick on in her bedroom and before she'd even got dressed. She did not look glamorous, sparkly and alive, like my mother did when she dressed up. She did not have my mother's lovely, smooth tanned skin, or have her hair curled and shaped smartly by Ruth Kingsley. Mrs Saunders' skin was white and a bit flobby-looking, and her curls were long and rather wild.

Cleonie Saunders was not up to my mother's required standard. She did not play bridge or mix socially with Mrs Saunders. Being Irish, Cleonie was a Catholic, another sort of Christian, not quite as bad as a Christian Scientist, but almost, because they believed particularly in the Virgin Mary. My mother had told me that Catholics washed their bums in holy water, and then did it again. I could never get her to tell me what the Catholics did, again and again, every week, after they had sat in the holy water.

One night, we were in the car, coming home late. My father was driving, my mother was next to him, and I was in the back, pretending to be asleep. Just as we approached the roundabout at the top of Windmill Hill, my mother spotted a couple very close together, clutching each other. They were only visible for a few seconds as the car head-lights swept round the curve and lit them up, but in those seconds, my mother knew.

'That's Cleonie Saunders,' she said with great contempt, 'the *kurve*.[8] It's Albert I feel sorry for. She'd have nothing without him. He's got her that lovely house, and this is how she repays him. She treats him like *drek* and he worships the ground she walks on. She's slept with half the High Street. And I'll bet you that was Mr Thompson from the carpet shop. I bet you they're *shtuping*[9]. I'll bet you anything.'

My father did not reply.

*

[8] Prostitute – pronounced 'koor-veh'.

My father often did not reply.

'Your father is a sulker,' my mother explained to me.

And she was a screamer. But with reason, she felt. There is nothing more maddening than a sulker.

'He sulked for three days just after we got married,' my mother told me. 'I packed my bags and told him if that was what he was going to do, then I was off.'

In the long run this threat hadn't worked. A sulker is always a sulker. I could see it. As usual, my mother was telling the truth. My father would come in, turn the radio or telly off, sit down, read the paper, say nothing to any-body, and sulk. He couldn't help it. He had worries. He was an anxious person. The doctor explained it all to my mother when she went along there, worried about his odd behaviour. It was the anxiety coming out in odd ways: the sulking, flirting with other women – cleaning women, au pairs, nurses, neighbours. They all thought him charming, because he was tremendously dashing and handsome, rather like Errol Flynn, and amusing. His joke telling was top-notch, his timing exquisite, and he rarely sulked in front of visitors. A visiting woman could often perk him up out of his sulk, and he would chat away so that no one could believe what a sulker he was when they weren't there.

Which is perhaps why Blanche Walmesley, from a few houses down the road, tended to sit about in our house,

[9] Stuffing, i.e. having sex, not at that actual moment, but in the course of their suspected affair.

dressed smartly. Her own husband was elderly and rather dull, and coming to our house cheered her up. Here, life seemed thrilling, almost steamy and exotic. There were never long periods of silence as in her own stifling home. Someone here was bound to do something extravagant: cook, scream and row, laugh, crack a fairly vulgar joke, talk about money, be rude about the neighbours, criticize each other in a robust way, drink a martini or a whisky, eat unusual snacks – olives, chicken liver paté, chopped herring and chopped egg and onion on funny water biscuits called *matzos*.[10] It was all rather Foreign. Here Blanche felt alive and free. But she obviously couldn't stay here forever. She had to go home to prison.

Sometimes my father seemed to get rather bored with Blanche. He couldn't always be bothered to be charming when she was at our house, because she was here so often. He would come home from work knackered, all ready to slump down in his armchair and sulk until dinner time, and there would be bloody Blanche, sitting at the hatch expecting charm and a hint of flirtatiousness, which my father was very good at, being so handsome. But if he hadn't the strength or inclination to dredge any up, he would just go up to bed with a whisky, and not come down till Blanche had gone. As my mother did not want to offend Blanche – because she knew the real reason for his disappearance – she would tell Blanche that

---

[10] Unleavened bread, usually for Passover, but eaten at any time.

he was very tired and was having a rest. Or if she was fed up with his sulking, she would forget Blanche's sensibilities and moan about it, and tell Blanche that if she thought he was so marvellous, she should try living with him. The miserable bugger.

Sometimes my mother went upstairs to ask him to come down and talk to Blanche – to share the burden – because she'd been talking to her for an hour or so already, and listen to her *kvetching*[11] about her husband, and how she wished someone better would come along, but he would just say, 'Do me a favour,' and stare at his paper. So Blanche never knew the truth.

Grandma Davidson, my mother and me, 1945.

[11] Complaining.

2: MICE AND PEAS

It was a long journey to my new school for someone aged ten. Junior school was just round the corner, but my new school, Haberdasher's Aske's for girls only, was in Ealing. I had to walk down Windmill Hill to the station, get the Piccadilly line train straight to Ealing Common, then walk for ten minutes more to the school. Luckily, an older girl, Alison, who already attended the school, lived just across the road. She would take me a few times, then I could go myself. By which time I would have presumably made other friends on the train – lots of girls travelled that way – and I could go with them.

This was a favour for a favour. When Alison's mother had been poorly a year ago, her younger brother, 11-year-old Anthony, would come to our house for tea. Together we would sit on the lounge side of the hatch while my mother, on the kitchen side, would feed us.

'Would you like a sandwich, Anthony?'

'Yes *please*,' he would reply in an oddly deep voice.

'Another sandwich?'

'Yes *please*.'

'More?'

'Yes *please*.'

'Cake?'

'Yes *please*.'

'More cake?'

'Yes *please*.'

More this, more that? Yes *please*, yes *please*. To my knowledge, Anthony never refused anything, and soon, in his absence, we were all doing 'Yes *please*' for a laugh. Same deep voice, same accentuated, big, fat '*please*'.

Because that was more or less all Anthony said, until one day, when my mother was busy at the cooker, or didn't have her eye on us for some reason or other, Anthony told me something.

'I've got hairy legs,' said he, smiling proudly, and then he leaned towards me, closer than usual, as if it were a thrilling secret, 'and they get hairier and hairier and hairier all the way up.'

Each 'hairier' was louder than the last. I didn't tell my mother. Who knows what she would have done? It would have put her in a dilemma. Would she have wanted to feed a boy who talked to her 9-year-old daughter in such a way? But how could she refuse to feed a child with a sick mother? Experience had taught me that if I even had the slightest concern about what her response might be, the best thing was to keep *shtum*[12] and if I wanted to talk about Anthony, to stick to the 'Yes *pleases*' upon which we were united as a family.

Luckily the going-to-school plan worked. It had to. It was part of a grand plan to save me from the secondary modern. I had left our primary school two years earlier than my friends, so that by the time I was 11, I would have been trained up, ready to pass the eleven-plus exam, and so been able to stay at this grammar school. The secondary modern would then only ever have been a dreadfully scary place which I had to walk past on my way home from Bishop Winnington Ingram Primary School, where Pamela and I had met. Kathy was already Pamela's best friend, and lived in her road.

Large, fierce children, who were common and definitely all *goyim*, poured in and out of the gates of the secondary modern. What might those big children have done to me? Anything horrid. I wasn't sure what was wrong with them particularly, but I was frightened, when travelling alone past the entrance, of the way they came scudding out, running into the road screaming, with no uniform or teachers or grown-ups about to tell them off, or help me, should they come swarming round and scream or punch or push me over. But there was no other route home so I had to pass the gates of the secondary modern, full of poor and dangerous Christians who had failed their eleven-plus.

[12] Quiet. Keep your mouth shut.

In the end, I didn't pass it either. I couldn't do the maths part but, luckily for me, my father could afford to pay to send me to Haberdasher's school. It was definitely worth it, to keep me away from the dangerous *drek* in the other school. Why send your only child, upon whom all your hopes rested, to such a place?

By the time we were 11, Kathy, Pamela and I were going to similar girls' schools, all with uniforms, all a train journey away. Pamela's was Catholic, Kathy's was Church of England, and mine was too, but a quota of Jews was admitted. But we still had holidays and weekends in which to carry on our old life. We loved riding on Ruislip Common, we took Lusty for walks in the woods (Gaddy was by now too old for that sort of thing), we bred mice, we played in gardens and sheds, at Ruislip Lido (on the beach, in the rowing boats, on the model train), in my house and Kathy's house, but rarely in Pamela's. Occasionally we got into the kitchen for a snack, but usually we stayed in the garden, around the mouse palaces. If Pamela could play at all. Often she couldn't. We would knock at the front door and Mrs Saunders would open it.

'Pamela can't come out to play today,' said she, smiling at us, because she liked us so much. 'I'm sure you've both done all your homework, like the good girls you are, but Pamela hasn't finished hers yet.'

Or, 'Such lovely girls. Aren't you the clever ones?'

And we wouldn't see Pamela for days on end. Where was she? She was not in sight. Not standing next to her mother, or coming to the door herself. It seemed the days on which she couldn't come out were growing more frequent. How could we know what was happening to Pamela on those days? We didn't like Mrs Saunders much. She was a bit peculiar, compared to most mothers. And too strict.

Sometimes there was a stretch of days when Mrs Saunders didn't seem to care what Pamela was doing or where she was, as long as she was out of the way. Then she could come to the lido with me and Kathy or Jacqueline. To reach it you had to walk through the woods, but the snag about the woods was that a Tarzan had been spotted there. We heard that he would swing down from trees dressed in nothing but a leopard-skin loin-cloth. People were terrified. There was a woman, we heard, who'd been walking in the woods with her dog, she'd met a keeper, they'd had a chat about the Tarzan. He told her not to worry, it was probably only some student, then she left and two minutes later the Tarzan swung down from a tree whooping and screaming and gave her the fright of her life. It rather put the wind up us. We had gone into the woods in the spring with our baskets to pick bluebells, when suddenly we all, at exactly the same second, thought of the Tarzan, whispered it to each other, and ran out of the woods shrieking. So after that, we always took Lusty, who we hoped would attack the Tarzan if necessary. And if Tarzan didn't appear, then what about the mad old woman? These woods, after a bit of a walk, turned into Mad Bess Woods. Who was she? How mad?

But there were periods when Pamela seemed to be stuck indoors forever. Why? It was particularly odd and annoying during the holidays, because first of all, how could she possibly have work to do? And secondly, holidays were our best chance to forget our separate schools and see each other again. We lived just two minutes away from each other, the streets were safe and quiet, hardly any cars came along, and even my mother never seemed to worry about us wandering from one house to another, and so Kathy and I kept calling for Pamela, but her mother kept opening the door as usual and saying, 'Pamela can't come out today, she's busy. Kathy darling, haven't you got lovely curly hair?'

What was so lovely about curly hair? Pamela's hair was really the best. Kathy's was short, curly and brown, mine was straight, thin and brown, but Pamela's was thick, black, long, shiny and straight. She had big green eyes, and I thought that Pamela was very beautiful. The older she got, the more beautiful she looked, and already, at 11, she looked a bit like a film star.

What was Pamela busy doing? We didn't know. By now Kathy and I thought Mrs Saunders was almost hateful. There was something funny about her, and she was a *kurve,* after all, according to Mummy, which wasn't a very nice thing for a mother to be. We didn't know that when we'd gone, she'd go straight upstairs to the bedroom in which Pamela was locked with the blackout blinds down, and tell her, 'That Kathy has lovely curly hair, and yours is all straight and straggly, like a witch. You think you're so good-looking do you? Do you? Well you're not.' Or sometimes she'd go down to the cellar, if Pamela was shut down there, and hit her with sticks. But how were we to know? In 1953? How would you guess that your friend was locked up like that, if she didn't tell you? And she never complained about her mother, or about not being allowed out or hit. Never.

My mice had started off sandy coloured with white markings. They had four babies, which meant I had six. Kathy's had always been plain brown and she kept them in the garage. My big mistake was, after a few months of mouse-keeping, to become overambitious and see the mice as a business opportunity. I planned to sell the babies for sixpence each to the pet shop. The pet shop man had expressed an interest. Foolishly, I swapped one of my smartly coloured ones for one of Kathy's brown ones. From then on, all my mice gave birth to plain brown babies and the pet shop man lost interest. The increasing number of all-brown mice was becoming rather a burden.

Kathy's mice were becoming even more of a burden. One day she had eight mice, then she had tonsillitis, which meant she had to stay in bed for a fortnight, and wasn't able to check on the mice or clean them out, although she got her brother to feed them. By the time she was better she had 24. I went to have a look.

Phooey. What a stink. A great fat layer of mouse poo had built up over the two weeks and gone solid and wet, and on top of it were piles of mice: quite big babies at the bottom, medium babies in the middle and, right on the very top, a pile of tiny new ones, like little pink, bare, soft finger ends. Pamela and I helped Kathy to clean the cage and sort them out, into what we thought were families, using two old spare cages of Pamela's. It was a terrible job, because Kathy's mother, Gracie, had just left them. They were Kathy's mice, she said, so Kathy could clean them.

I knew that my mother would never have allowed this to happen – a great pile of poo in the shed. She would have intervened and cleaned it up. It wasn't Kathy's fault. If you were ill, you couldn't clean your mice out. Although I loved Gracie, I was surprised by her neglect of the mice because it was rather cruel. No mouse should have to live on a mountain of slimy filth, crushed by layers of more babies.

I was pretty certain that I should not report this bit of dirtiness to my mother. It would have thrown her into another dilemma. How would she cope with an unclean friend? She was very hot on hygiene. I had to clean my mice out regularly or there was big trouble because my mother also had a very acute sense of smell. The slightest whiff of body odour, or bad breath, or wet dog, or lavatory, and she would have to tell the person responsible to do something about it. Mr Clanfield, the stinky chicken farmer who delivered our eggs, may have smelt unpleasant to many people, but to my mother the smell was torture. Luckily, she seemed not to have smelled the mice so far when visiting Gracie's house but she had noticed, and pointed out to me, that Gracie did not clean her cooker, which was bad enough, even without the mouse slum.

'Have you ever seen anything like that?' my mother asked me as we walked home from Gracie's after a visit. 'Christ knows when she last cleaned that cooker. It's covered in grease. She'll never get it clean now. If you don't clean things straightaway,' my mother warned me, 'the *drek* will all go hard and you'll never get it off.'

She was right. Even I had noticed that the cooker was dark and greasy-looking. It wasn't just that my mother's cooker was much cleaner than Gracie's. The worrying thing was that everybody else's cooker that I had seen was much cleaner. And Gracie didn't bother with Gaddy the dog much either. She let it do as it pleased, and rarely walked it, but as it was rather old, it just lay about outside the house on the pavement in the sun, when the weather was warm.

'Gracie is letting herself go,' said my mother ominously.

What did she mean? Letting herself go where?

No one at the new school kept mice. The new friends I had met on the train had other interests: tennis, lacrosse, hairstyles, even boys. Shirley was my proper friend. I wished that I looked like her. She and her two sisters and her mother all looked very English. What lovely, creamy

skin they had, with a slight flush on their cheeks, and
shapely, angular faces, blue eyes, blonde hair, straight backs,
and they were ever so good at games, particularly netball.
Shirley could also cradle with ease in lacrosse, whereas I
always found it a struggle. Asthmatic, especially in the cold
weather, I ran wheezing about the field, red-faced,
exhausted, dropping the ball, but there would be Shirley,
calm, pale, athletic, gliding across the pitch, catching,
cradling, goal-scoring, sometimes slightly flushed, in a
healthy rather than sweating way, in the team and popular.

I would never reach that standard, but in another area
I was her equal, if not her superior: the Hartley's peas
competitions. If you bought a few tins of Hartley's peas
and kept the labels, you could enter a competition which
asked you to find the mistakes in a picture. You were also
given a correct version, which you had to compare and
contrast. The person who found the most mistakes won
a £1 10s gift voucher for the shop. We won several times.
Then we shared the winnings. I spent the bulk of mine
on small packets of chocolate raisins. Rationing was over.
I could buy unlimited chocolate raisins.

But then a problem came up. I had bought the tins of
peas. Shirley would not pay for half of them. Why should
she? She hadn't eaten them. But I hadn't eaten them
either, because in our house we never ate Hartley's tinned
peas. Only frozen or freshly shelled. To my mother,
Hartley's peas were in the *drek* category. So all right,
Shirley could have her peas. I put them in a jar for her.

Her share. But she didn't want them. Nor did she want to meet me on the train any more. Nor did her friends Stephanie or Rita. They promised to get in the second compartment from the end, but they got into the third one. They were avoiding me. And I felt, although no one had said it, that they thought I was mean and greedy, because I was a Jew. I had kept all the peas for myself.

Perhaps I was mean. Even though I did all the work and organizing, went to the shop, paid for them, never ate them, offered to share them and shared out all the prize money scrupulously, and all Shirley did was sit and stare at the pictures with me looking for the mistakes, I was still in the wrong. I went to school on my own again.

Me aged 10. A nice grammar school girl.

3: THE BURDEN OF ALWAYS
BEING RIGHT

Every day my father drove to work up Western Avenue. About half-way along on the left stood the Hoover factory, a rather wonderful building – white with stripy coloured bits, set back among its own lawns, and with a relatively small, matching but separate part at the side. It was my father's dream to possess this separate bit of the Hoover building, but it wasn't available, and instead he had to make do with a factory in Poland Street, Soho, where he made ladies' accessories – mostly belts.

He had changed his name from Adolf to Arthur David. Who wanted to be called Adolf through the Second World War? No one. He had a business partner, Dennis, who my mother disliked – a *yok*[13] and a *drek,* in her opinion. She never trusted him. My father and I tended to float through life, encountering this person and that, thinking they were fine, blindly trusting most of them,

[13] Male Christian – pejorative.

him employing some of them, me making friends, as I had done with Shirley, and being disappointed. But my mother lived on red alert, always on the lookout for anyone who might be taking advantage of our good nature. Take the Andrews and the story of the sugar mouse for a start – the perfect example. You give, they do nothing in return. You feed their children, they starve yours. And it wasn't so much my mother's own friends that she felt she had to beware of. It was ours – mine and my father's – because we were incapable of looking out for ourselves.

Without my mother watching over us like a hawk, we could do nothing properly: feed and clothe ourselves, exist safely out of her sight, or choose our friends and employees wisely. Without her we were bound to make mistakes. Even worse, once we had made a mistake, we refused to listen to her criticism or act upon her advice, but she never gave up – watching, listening, trying to protect us from the world and ourselves. Imagine her frustration. She could see it coming and she couldn't stop it. She must sit helpless and watch us both walk into the lion's den.

She was right about Dennis. As usual, her suspicions were justified. Dennis was a handsome sponger. He was the spit of Errol Flynn, whereas my father just looked rather like Errol Flynn. It didn't take long for my mother to detect that my father was working like a slave, morning noon and night, racing about town and country *schmoozing* the buyers, keeping the business going, keeping the staff happy, coming home late and exhausted, while Dennis left punctually at 5 p.m. to get home to his wife and an early supper. She liked to eat at 6.30 p.m. But did it matter what time my mother liked to eat? Did it matter how many meals went cold and were ruined? No it did not, because The Business Came First. And if my father had done what my mother had asked for in the first place and made her his partner instead of bloody Dennis, then he wouldn't be coming home fit for nothing. Better still, she wouldn't be stuck at home with no outlet for her considerable talents and energy other than flower-arranging classes, art classes and bridge. And gardening and cooking and looking after the dog, and me, and him, and stuck in the bloody kitchen for the whole of her life. No wonder she became a screamer.

We were let out, and she was stuck in, and it was us, free as birds, who made the mistakes, and she who knew we would. So Dennis was the first of a series of partners and managers who ripped my father off, because he had trusted them too readily. My mother had distrusted all of them, except for one, who would fool both my parents, but her warnings put my father in a difficult position. You cannot sack a person just because your wife dislikes them. You tend, instead, to stick up for them and point out their virtues, as I did with my friends. While busy doing this you may be blinded to their faults, which you do not wish to acknowledge, and then in the end you have to, because my mother was nearly always proved right.

But there was one person against whom both my mother and father were united. Auntie Celia. She was their common enemy and brought them together. Because she had bad-mouthed my father to my grandma, and filled her mind with worry and doubts about my father's character. And although my mother felt herself entitled to criticize my father and me, no one else was allowed to. She was at the front, charging in like the Light Brigade, fearless, guns roaring.

The trouble with that method was that she could not always use it. My mother couldn't just let rip about Celia whenever she pleased, especially if Grandma was around, because Celia was Grandma's favourite. And she was my mother's sister, after all, and you cannot fall out with your sister, even if she is a fibber and a stirrer. So my mother had to keep on repressing herself, which was particularly difficult for her, being a person who liked to come straight out with things.

My father, on the other hand, had no problem repressing. He had problems with letting rip, but his method was sometimes more effective. Especially with Celia. My mother could not allow herself to scream her real opinions at Celia but he could drive Celia mad by doing nothing at all – no speaking, no arguing, no shouting. Nothing. He would behave as if she wasn't there. And he could do this for as long as it took. That is the power of the sulker. If he had to drive Celia somewhere, he would drive her. But he wouldn't speak en route.

Once he was required to drive her all the way to Cannes in the South of France. My mother and I were already there; he was joining us later in the holidays, and bringing Celia with him. It was usually a three-day trip in those days. We would drive for a day, stop at a little hotel, take it easy, drive on, stop again, make for Avignon, go over the bridges singing, stop for lovely picnics with baguettes and jambon. But this time, with Celia, my father just drove. He drove from Calais to Cannes in one day without speaking. Or stopping. Celia had to beg him and beg him to let her out to the lavatory. By the time he did she was bent double and weeping. When my father reported back to my mother she was thrilled to bits, and The Day That Celia Was Not Allowed to Talk or Pee became another of her favourite stories, along with The Bateses' Cauliflower Cheese and The Andrews' Refusal to Feed Me. To my mother's knowledge, no one else in the world was able to stop Celia talking, but my father had done it. In my mother's book, he deserved a medal.

But it is one thing to sulk effectively for a day at someone who deserves it. It is quite another to sulk daily at people who love you and, to their knowledge, have done nothing wrong at all. Sometimes, if my father had particularly desperate worries, he would only work and sulk. And read the racing pages. So my mother did everything else. But that's what wives did in those days: housework, shopping, cooking, children. Husbands went to work and came home and were waited upon. I didn't often see a husband and wife happily chatting. Not Kathy's parents, not Pamela's parents, not the Andrews, not Mr and Mrs Bates. Jacqueline's father was a shouter, Kathy's was a bottom-pincher, Pamela's was a mouse-cage maker, and mine made ladies' belts and accessories.

But when he wasn't sulking, my father could make everyone laugh. There is a special way of telling a Jewish joke. The voice, the timing and the expression have to be just right, and my father could do it. Listeners would sit spellbound, however long the joke took. And he would, when not sulking, wash up immaculately, often with his sea-captain's hat on, while using naval terms.

'Clear the decks.'

And once, at a time when he was working particularly hard, my mother made him a pair of donkey's ears from a bit of old fur coat, attached to a sort of metal, Alice-band fixture, which fitted over his head, and he would sit at the table, or watching the telly, or even driving the car along, with his donkey's ears on, which was meant to imply that he worked like a donkey. My parents laughed like drains when the ears were on, and I felt rather proud of him. It was not everyone's father who would wear ears, never mind indoors, but out in the car. Being handsome on top of all this was, in some ways, not a plus. Because women found him charming. They did not believe, however much my mother told them, that he was only charming sometimes.

So my mother threw herself into bridge, the garden, which she looked after all by herself, and Latin American ballroom dancing, which she was very good at and for which she won a silver medal. But unfortunately for her, my father had no rhythm. He moved about a bit, still managing to look rather elegant and film-starry, while my mother swirled around him, doing the Paso Doble.

'Look at him, the *potz*,[14]' my mother would complain, almost fondly. 'He's got no bloody rhythm.' She was right again.

My mother and father dancing at the Orchard Hotel,
Ruislip, circa 1956.

[14] Penis. Vulgar.

4: THE OTHER SIDE OF THE FAMILY

My father had two brothers and five sisters. Phil, Dicky, Annie, Fanny, Millie, Rickah and Leah. Phil was a doctor, Dicky was a Communist. All the sisters, my aunties, were thin. Annie was very glamorous, because she had been a film starlet, with small parts; a woman in the concentration camp in *The Diary of Anne Frank*, and other things. And also, a very famous television producer had fancied her and asked her out. She, and Millie, who was also fairly glamorous, had a bendy, sideways way of standing, as film stars tend to do, and they both had dark hair, also swept sideways, in waves or swirls, and together they would go swimming at the Hampstead Ladies' Pond, in swimming costumes with some sort of sideways design, which my mother called asymmetrical. There was something artistic about asymmetrical things. My mother, whenever she arranged flowers, would ensure that they were asymmetrical, and she admired Annie's and Millie's clothes, but otherwise, as far as she was concerned, they were a bit simple.

She preferred Fanny and Leah, an altogether sharper pair, and both excellent seamstresses. They worked in their husbands' shops: Leah in a tailor's shop in Ruislip High Street, Fanny in a tailor's trimmings shop in Tottenham Street, off Tottenham Court Road. Sometimes I would have to accompany my mother to the Ruislip shop while she had a suit fitted, or a skirt or jacket altered. What a boring place to be. There were no bits and pieces to look at, no dogs, no garden, no snacks, just a couple of dark, finished suits in the window for show, and more inside, half-done on headless, armless dummies. You couldn't even see out of the window to the High Street, because it was closed off. There was hardly any sound in the shop, except for my mother's voice, which was louder than Auntie's.

Auntie Leah was a quiet, sweet-natured woman and never cross or rude to anyone, unless they really deserved it. One day, worn out with working in the shop every day for years and years, she took a little holiday by herself to a hotel with mainly Jewish clientele, on the south coast. But could she get any peace? No. The minute she sat down in the lounge or dining room, some woman or other would come up to her and ask her her business. Where did she live, how many children did she have? Were they married yet? Grandchildren? What did her husband do? Always, what did her husband do? Eventually a particularly annoying *yakhne* approached her as she sat in the conservatory. The usual question.

'What does your husband do?'

But this time Auntie had had enough. She leaned towards the woman and spoke quietly into her ear.

'My husband's a burglar,' said Auntie. Off went the *yakhne,* who probably blabbed to the whole hotel, and Auntie was shunned for the rest of her holiday. Bliss.

Then it was back home to the regular routine. Every day, in the shop, Auntie gave Uncle Charlie two boiled eggs for his lunch. With toast. I never saw the two eggs, but my mother told me about them, because in her opinion, two eggs every day was not a good idea. Everybody in our family knew what two eggs a day did to a person, especially if they were hard boiled, so my mother treated them with caution. God knows what they were doing to Charlie's bowels. She told Leah what she thought. She warned her, but did Leah take any notice? No she did not. Uncle ate two boiled eggs a day until the end of his life, which came relatively early. Could it have been the eggs? Nobody knows. But while he was alive and working at the shop, he didn't seem to say much. He probably tailored for the men customers. It was Auntie who dealt with my mother's fitting, drawing lines on the cloth with flat, square chalks, putting pins everywhere.

Then, one awful day, I had to have a frock fitted. I was to be a bridesmaid at my cousin Isabel's wedding. Isabel was Leah and Charlie's daughter and she was to have three bridesmaids. Did I want to be a bridesmaid? Did anyone ask me? Did anyone tell me about the frock? No to all of it. Did they care that I didn't want to go to a wedding on a Sunday, when I could instead have been riding over Ruislip Common on a horse with Kathy and Pamela? Did they not care that I hated frocks, and especially this one, made of organdie and net, in pink and pale blue, with a little round neck and itchy little puff sleeves and, to match the puffs, there were three more circles of net puff, three sausages of frill, around the bottom of the long skirts, which looked horribly soppy. So it was my turn to stand still and be chalked and pinned, for ages and ages, in front of a mirror. Hateful.

A line-up of aunties. My father with, from left: Millie, Leah, Great Auntie Rosa, Fanny.

Standing and standing. It brought on a sort of dull stomach ache, hardly a pain, more collywobbles, where you don't need to lie down, but you feel that if you could just scream and scream and run about, the ache would go straightaway. And there would be more of these fittings, and then the hairdresser.

'Any other child would be happy,' said my mother in a fury, 'to have such a lovely dress. What's the matter with you? Stand still. It looks very pretty.'

Then to Leah, 'I don't know what's the matter with her. I can't get her to wear a decent dress.'

'Leave her alone, Clarice. She'll get used to it.'

'She'd better.'

5: GRANDMA'S ENORMOUS TRAGEDY

My cousin Olga and I were both only children, born six months apart. She was my mother's brother's daughter and the cousin I played with. All the other cousins were on my father's side and much older than me, so Olga was my favourite. We had our ups and downs. As infants, we squabbled over ownership of the moon, pointing at it and each claiming it.

'It's my moon.'

'No. It's my moon.'

Our parents often reminded us of this argument. It was their favourite. But for the most part we were good friends. It was some years before we learned exactly how much and why our grandma loathed Christians, or why and how deeply she disliked Olga's mother, Auntie Betty, or why I was her favourite grandchild. We knew vaguely, because bits of information had seeped out, usually via my mother, but Olga and I had other things to worry about, mainly the unfairness of Olga's boarding school. They had a rule that all sweets sent or given to pupils must be shared out, which meant that there was no point giving Olga a supply of her favourite chocolates at the beginning of term, because they would just be put into the communal pot, and she would end up with something she didn't like such as sherbet lemons or flying saucers.

To us this was fearfully unjust. But we had a plan to sabotage it, or at least wreak a terrible vengeance. I would send Olga some chocs in an envelope with a letter, they would be taken from her and given to someone else, but secretly I would have cut a tiny slot in the bottom of each one and pushed in a cascara pill. Pity the poor person who got it. But serve the school right.

The boarding school also meant that we only saw each other in the holidays, when we had the mice in the shed to look after, Jokari to play, the dog to take for walks and train, and our clothes to sort out. And our other friends to introduce each other to: Kathy, Pamela and Jacqueline down here in Ruislip; Lorraine and Esther up in Barrow-in-Furness.

Why had my grandparents ended up in Barrow? To me it was a dull and rather backwards place, where people talked much more slowly than London people, and stared at Olga and me if we wore anything modern – like our best brightly coloured, stripy, spotty, tight, matching trousers (we chose the material, Auntie Betty sewed them up) or our swirly skirts. But my grandparents hadn't necessarily chosen Barrow. They'd left Poland in a hurry at the turn of the century, boarded whatever boat they could, and they'd happened to get one that was going there. Perhaps they were hoping for New York and Coney Island. Instead they got Barrow and Walncy Island.

But I did know from my mother, who, if she didn't directly tell me, at least told everyone else out loud, so I was bound to hear, the reasons for Grandma's low opinion of Christians. They had their uses but she did not mix with them socially and she certainly had no Christian friends, as my mother did. They were even more dangerous to Grandma than they were to my mother. My mother had only been through one war when people hated and murdered Jews, but Grandma had been through two. She had run away from Sudwalki to escape the murderous Christians, and arrived here, in Barrow, and less than 40 years later, when she thought she was safe, along came another lot, attacking our shores and chasing all over Europe after the Jews. The Germans had been particularly keen to have a go at Barrow, because of the Vickers Armstrong shipyards there.

We had enemies everywhere. Directly opposite Barrow, just across the Irish Sea, Grandma knew that those Irish *mamseyrim*[15] were leaving their lights on at night, all through the blackout, so the Germans would be able to tell where Barrow was and bomb it and its shipyard to

[15] Bastards (*mamser* – singular, *mamseyrim* – plural).

buggery, because the Irish hated the English and the Jews. Nearly everyone hated the Jews, Grandma knew for a fact, which is why they had to stick together, because no one else could be trusted. So naturally she had as little to do with Christians as possible, although she did have to employ them in her shop. They made good shop girls, but that was as far as it went. She certainly did not want them in her family, but bad luck, she had got one – my Auntie Betty. And it was Grandma's own fault. She had brought it on herself. She had hired Auntie Betty as a shop girl, and in Grandma's very own shop, Cyril had met Betty and fallen in love.

Even though Uncle Cyril loved her, even though she was my favourite auntie, even though her family were honest and terrifically hardworking, even though she had converted to Judaism, it made no difference. Betty's brother was a butcher, her father was a labourer and her mother bred chickens and had an allotment, and so all through the war they had fresh eggs, chicken and veg-etables, but to Grandma, Betty was common. Poor. Working-class. Not good enough for Cyril. But worst of all, she would always, in my Grandma's eyes, be a *shikse*. She could never be a proper Jew.

This was a tragedy of enormous proportions to Grandma. Once it had happened, she could never be really happy again. Nothing could cheer her up. Not even me. Not even the marvellous news that my mother, after seven years of trying and at the advanced age of 35, was finally pregnant. How could Grandma be thrilled by my arrival if only six months earlier, my cousin Olga, the bastard child of Cyril and Betty, had arrived?

This is why Grandma had always planned to leave her money to me, not Olga, and why I was to be the heiress.

'Everything is to go to Chuckles,' my grandma had said, because she thought me a happy, chubby baby. And although my father was not, in my grandma's opinion, up to scratch, he was at least Jewish, and therefore so was I. Properly Jewish and Olga was not. But obviously I was not to tell Olga all the details. They were too hurtful.

'Aren't you happy for me, Mammy?' my mother had asked Grandma, when she'd given her The Marvellous News that I was on the way. But Grandma had only stared at her, red-eyed and desolate. At that time she could think of nothing but the tragedy of Cyril's marriage and the arrival of my baby cousin Olga, which more or less sealed his fate ...

'I only want the *mamser* to die,' wept Grandma. 'Then Cyril will leave that cow of a *shikse* and come back to me.'

What a terrible thing to say. My mother reported this to me word for word, several times. She had never been able to forget it, but I was not on any account to tell Olga. Of course not. How could anyone tell her that her grandma thought her a bastard and wanted her dead?

Olga knew that Grandma had not been thrilled about her mother starting life as a Christian, but she had been shielded from the whole story, in all its horror.

My mother waited until she herself was almost dead, over 50 years later, before she filled Olga in with the details, which cleared up a lot of Grandma's mysterious behaviour. As a child, Olga had wondered why Grandma always gave her mother the chicken's wings at dinner. Everybody knows there is no meat on chickens' wings, they are not meant to be used as a dinner portion, but just to make soup. But Betty cleverly pretended that she liked them. What was the point of doing otherwise? She ignored Grandma's slights and rudeness and was never rude back, and that's how she managed.

There had been a time when Betty had given up on the idea of marrying Cyril. She had run away, pregnant, to Carlisle, determined to manage on her own, instead of causing ructions with Grandma, but Cyril had run after her, found her, brought her back and insisted on marrying her, and they lived happily ever after, despite Grandma. They took over the shop when she was poorly, played bridge, played golf, never argued and never moaned. Why bother? And eventually Grandma's fury turned from a rolling boil to a bitter little simmer, which never ended, but led her to favour Auntie Celia. Because not only had my mother married a potential gambler and wastrel, she had also stuck up for, and sided with Cyril and Betty all the way along. Grandma had never quite forgiven her. But she still visited us. Celia was always busy, off to South Africa or Cannes, or cruising round the Mediterranean. And how could Betty stay with Cyril? And anyway, she loved me. Chuckles. Her favourite and only official grandchild.

Grandma Davidson came to visit at the beginning of the summer holidays, when the weather was mild enough to travel, and while she still had the strength, arriving with a small case and a big string bag busting with food – a large *vorsht*[16], fruit, fresh eggs, and some salt-beef, already cooked. Grandma, like my mother, liked to have plentiful supplies of food, especially meat, which was still difficult because of rationing not quite being over, and even more difficult to make sure it wasn't *treyf*[17]. Or perhaps she didn't always insist on that. You couldn't always be certain. There was one shop that used to just stamp the raw meat all over with their shop stamp, and if you didn't look carefully, you could just assume it was the stamp of the Beth Din.[18] If you chose to. Who knows what Grandma chose? But she had always managed to get hold of more than enough meat all through the war, somehow or other. Having a shop, she could swap produce with the butcher and the farmer, and the fishermen

[16] Kosher salami made of beef, not pork.
[17] Forbidden food, not kosher, i.e. not prepared according to regulations.
[18] Official body which inspected food to ensure that it was properly produced in a kosher manner.

on Walney Island, which got round the problem of coupons and ration books.

She had come down to London on the train from Barrow, changing at Crewe, and because this time she was coming on a Friday, for the weekend, she had taken an early train so as to arrive before *shabbes*[19]. Jews may not travel on *shabbes* – another reason for Grandma not to travel until summer, because she liked to come for the weekend and the winter Fridays were just too short. She could barely make it from Barrow in time. I got home from Shirley's house and Grandma was already in the kitchen, sitting in the corner seat at the table waiting for dinner. Grandma felt that she could have made the dinner better herself, but now she had to eat what my mother had cooked, just giving a little advice here and there and adding salt. Two *shabbes* candles were alight at the table.

'My chuckly-bubbly,' shouted Grandma. 'Come and give your grandma a kiss. Ooh I love her. Look at her! *Kenenehora.*[20] What a *ponim*.'[21]

Then I had to sit next to Grandma on the red, padded leather corner seat to be kissed and adored. My mother had made fish. The kitchen was baking hot, the side door open to let out the stink, the fish laid out on layers of

[19] Sabbath.
[20] Magical phrase uttered to ward off the evil eye ... reflex [action] to protect a child or loved one, according to Leo Rosten, *The Joys of Yiddish*.
[21] Face.

brown paper bag, and now that I was here, and my father was about to arrive, she began to get the chips ready. Grandma was asking for *khrayn*[22]. She couldn't eat her fish without *khrayn*. She drew her hands across the candles as if pulling holy air towards her, then cupped them over her face and mumbled.

'*Borukh ato adonoi,*[23] *something something something . . .*'

I only recognized the first few words. I felt rather embarrassed by this praying and religious observance. Only Grandma did it, so I wasn't used to it. Sometimes Mummy did it very quickly at festivals, but my father didn't seem to bother with it much. Nor did he always wear his *yarmulke*[24] when he ought to have done, but instead balanced a paper napkin on his head for a laugh. But when Grandma arrived it was serious. Numerous things and events had to be blessed when she was here: dinners, wine, first fruits of the season.

'First raspberries,' cried Grandma, holding the relevant fruit in front of my mouth, because I must eat one. I must have the best, ripest one, and I, Grandma's favourite person, must have it first.

'Taste. Taste one. *Borekh ato adonoy . . . blah blah . . . borey pri ha eyts*[25] *blah blah . . .* She can taste my wine. It

---

[22] Horseradish and beetroot sauce.
[23] Blessed art thou oh Lord . . .
[24] Skullcap worn by Jewish men at festivals or religious occasions, or all the time if they were very *frum* i.e. orthodox.
[25] The fruits of the tree.

won't do her any harm. Give her a taste. *Borekh ato ...*
blah blah ...'

Grandma wanted me to repeat the words but I could
hardly bear to do it. What embarrassment. So I mumbled
the words very quietly. What if my friends could see?
Kathy or Pamela might call round while Grandma was
here, and Grandma would go on doing the praying in
front of them. I knew she would, because she was not
ashamed, but luckily it hadn't happened yet. So I said my
own little prayer. 'Please, oh please God, do not let my
friends come.'

It was more difficult, when Grandma was staying, to
get out of the house. Because first of all she wanted me
with her for as long as possible, and secondly, she would
worry about me, a girl of 11, going out alone, which
made two levels of worry: my mother's and hers. They
would infect each other. Something my mother had
hardly been worried about would become a death trap
once Grandma had examined the possibilities for mishap.
She knew that if anything was going to happen to anybody's grandchild, it would be hers, if she took her eyes
off me for a minute. Then it would be her fault. God
would never forgive her. Constant watch must be kept
over me by one or the other of them, so that if I did,
kenenehora, absolutely have to go out, then at least I
should go only with friends who could be trusted. Who
were these girls, Pamela and Kathy? What sort of family
did they come from? Catholic and Church of England!

Why? *Two shikses?*[26] Did I have no Jewish friends? Why not? Here were some more Christians threatening to wreck her family again, because those girls would have Christian friends, and some of them would be boys and I would meet a *yok,* and then it would be Cyril and Betty all over again.

'Because she hasn't,' said my mother. 'Don't ask me why. How should I know? Don't *hak mir in kop.*[27] She just hasn't.'

Grandpa and Grandma, Saul and Queenie Davidson, Celia (left), my mother Clarice, and Cyril, Barrow-in-Furness, 1919.

[26] Non-Jewish girls/women.
[27] Nag, drive me mad, lit. 'bang me in the head'.

6: THE WEDDING

It was time for the wedding. I had to go, wearing the horrid, frilly, scratchy dress, and have my photograph taken in it twice: once with my mother, once with the two other bridesmaids. Throughout this ordeal, a whole day long, an endless summer day, I dreamed of Ruislip Common, where my lucky non-Jewish friends were galloping about freely, in jodhpurs. Along woodland paths, over the open grasslands, trotting, cantering, breathing the warm open air, while I was stuck here indoors for the whole day, firstly in the synagogue, standing behind the bride and groom with the other two bridesmaids. But I was really alone, because the other two had known each other for ages. They were friends. They whispered together. Their dresses, although identical to mine, looked different. Theirs fitted nicely and smoothly, they looked pretty, whereas I looked crumpled and didn't stand up as straight. And this was a rather grand synagogue, nothing like our prefab one in Ruislip. This building had a high ceiling and was made of dark shiny wood, with high balconies and tiers of seats, and we were down in a space in the middle of it, standing behind the *bimah*[28], listening to the burbling Hebrew, watching my cousin Isabel's future husband stamp on the customary glass.

We were a group on show, a tableau, on a stage, separated from all the other guests by yards of shiny wooden floor, and then gradually, I realized I was in trouble. I had wind. I could feel it building up, wanting to come out. I wasn't going to be able to stop it, but I must, must, at least make it be quiet, which I did, but there was still the smell. A horrible warm smell which drifted up and across, until it reached the other bridesmaids. And they knew it was me. Because they knew it wasn't them. They managed a tiny whisper and giggle. They knew, they knew. Not only did my dress look silly, but I stunk. I was an outcast. This was the first time that I had felt so odd and not normal. I was a weird girl with no bosoms who didn't talk about boyfriends and smelled bad. What shame. And nobody could save me, until the end of the ceremony, which was a long way away.

At last it came. But just as we were leaving the stage area, my cousin David, brother of the bride, waylaid me.

'Hallo Mish,' he said. 'How you doing? All right?'

'Yes.'

'See you at dinner. Then we can have a dance, can't we? Will you have a dance?'

---

[28] Canopy beneath which the bride and groom stand.

'Yes.'

I liked David. He was my friend, and only trying to smooth things along, but I couldn't answer him properly, because now he'd accidentally made things worse. He'd detached me from the other bridesmaids and I was left behind. Where was I meant to go now? Where were they? Not only had I made the horrid smell, but now I was lost and late for wherever we were meant to go next. Then my mother found me.

'What you doing now? What's the matter with you? You're meant to be over there. Come on.' She grabbed my hand and pulled me in the right direction, and a thick cloud of Secret of Venus by Zibeline, her favourite perfume, swamped me and blotted out any lingering trace of the other smell. I have loved that perfume ever since.

'It was David. He wanted to talk to me.'

'He can talk to you later, the *drek*. Come on.'

There they all were, outside getting into the cars. My mother shoved me in in the nick of time, squashed up against the other two bridesmaids in a car full of organdie and net puffs. And it wasn't even nearly the end of the wedding. There was still the reception to endure: a huge banquet loads of courses long, with a lemon water ice in the middle to get you through the next marathon of courses, and little packets of six brightly coloured Sobranie cigarettes for the men, and tiny net frilly bags of sugared almonds for the women, and dancing with an old uncle with fat, purply-red sausage lips, and women rustling in silks and organdies and satins, and older cousins in shiny frocks, but at last something pleasant happened. Little pots of ice-cream came round on trays: vanilla, strawberry and chocolate. My favourite was chocolate. If I could have one of those, I felt that I could last out.

Round came the tray to our table. But what a horrible disappointment. There was no chocolate left. For me that was the last straw. I began to cry. Just over a chocolate ice-cream, my mother thought. Now it was her turn to feel shame. Because she didn't know what had gone before: the isolated standing, the fart, the humiliation, the dreams of Ruislip Common. It was difficult for my mother to keep her feelings concealed. She was in a boiling fury. Disappointed, humiliated at the family event of the century, because I, unlike any normal girl, had hated the frock, the curls, the dancing, the dinner, and now here I was, looking *farpisht*[29], because I couldn't have a *farkakte*[30] ice-cream. My poor mother was ready to bust.

But help was at hand. I was rescued by the waitress, who had spotted my blotchy red face and busting mother.

'Come with me,' she said, 'I'll find you a chocolate one downstairs,' and took me away, down to the kitchens, where, spread across a huge table, was a sea of pink, white and, here and there, a dot of brown – the ice-cream

[29] Piss-faced.
[30] Shitty.

waiting to go upstairs, and before it did, the waitress saviour reached across it and bagsied me a chocolate one. I sat on a stool and ate it, among the servants – an altogether jollier crew than the guests, I thought. How relaxed it was down here. I felt at home. Here was the difference between the rich upstairs and the workers downstairs – my first real look at the difference, and I preferred the downstairs. It seemed like a happier world, all camaraderie, with friendly people cracking jokes, being nice to me, not having to stuff themselves with twelve courses, not having to wear itchy frocks, but all dressed in comfy white chefs' clothes or plain waitress dresses. To me, in the sub-wedding catering community, life looked easier and warmer. I never wanted to go upstairs again ever. But, after the ice-cream, I had to.

7: MOONFACE THE FIBBER

It is perhaps a good thing to be an only child. Not all sisters and brothers are fun. My mother loved her brother, Cyril, but she hated her sister Celia. Look at the contrast between Celia and Cyril. One, greedy, selfish and deceitful. The other, kind, generous, good-natured and scrupulously honest. How could two children of the same parents be so different? my mother would ask. I couldn't understand it either, but I could see why my mother loathed Celia. And if Mummy thought I couldn't clearly see why, or didn't seem adequately bothered, then she would explain exactly why Celia undoubtedly deserved her criticism, so that I knew and reacted appropriately.

Some people believe you should shield children from some of the nastier truths and goings-on in life; that you should not burden your child with your grown-up hatreds and anxieties, but my mother didn't see it like that. She reported her feelings and reasons and everybody's failings to me, because that was the truth, and the truth, again, was the one thing you should adhere to and spread about.

And it was important that my mother impart the truth to me, because she needed a close ally, supporter and sympathiser regarding her sister. My mother needed her fury to be appreciated and understood, and I did understand. Auntie Celia was maddening. Besides always having to wait for her, because she was never ready and always late and often waiting for the *kak,* we also had to listen to her saying things over and over again, often accompanied by a soppy, simpering look, which she put on when someone was getting cross with her, as if she were a helpless innocent.

But she wasn't helpless, of course. She was scheming, manipulative, greedy and mendacious. I knew because my mother's tuition had worked. I knew all of Celia's tricks. How she fooled Bill (her husband) into thinking she was a virgin when she married him was perhaps the most audacious and successful fib of all. How did she get away with it? What a lovely man he was. A *mentsh.*[31] How the hell he fell for Cissy, God knows. And then there was the dreadful occasion when she and my mother went on a trip to Belgium when they were only 20 and 22 and Cissy buggered off with all the money and tickets and left Mummy £1 to get home. *How selfish could you get?* But however selfish, scheming and untruthful she was, it never seemed to do her any harm.

*

[31] A decent man.

In the early 1900s, all my grandparents had come here to escape the pogroms: my paternal grandparents from Russia, my mother's parents from what is now the edge of Poland, near Latvia. By the time I visited Barrow, my family had made it. They had a large ladies' dress shop in the main street – Dalton Road. My grandma had given up working and lived over the shop, my Uncle Cyril and Auntie Betty, parents of my cousin Olga, ran the shop and lived in the swankiest part of Barrow, rather like us in Ruislip, where the houses were all large, detached and individual. We had all made it. Our fathers were self-made men. My cousin Olga went to her girls' weekly boarding school because her parents were always slaving away in the shop. But when my grandparents arrived they had nothing.

Grandma worked tremendously hard. She started off by buying a bale of material, made it into aprons, sold them at the market, built up her business from there, until she had a grand shop and the first bath in Rawlinson Street. A triumph. And she did it alone. Grandpa had done nothing to help her. Less than nothing. He had been a charming gambler and wastrel. I can't remember him, only the bits I was told, about him sitting playing cards with me on his knee as a baby, and telling his friends how clever I was.

'She's got more brains in her little finger than you lot have got put together.' A phrase that my grandma often repeated, so naturally I think of him fondly. I knew nothing, at that stage, about his gambling or his mistress round the corner, or why he'd been sent away to South Africa, where we had relatives, or why, when he left and asked Grandma if she was going to kiss him goodbye, she only replied 'kush mir in tokhes'.[32] Or why, when he returned, she wasn't pleased to see him.

He had been no help to Grandma as she worked hard to build a better life. The struggle was all hers, with some help from her children, mainly my mother, who was the eldest. But when they were girls, my mother and Celia had good times together. They were a daring, adventurous and glamorous pair – the Davidson girls. Both tall: Celia the blonde, my mother the brunette. They did things that the ordinary Barrow girls rarely did. They wore slacks, they rode horses and motorbikes, they had their hair cut in stylish, matching Eton crops or finger curls, they even designed and made their own clothes in the very latest fashion. They went to Morecambe Bay in a crowd, posed and rolled about and leapfrogged over boys on the beach. They laughed, flirted, smoked, shrieked and danced and shimmied in beaded frocks. They even went to Belgium for the weekend, and although Celia buggered off with a handsome man and all the money and left Mummy stuck with only £1, they still managed to be friends, until they grew up, married, and Grandma decided to retire.

[32] Kiss my arse.

Upon her retirement, Grandma had given the shop to her three children – my mother, Uncle Cyril and Auntie Celia – to share. And just before the war she had given Celia another shop in Manchester. Notice that Celia had a shop all to herself, as well as her share of the main shop. Why was she favoured when she had been the worst-behaved child? No wonder my mother felt bitter about this. During her childhood, being the eldest, she had looked after her brother and sister while her mother worked.

And what terrible things Cissy had done during this period. Once, she had taken a cotton reel from the sewing machine, told baby Cyril to shut his eyes and open his mouth and see what God would send him, then she had rammed the cotton reel down his throat, making him choke and go red, so that Mummy had screamed for help. Grandma came running upstairs from the shop, took Cyril by the ankles, held him upside down, shook him and ran with him like that, dangling and choking, all the way to the hospital, where they got the bobbin out. Cissy had nearly killed her little brother. And what did she get for that crime and all the other hundreds and thousands of spiteful, wicked things she did as she grew up? She got her own, whole shop.

Manchester was a good place to have a dress shop just before and during the war. It wasn't far from Barrow, which was a large port, the military were about, and where there are soldiers there are prostitutes. Prostitutes need dresses, and what's more, they can afford them, somehow without coupons. They were about the only women who could afford extra black-market dresses, and didn't need to stick to the one or two measly dresses allowed by rationing. They could buy as many dresses as they wanted, and they could buy them from Celia, which meant that she did tremendously well with her dress shop. She sold it for a fabulous profit. But with someone like Celia, one fabulous profit is not enough. Once one has a taste for luxury, then one likes to have more, and so Celia wanted Uncle Cyril to buy her share of the big shop for much more than it was worth. This was the turning point for my mother – the ghastly bit of behaviour that she couldn't overlook – taking advantage of your own brother. It finally snuffed out what was left of my mother's affection for Celia.

Cyril had already bought my mother's share, for a fair price, but he now had to pay through the nose for Celia's share. But one thing he didn't have to do was to ever speak to her again. Lucky him, whereas my poor mother felt that she had to, because once Celia knew Grandma was thinking of leaving all her money to me, my mother felt that my position as heiress was under threat.

'That's a lot of money for a little girl,' Celia had said when she heard the news, opening her eyes wide. 'I hope *somebody* will look after it for her.'

Why would she say that? What business was it of hers? My mother didn't like the sound of it. She knew, as soon as she heard it, that Celia was plotting something, and it would be something horribly unfair, and Celia would get away with it unless my mother kept a close eye on her and sucked up. Her greed and ruthless treatment of Cyril was a worrying indicator of what she might do to me. She had stolen from him, why not from me too? My mother's fears were not hysterical fantasy. They were based on bitter experience.

Celia's successes had taught my mother from an early age that life was not fair. She had been truthful and hard-working, while Celia Moonface had always been a liar. But she had been a very good liar, and she had somehow always had money, even when she was eight. My mother had had no money, so where had her sister got it from? My grandma gave neither of them, nor little brother Cyril, any pocket money. If they needed any for something, they had to ask and specify what it was for, then she would give it to them from the shop till. So one day on the bus my mother asked Celia Moonface for an explanation. She got such an extraordinary one that she remembered it by heart for the rest of her life, and was able to report it to me, word for word, exactly as it happened.

'You know that cat that lives behind the bins on the corner of Rawlinson Street?' said Moonface.

'Yes.'

'Well you know it's got kittens?

'Yes.'

'Well it gives me pocket money to look after its kittens.'

'Cats don't have money. Where does it keep its money then?'

'In its pouch. It's got a pouch on its tummy like a kangaroo, and it keeps its money in there.'

'You're a liar. You took that money out the till, didn't you? You did, didn't you?'

Moonface stretched her blue eyes open wide and swore she did no such thing. But it wasn't so much the stealing from their mother's shop till that shocked my mother, although that was bad enough. Nor was it the lie about the mummy cat. It was the awful realization that she had believed Moonface's lie at all. She had only believed it for a second or two, but she had believed it, because Moonface had looked straight at her while she told the story as if it were an absolute truth and Mummy had followed it along and even imagined the cat handing money over to her sister. She could see it happen, just for an instant.

Could anything demonstrate more clearly what an accomplished fibber Auntie Celia was? If I were to fib, warned my mother, I would grow up like Auntie, and I didn't want that, because I knew Celia for what she really was, but to the rest of the world, she may well have looked a success. She had sold her prostitute dress shop years ago, married Bill, a wealthy man, and now lived just off Park Lane, on the second floor of a block of flats directly above the tube station.

This is where my mother and I went to meet her in town, and where we often had to wait and sit about until

she was ready, because you could bet your life that whatever time you told her you were coming and however
many times you warned her, she would never, ever be
ready to go when you got there.

'She'll still be *kakking*[33] about,' said my mother. And
she always was. Every time. But by then we were there
and stuck waiting, and once you were inside her flat,
there didn't seem to be an outside world any more.
Although thick streams of traffic swirled past it night and
day between Marble Arch and Hyde Park Corner, the flat
was silent, all outside sounds muffled by thick carpets,
heavy curtains and silken walls, so that you felt, when
you visited, that you were stuck in China. The whole
place felt foreign and a bit creepy, full of dark, lacquered
cabinets decorated with Chinesy patterns. A dim light
shone in a tank of Chinese fish, Auntie drifted around in
silky Chinese robes and slippers. Only in the big front
room overlooking the park was there any brightness and
you could get out onto a small balcony and into the air.

On a ledge in an alcove in the hall sat the model of an
oriental-looking fat, bald man, dark red all over, sitting
down with his legs crossed. He had no clothes on, as far
as I could see, except for a cloth, presumably where his
knickers ought to have been, but only the sides of this
cloth were visible, because his enormous round stomach
hung over and obscured the front part. I suspected that,

---

[33] Literally 'shitting about' but in this instance – messing about.

had this man had his normal clothes on, he would have looked just like Auntie Celia's husband, Bill. So perhaps, if Uncle Bill, under his clothes, looked like this statuette, that was the reason for Auntie Celia having no children. Once I knew about the mechanics of this business, I reckoned it had to be.

We had just learned about it in biology class, taught by Miss Matthews, a young rather shy woman, with longish frizzy curls down to her shoulders, and check suits. As far as I and my friend Naomi were concerned, this lesson was about rabbits and the way in which they reproduced. Body parts with Latin names were mentioned, and while Miss Matthews was describing these parts and how they connected, I noticed that the rest of the class was laughing behind me. And Miss Matthews had gone pink. What was so funny? Then we both realized exactly how the rabbits were doing it. Erk. And then, Barbara Wyatt, who had a grown-up married sister, had told us even more about how people had babies. What a terrible thing for people to do. But if they really did, then as far as I could work out, there was no way that Uncle Bill could reach Auntie Celia to do that, with the enormous stomach in the way.

Now here we were, waiting for Celia as usual. It was her birthday and we were going to the Carvery at Marble Arch, Auntie's favourite place, because you could help yourself. That meant you could take as much as you liked for a set price. We needed to be there in twenty minutes, we had booked a table, but Celia was still in the bathroom.

'Will you stop faffing about Cissie, and hurry up.' My mother was losing patience. 'Haven't you *kakked* yet?'

But we couldn't hear an answer. The bathroom was closely sealed shut, and if Celia had heard us and answered it would have made no difference. If we were late, we were late. The managers of Auntie's favourite restaurants knew of her and her lateness, and they would excuse her and pander, because she was so grand and rich. She knew none of them would dare be cross, and neither could we, with The Threat hanging over my mother. All we could do was to pray that the prunes would work.

Auntie Celia, Queen of Fibbers, circa 1930.

8: THE CARVERY

In the Carvery you took your plates and went up to a big chrome counter. All around this counter, in hot silver trays, were different roasts: beef, lamb, pork, deep trays of vegetables, roast potatoes, carrots, greens, and there were jugs of gravy, pots of sauce, Yorkshire puddings – everything you could possibly want for a roast dinner, and you went round helping yourself, carving your own meat, while across the counter, inside the square, stood several chefs in tall white hats, ready to help carve if you couldn't manage it.

Here in the Carvery I saw greed. I recognized it because my mother had taught me that, like fibbing, being greedy was a horrible thing to do. You helped yourself modestly, you finished your dinner, and if you were still hungry and wanted more, you asked for it and you got it. You did not behave like a *khazer*[34] and *khap*[35] more than you could eat, you did not allow your eyes to

---

[34] Greedy pig.
[35] Grab.

be bigger than your belly. But many people did it here. While I was queuing for the lamb, I naturally watched the people ahead, just to get an idea of how to do the carving, and noticed the man next to me at the front of the beef queue cutting the meat oddly. It was a round roast, solid meat in the middle and a ring of fat and skin around the outside. This was not how my mother did it when we had it for lunch. She would cut across-ways into thin slices but this man took the carving knife, and instead of slicing across, he dug the knife straight down, digging between the meat centre and the outer fat, loosening the fat, then he cut across, deep down, and brought up a giant slab of pure meat, inches thick, leaving the empty shell of fat with a gaping cavern in the middle.

From the other side of the counter, a tall chef, his arms folded, stared at the beef carver, smiling like God, I thought, because this is what God must have felt like. He creates the world, He lets us go in it, He leaves us in charge and then we take advantage. (Another sin my mother often warned me against − taking advantage.) Then God looks down and sees things like the man taking all the beef for himself, but God has done his bit and washed His hands of us. If we want to behave badly then there's nothing more He can do. He's at the other side of the heavenly counter, His hands are tied. For Him it has all been an experiment, which he half expected to go wrong. It must have been painful to watch, but in the grand scheme of things, did it matter? Not to Him.

Only to the chef, who was right there. He could have put out his hand, grabbed the greedy pig's carving knife and stopped him and shamed him, but the rules of the Carvery did not allow it. He had put out the roasts and the rest of it and now he must stand back, and watch it being wrecked. I wanted him to know that I had seen and been disgusted and appreciated the horror and helplessness of his position, and so when the beef carver had gone, I asked the chef, 'Wasn't that man a bit greedy?'

His expression changed. The stiff smile had gone, his face had sunk a little and he spoke with a faraway, half-despairing, half-baffled and slightly bitter look.

'You should know the greed I've seen here.'

It was still shameful for me to see such greed at my own table. On Auntie Celia's plate was a meat mountain. However would she manage to eat it all? But she wasn't planning to eat it all straight away. She was planning to take a few rolls, put the meat in the rolls, wrap them in paper serviettes and put the rolls in her handbag. Then she'd have them for tomorrow's lunch, and dinner, which meant she'd have had three meals for the price of one. So she stuffed two rolls with a big wodge of beef, wrapped them up and stuck them in her especially big handbag under the table, but she really needed another roll to put the rest of the meat in. She called the waiter for more rolls.

'For Christ's sake, Cissy, stop it. That woman over there's watching you. You've got enough already.'

My mother was ashamed, and so was I. More so because Auntie did not need to steal. She was rich, she lived in Park Lane, she drank champagne every day, her cupboards were stuffed with champagne and smoked salmon. But it still brought her joy to get something for nothing, and so she did this on every visit to the Carvery and put my mother and me through the same torment and embarrassment.

I had another auntie on my mother's side – Auntie Emily. Some of my mother's family, when they fled Sudwalki, had gone to South Africa on a boat, rather than Barrow, and Emily was one of them. She was not really an auntie but some sort of cousin of my mother's and according to my mother had led a pampered life in Bloemfontein. Out there, said my mother scornfully, Emily never lifted a finger. Black servants did every single thing for her. She didn't even know how to boil an egg. She would sit on her verandah and ring a little silver bell whenever she needed anything, and her servants would come running – 'Yes Madam, thank you, Madam, yes Madam' – and run and get it for her.

But the Mau Mau were rampaging about Africa and Emily came over here for a short holiday. She was a little, plain woman with mousy hair, short and a bit frizzy from her perm. She wore mousy, beige clothes and would often sit on our lawn rather helplessly on a relaxa-chair, while my mother ran backwards and forwards, bringing her everything as if she were a frail invalid. And in a way she was, because she didn't understand the world.

'Where has the sun gone, Clarice?' she asked on cloudy days when she had to stay indoors, because in Africa the sky was always blue and the sun always showing. And she'd never seen a television. To her the television was magic. How did the little people get inside it, Auntie asked, and got up from her armchair to go round the back of the television and have a look. She stared at it, enraptured, with her feet up on a pouff and us all bringing her snacks and tea in china cups, to be placed on a little table at her side. And when the telly was off and the sun hiding, Auntie would talk to my mother about her South African cousins and life in Bloemfontein. Then my mother would tell me.

Among her servants Auntie Emily had a house-boy called Johnny. Really he was a grown-up in his twenties, but Auntie called him her Boy. One day she returned from a little outing to the shops and found a terrible thing going on. Johnny was using her lavatory for a tinkle, said Auntie. He was absolutely not allowed to do this. Auntie lived in a tall block of flats and if Johnny wanted to go to the lavatory, he was to use a special lavatory for blacks up on the seventh floor. She told him off very strictly, and he never did it again, but usually they got on very well.

She was a bit frightened of the Mau Mau, but not of Johnny, so when she heard of all these blacks killing whites, and even their white masters and mistresses, she asked Johnny about it.

'You wouldn't stab me, would you, Johnny?' she asked.

'No Miss,' said Johnny, 'but next-door's Boy would stab you, and I'd stab next door's.'

Which is when Auntie took her little holiday over here.

'Bloody idiot,' said my father, and went up to the bedroom as much as he could, away from Emily. Sometimes my mother would join him and call him Johnny. They were both very keen on the stabbing story, and often repeated it, which is how I learned it by heart.

9: NAUGHTY JEWS

My second Christmas at the new school came round and the Hartley's peas upset had long ago blown over, but I was still a bit of an outcast. Jews were not allowed to sing in the school carol concert. During the final rehearsals, we could watch from the balcony. From there, I could look down at the Christian girls, singing and fainting below.

Look! There goes Pamela Moodley, suddenly sprawled on the floor. It was always poor Pamela Moodley. Adjacent girls carried her out. Every now and again there was another kerfuffle, the neat lines of girls were spoilt as another one fell and was carried out. They'd all been standing up for too long.

Sometimes, worse still, Pamela Moodley wet her knickers. A puddle spread out around her on the shiny parquet floor of the school hall. Watching from our balcony we knew what she'd done because the other girls shrank away from the puddle, creating a sudden space. No one wants to get wee all over them. How awful to be

Pamela Moodley. No one likes a girl who wets her knickers.

I know. I did it once at nursery school, and had to sit on the radiator till they dried. Then nobody would play with me at playtime. I might have forgotten this, but I didn't, because my mother was secretly keeping watch and saw me through a small hole in the school fence. There I was standing by myself and another horrid girl was shouting at me, 'Err. You've got green teeth.'

Imagine my poor mother on the other side of the fence. She could see me in trouble and she couldn't help. For the first time, she had to leave me to fate. And now Pamela was the outcast. No friends, no mummy to help her. And it wasn't just the once, like me. It was over and over again. She fainted when the Christians were standing and weed when they were sitting down in their neat rows, legs crossed, hands on knees, for hours and hours, practising away at the carols.

So being an outcast had its plus side. I was pleased, in a way, that I wasn't a Christian. Jews did not faint and wee, except for that one time at nursery school. We did not even have to go into prayers. We arrived in single file with the Catholics after prayers and in time for the notices. Until then, while everyone else was praying, we could stay in a classroom next to the hall and finish our homework. What luck! An extra half-hour. So why must some Jews always be naughty? I got fed up with them. Why were Becky Costa and Yvonne Schneider always making a noise and climbing on desks and giving us Jews a bad name?

Because of them, I did not want to be with the Jews. Or be Jewish. Then I needn't have been stuck up on the balcony, but could have been down in the hall, singing the heavenly carols, gazing up at the organ pipes and the galloping white horses of the pretend Parthenon frieze, which stretched along the top of the whole front wall of the hall, above the platform upon which the headmistress stood at assemblies or ceremonies. What grandeur! There was no grandeur in Ruislip synagogue. There was no wonderful, uplifting, holy-sounding singing, only mumbling and shuffling from the men at the front and subdued yakking from the women at the back, behind the wooden screen with the little net curtain on the top.

But I couldn't join the Christians. Except for the lovely carols, there wasn't anything much else that I envied. Some of the hymns seemed rather gruesome, particularly 'There is a Green Hill Far Away'. I could hear it from our homework classroom when it was sung towards the end of prayers. That horrid discord on 'crucified' gave me the creeps.

The previous summer, as Mummy and Daddy and I drove through France on our way down to Cannes on the Riviera, which we visited annually, we had come round a corner and there, all of a sudden, hanging up, far bigger than life size, was a giant technicolour crucified

Jesus with blood dripping from a big wound, the nailed bits and his forehead. What a shock. I screamed with fright.

That Jesus was the sort of thing that stuck in your mind. I remembered it for ever. Every now and again the tortured Jesus would pop back into my thoughts, in colour with his ribs sticking out and his blood dripping. And then I would thank goodness I wasn't a Christian, because then I'd have had to say my prayers to him, and look at him regularly, in church, outdoors, indoors, on walls, in homes, in schools, even in my own bedroom. Pamela had a Jesus in her bedroom.

But the carols did not refer to this grown-up Jesus. Only to him as a baby, before he knew what was coming. There was nothing about him dying to save people and no horrid discords, just something pure and cool that I loved about these Christmas songs.

I wanted to join in. Why couldn't I? They were only songs. I didn't have to believe Jesus was the Son of God. How could I when I still couldn't work out God's actual shape? God was everywhere, all at once, said the Christians. But how could He be? How big, for example, was His toe-nail? Did it cover Ruislip? I couldn't really believe their theory. It seemed to me that God was more likely to be constantly on the go, visiting this or that area, and if you were in luck, He might be over your area when you needed Him. But it was very hit and miss. However I assumed that He did have a pretty firm grip on the situation as a whole and a fairly all-encompassing overview, so that if anything absolutely terrible was going on in any particular area, He could get there pretty quickly and Act.

But it didn't matter what I thought. Joining in the carols wasn't allowed. After the first year stuck up in the balcony, I nagged and nagged, beginning in September, until my mother wrote an imploring letter to the headmistress, asking that I be allowed to sing carols, but the headmistress sent back a crushing reply.

'It is all or nothing, Mrs Hanson,' she wrote strictly. So that was that.

My mother was mortified. She had had to beg for her daughter to take part in a *goyishke* procedure, and she had been rejected. The Christians demanded a huge price before they would give the tiniest crumb away. What a *chutzpah*. Now she was ashamed of herself for having asked for such a thing. She sweated thinking of what she had done, abasing herself before the Christians. She told me exactly what she felt, what a fool I'd made of her, and you can bet it would be the last time she would ever ask them for a favour again.

10: THROUGH THE HATCH

There was another way that I could still get a little of that pure, clean, Christian feeling. I could play the piano. When I practised the piano, I was miles away from shouting and the bloody headmistress, and what I'd eaten, and what my bowels were up to, and I must be left alone. Because a child who was practising the piano could not be disturbed. She was going to be talented and raise herself above the rabble and become a genius. She was climbing on her parents' hardworking, slaving, cooking, shouting, crapping, struggling backs and getting to a higher place: to college, to university, to levels of cleverness and attainment never before reached in her family.

So that's what I would do for peace. I would say, 'I'm going to practise', then I could shut myself in the piano room and practise for hours and hours and be given privacy.

'She's practising,' said my parents proudly, explaining my absence to visiting adult friends and relatives.

Then they all shouted among themselves in the

kitchen, or through the hatch, sitting at it like a bar, having gin-and-tonics and whiskies and salted nuts, on its Formica surface, which could be easily wiped clean. Why bother with tablecloths that you had to keep washing? This way, my mother could be in the kitchen cooking but also be a part of life in the lounge. She could see or hear the television, she could observe the back of my father's head as he sat in his armchair reading the paper, she could call people to the hatch for dinner when it was ready, and she could serve it from the kitchen side without running from room to room. A brilliant device. Or visitors could just sit at the hatch having a drink, or tea. But while I was practising, I was in another lounge, on the other side of the hall, behind a closed door, away from life on either side of the hatch.

When Blanche Walmesley came visiting she would sit on a stool at the hatch, her favourite place, sometimes on the kitchen side, sometimes on the lounge side, if my father was in the lounge. If only my mother was there, Blanche could sit on the kitchen side and talk to Mummy about her marriage, in which she was stuck and miserable, and her husband, who was old and dull. My mother felt sorry for Blanche. But despite her miserable life, Blanche wore elegant clothes. She did not *shlump*[36] around in a pinny and an old frock like my mother often did. She had a rather striking dark blue dress with white

[36] Slob about, let yourself go, look like a drudge.

polka dots, fitted, and sleeveless, for wearing in the summer, and her dark hair was swept up into a loose, fat and voluptuous bun, making her look Spanish.

Blanche's husband hadn't touched her for years. Heaven knows why she stayed with the miserable bastard, but then she had her daughter to think about. You can't just leave a marriage and your child. You can't take a child away from her father.

My mother knew because she had tried it. She'd got fed up with my father when I was little and threatened to leave him.

'And do you know what he said to me?' she asked.

'No. What?'

'He said he'd keep you.'

In those days, men could do that. So that was why my mother stuck it out. For me. Same for Blanche, when she probably wished she could meet someone handsome and dashing and more exciting, who would just sweep her off her feet and take her away.

'She can keep wishing,' said my mother, knowing from experience that such a dream was hopeless.

My mother sympathised with Blanche because she knew what she was talking about. My father never touched my mother either, although she didn't tell Blanche this. He had not done so for years. He never even put his arm round her. He came to bed very late; he turned his back and went to sleep. I didn't like to think what else he did if he was touching her. Now I was learning about all that, I most certainly didn't like to think of it. But it bothered my mother and during this no-touching period, which lasted for years and years, she had rather let herself go. I sort of knew about it, because she had left a letter, that she was in the middle of writing to her cousin in South Africa, in the typewriter on a table in front of the bay window in the hatch lounge, and I had read a bit of it. The bit was about the not touching. But she didn't tell me any of this properly until I was older, of course, and when she had come to realize how much she had given up on her appearance.

Not everyone thought my mother looked shocking. People hung around. They wanted to talk to her. She couldn't get rid of them: Mr Clanfield the chicken farmer, Horace the coalman, Miss Hilary, the vet. Mr Clanfield was the worst visitor. What a huge stomach he had, and what a stink of chicken shit he brought with him. My mother would sometimes ban him even from entering the kitchen. He would come round the side door, which cleverly opened in two parts, like a stable door, so Mr *farshtunkener*[37] Clanfield would have to stay outside, if he was particularly shitty that day, and just lean over the top part of the door like a horse. But in winter my mother couldn't enforce her ban, it was too inhospitable. She would feel obliged to invite him in, and he

[37] Stinky.

would sit at the hatch, kitchen side of course, on a stool, with his enormous, round stomach sticking out and his corduroy trousers spattered with chicken droppings, stinking and drinking tea, and looking at my mother and telling her what a good-looking woman she was, until she ordered him out again, calling him a stinkpot, or a dirty old sod.

'Pfaw! What a pong!' But he didn't seem to mind. So long as he could sit there for a bit.

Miss Hilary also liked to sit about and have a whisky, even if there was nothing wrong with the dog. Of all the visitors, she was my favourite. There was nothing wrong with her. She was a nice woman, a wonderful vet, but she didn't make the most of herself, my mother said. She looked just like a man, but what was wrong with that? I would have liked to have looked like her – in jodhpurs, boots, no brassiere (she was completely flat-chested, and that would have suited me, to never, ever have any bosoms) – a white shirt, yellow tie with horse-shoe pattern, waistcoat, hacking jacket and her hair smoothed down flat and shiny, with Brylcreem. What else could a vet wear? You wouldn't want to be wearing a frock in that job, but she came as a shock to some people, like my mother's best friend, Ruth, the hairdresser.

Ruth popped round one morning when Miss Hilary was visiting. My mother introduced them out in the garden, because this time, Miss Hilary had just been looking at the dog's eye. It had an ulcer, which Boxers often get because of their bulgy eyes. Now Miss Hilary was sitting on a deckchair on the patio with a whisky and soda, having a little break before she went back to work. She swirled her glass a bit and made the ice clink.

'Ruth, this is Miss Hilary,' said my mother.

Ruth looked rather startled, but my mother had wanted them to meet because she thought Miss Hilary could do with a blow-wave, which Ruth's shop was good at. Now here was her opportunity.

'Couldn't she do with a blow-wave, Ruth? To give it body.' My mother turned to Miss Hilary. 'They're only down the road. Go down there and have one, on your way home.'

But Miss Hilary only laughed. At least she didn't take offence. People often did if you criticized their hair.

Aperitifs at the hatch, 1960.

11: THE PERILS OF BEING
A BLABBERMOUTH

The older Grandma became, the more my mother worried about my inheritance. It was clearly mine now. Everybody knew. Grandma's despair about Cyril marrying out had never really abated, and the closer she got to her death-bed, the more vital it became that she ensure that Olga the *mamser* got none of her money. Because Cyril had done a terrible thing. What if everybody did what he had done? Soon there would be no more Jews left. Why did Hitler bother? Grandma asked; these marrying-out Jews were doing his work for him. And what shame that my grandma's own son had done it. Her only son. He had ruined her life. Betty's conversion to Judaism counted for nothing.

This is an unusual thing about Jews, and one way in which they seem to differ from the rest of the world's religions. They absolutely do not want any converts. They just want to hang on to what they've got. Although this had caused terrible difficulties in my family, I was always rather proud of this bit of Jewish behaviour. It seemed much better, to me, than doing what the Christians and Jehovah's Witnesses and Catholics did, which was to go round knocking on people's doors and nag them to join up and be one of them. My parents didn't think much of it either. My mother would just slam the door, shouting, 'Bloody *chutzpah.*' But my father liked to engage with them, pretending that he was interested and might join, asking them endless questions and arguing with the answers, for so long that in the end my mother had to stop him. She had various methods: shouting, calling that his dinner was ready, and – if none of that worked and she was in a jolly mood – throwing tennis balls at him from the kitchen while he argued. In between throws she would hide round the corner with her legs crossed, as if she might wet herself at any minute.

But religion wasn't a laugh for Grandma. To her it was deadly serious. If Betty wasn't a Jew, then this couldn't be a marriage, and if it wasn't a marriage, then Olga wasn't Jewish. Luckily for Grandma, to confirm her decision, something else terrible had happened which meant that Olga could never be other than a *goyishe mamser*[38]. The rabbi forgot, upon the occasion of Betty's conversion and ritual dunking in the *Mikveh*[39], to dunk Olga with her. And if baby Olga had not been dunked, that was it. She

[38] Christian bastard.
[39] Ceremonial bath.

was not, and could never be, Jewish. Then no one could say Grandma was making a terrible fuss about nothing. It was the rabbi's fault that Olga was not one of us, and the child of a non-marriage. Once she knew that, Grandma's decision was set in stone.

But she still had worries about leaving her money to me, because a) I was only a child, and b) she wasn't sure she could trust my father. And these worries had been confirmed, or perhaps even implanted, by my Auntie Celia, a.k.a. Moonface the Fibber, as my grandma lay on what she thought might be her death-bed. She should have been at peace, but instead she was in turmoil. Her mind whirled round and round.

Perhaps Celia was right, my grandma thought. How could she be sure of my father? Celia had pointed out that a business always needs money, my father might use the money for his business, and then the business might go down the drain and I'd never get my money back. Anybody could go bust. Why not my father? And what did she know of him? Nothing really. He never said much. She knew he went to the betting shop, that wherever he was, he would find a betting shop. She knew because my mother told her.

Why on earth did my mother tell? She, like me, knew that she had to be careful what she told her mother, because once she had bad-mouthed someone, even if it was only a tiny bit, then Grandma was on the look-out for sponging and advantage-taking and personal faults.

But sometimes my mother just couldn't stop herself from blabbing out something that was worrying her. She had to speak. She was busting, like a pressure cooker, with some terrible knowledge or other, and it would suddenly spurt out and cause even more problems. So now Grandma was aware of my father's penchant for betting and, for all she knew, my father could gamble the money away. Anyway, she had never quite trusted him. Why should she? Her own husband had been a handsome wastrel and gambler. Why should he not end up a wastrel too? Arthur was handsome and a gambler. She only needed a tiny push from someone to confirm her fears and set her against my father. Celia provided that tiny push. To make sure, she kept up a drip of regular, stronger pushes. So Grandma decided, instead of trusting my parents regarding my money, to put her trust in Celia. Then, should she become *farmisht*[40] in her old age, Celia would know what to do.

I knew all this, because my mother had told me, and she knew all this, because Grandma had told her.

She had also told my mother, 'Celia knows what to do with the money.' That was all. But what was Celia meant to do with it and when? My mother knew that Grandma wanted me to have the money, but how could she be sure that Celia also wanted me to have it? Celia might want to keep it for herself. This was The Threat. This was the

[40] Mixed up emotionally. Confused.

worry that my mother would have burdening her for the rest of Celia's life, or until Celia spoke of her intentions. But since when did anyone ever get Celia to tell them her plans? Never, ever, ever. And even if she did tell, could you believe her? Not the tiniest, weeniest chance.

What a fool Grandma had been to trust Celia, but that was the trouble. She had always fallen for Celia's tricks. She had never been able to believe that Celia was deceitful. To Grandma, said my mother, the sun shone

Auntie Betty with Olga, my mother and me, 1944.

out of Celia's *tokhes*. She pissed port wine. And now my inheritance and my mother's peace of mind would be subject to Celia's fancy. For how long was Celia meant to hang on to the money? And when was I supposed to get it, if ever? In ten years? Twenty years? When Celia died? This was the beginning of my mother's sentence. She must now, for God knows how long, be nice to Celia, otherwise there was every chance that Celia would turn nasty and I would never get my inheritance. It is not easy to be nice to a scheming, greedy, lying, selfish bitch of a sister who has driven you mad since almost the day she was born, but this is what my mother would have to do. For me.

12: POOR TOAD

What about my other grandma, grandma Nathanson, my father's mother? I think I saw her once or twice, lying in bed. She spent a lot of time in bed, so my mother told me. She rarely lifted a finger to look after her children. She didn't even give them any breakfast, but sent them off with a penny to buy a bun on the way to school, and then they were bullied all the way up Camden Road until they got there, on a more or less empty stomach. Luckily my father had a big brother, Phil, to look after him, but still his childhood was not easy. Two awful tragedies happened when he was a boy:

Number 1) He had a pet toad living in the coal hole. He had asked his mother repeatedly to warn him when the coal men were coming, so that he could save his toad, if it was still down there hibernating. She did not warn him. Poor toad.

Number 2) His dog *Ganuf*[41] jumped over the fence

[41] Thief.

and stole next door's Sunday roast. They poisoned Ganuf in revenge.

As if that wasn't bad enough, there were the continual hardships of everyday life: the lack of breakfasts, the bullies, and once, when my father was little, he asked for pears. Just that particular day, he felt desperate for pears. He probably nagged for them.

'Pears he wants, pears he'll get,' said his mother, and gave him a *frusk*.[42]

My mother often reported this event, because what really shocked her about Grandma Nathanson was her lack of food provision. Such behaviour in Christians she was used to. It was almost the norm. But for a Jewish mother to fail in this area was unspeakable. Grandma Nathanson was a tremendous let-down to the team. No breakfast for children was shocking enough, a smack instead of a pear was nasty, but even when her children were grown-up and earning money and some of them still living at home, Grandma's behaviour regarding food was close to sub-human. Leah, Annie, Fannie and Millie would go out to work, buy fish and bring it home, Grandma would cook it, and then – horrors – she would charge my father and his brothers to eat it. Her own children. And she hadn't even paid for the fish.

---

[42] Smack round the ear, back-hander. You can give someone a *frusk* anywhere, but this one was round the ear.

I don't know what my father thought of her, but he did love his father, my other grandpa, who worked very hard in Camden Town as a tailor and cutter. He died when I was a baby, so I don't remember him, but Grandma lingered on, a miserable shadow in our background, who rarely left her house.

Luckily Grandpa left his mark on my father. Grandpa had liked to have a laugh, so did my father. The sulking he probably got from Grandma, but the jokes he got from Grandpa. They had played a good one on my Auntie Fanny's husband, who they weren't very keen on. He ran a tailor's trimmings shop in Tottenham Street and sometimes Fanny helped him in the shop. She was sitting behind the counter one day, with a few customers in the shop, when suddenly three gangsters came running in, wearing fedoras and with handkerchiefs tied round their faces, in the style of Al Capone. One pointed a pretend gun and they wrenched the till right off the counter.

It was my father, his brother Phil, both in their twenties, and my grandpa, still young and handsome, all having a laugh. Auntie recognised them, but the customers didn't. What a fright they got.

'Stop it, you bloody idiots,' shouted Auntie. 'Leave it alone.'

She tried to hang on to the till, fighting bravely while the ashen customers stood frozen with fear. One fainted. But it was three against one. The gangsters dashed out of the shop with the till, ran round a corner and sat on the pavement laughing like drains.

Grandpa's death upset my father terribly. And one of the awful things about it was that my father laughed at his funeral. He didn't know why, but he couldn't help it and he felt ashamed of himself forever for doing it, then after the funeral he couldn't bear to go out for a year. He went

My parents circa 1938. Happy days.

to work, but that's all he did. In the evenings and at weekends he just came home and stayed in. His brother Phil begged him to go out. He tried and tried to get my father out of the house – to the cinema, to a dance, to the dogs or horses, for a drink – anywhere, but my father would only stay home and mope. Luckily Phil never gave up, and at last, after a whole year of staying in, he managed to drag my father out to a dance.

My father didn't plan to join in. He thought he'd just go to keep Phil quiet, and sit at the edge. But then he saw my mother. She was wearing a dress with a neckline that was cut in a very low V at the back. My father saw my mother's back and that was it. He got up and asked her to dance, and his heart was beating rather fast and so loud, my mother told me, that she could hear it, and that was the end of his horrible year.

13: CANNES

My father grew into a man who could afford summer holidays in the South of France. He and my mother had been visiting Cannes since 1935, then the war put a temporary stop to that, and we started going there again in 1950, when I was eight and the world was more or less back to normal. We would drive down to the Côte d'Azur with its golden beaches, blue sky, baking sun and a real azure sea, just as it said. In those days not many people went to the South of France for their holidays. We were the avant-garde, crossing the Channel, driving to new and exotic places. Cannes had long stretches of modest, public beach, two casinos and the most wonderful ice-cream parlour in the history of the world – the Alaska, on the Rue des États-Unis. Cannes had something for all the family. And another good thing. The Mediterranean cured my asthma.

The asthma would come and go, sometimes lasting for two or three weeks. It was often brought on by particular events: smelling sulphur in science class, the smell of stink bombs, fireworks, breathing in sparkler fumes, having to play lacrosse in the cold, running in the fog, any outdoor exercise, even swimming. It had its plus side, for a girl who hated playing lacrosse. When the asthma came, I had to go and sit indoors in the lovely warm changing rooms. But then came the long bouts when I wasted weeks in bed, too weedy to do anything, doing my diaphragmatic breathing exercises – breathe out while squeezing the ribs in, breathe in while they expand – unable to go out to school or play, unless it was holiday time.

Then I would be carried to the car and driven south, to Cannes. There was a strap across the car ceiling, which secured the luggage rack, and from this strap my mother hung pairs of cherries, so that I could flop there, eating cherries, wheezing, gently doped by Piriton, until we reached the Riviera, got to the beach and into the warm turquoise water and then, like magic, the asthma went away.

But there was one thing my mother could not escape this year. Auntie Celia. She was there already. If she wasn't cruising the Mediterranean or all the way to South Africa where we had relatives, then she would spend much of the summer in Cannes, and she always stayed, with her husband Bill, in the swizzy Hotel Martinez, the second best and most expensive hotel in town. The best was the Carlton. Both hotels were close to each other and mid-way between both casinos: the old Casino in the old part of town, and the new, film-starry Palm Beach casino, Celia's favourite, because she too was a gambler.

Oddly enough, this didn't seem to worry my grandma. She still trusted Celia with her money, yet Celia was a big-time gambler. Much bigger-time than my father. She didn't bother with betting shops, but stuck to casinos, in which she could spend whole evenings in her best dresses: long, sequinned numbers, or clinging black, silk jersey creations by Worth, worn in the cooler evening with a short mink jacket – a box-shaped one, or a little cape one – to keep her shoulders warm.

The Palm Beach casino was surrounded by palm trees, illuminated romantically in the evenings by spotlights, so that we could see the gamblers like Auntie Celia and Uncle Bill, in long, sparkly dresses and evening suits, swanning in and out. It stood at the end of a promontory, with beaches on both sides: one side having swankier beaches and cafés, where the sun shone all day, and on the other side, the free Symphonie Plage for poorer people or the French, with no cafés – you had to take your own picnic – where the sun stopped shining at about tea-time and then the beaches were in shadow.

Celia had no need of these public beaches. She stayed on the Martinez beach, with its endless sun, and matching green and white umbrellas, deckchairs and sun-beds, all spaced equally with no crowding. From her own, personal beach station, with umbrella, sun-bed, deckchair and small table, Celia would order drinks in tall glasses tinkling with ice and the odd snack for herself and Bill from the beach restaurant, and lie in the sun for hours, or partly in the shade just leaving particular parts out in the glare, gleaming with dark-brown, oily Ambre Solaire, for a little more browning. Bill usually remained in the shade. He burned more easily.

Occasionally Celia would walk slowly down to the sea, sinking elegantly into its warm, crystal-clear water, swimming a few sidestrokes very carefully, Esther Williams-style like my mother, barely disturbing the water, so as not to wet her chignon, then rising slowly and gracefully, beautifully cooled, and drifting back to her place, gazing around on her way, to see if anyone worth noticing was about. She once spotted Tommy Steele, and introduced him to my cousin Olga, but he didn't say much and just went on chewing peanuts. I didn't like Tommy Steele anyway. By then I preferred Elvis.

We could visit Celia there, if we felt like a bit of posh beach, but personally, we liked our own little beach, the Bijou Plage, further down towards the Palm Beach casino, on the sunnier side but where anybody could go, and which had a small café, with a sandy, wooden slatted floor and a rattan roof, which let in little shreds of sun, and shaded a table football. A small stone jetty stuck out into the sea, short enough for me to jump off the end and swim to shore. After a few years of repeat visits, my mother knew the café proprietors and locals. Here she was in heaven. She could sunbathe, swim, relax and, best of all, talk French loudly with a tremendously French accent.

There was something about the French people and language which made my mother feel more at home than in England. Here she could shout, make a noise, talk more or less non-stop, crack jokes, have a laugh, repeat herself and eat the lovely food. How heavenly this food was – so unusual and foreign – the sort of thing you only found in England if you went to Harrods or the Dorchester, like Celia, but which rarely appeared in Ruislip or normal life: fresh sea-food, *crevettes*, langoustines, *moules marinières*, and fish soup and octopus. French people even ate octopus, in rings, and squid with their suckers showing, or the four little pink bits inside sea-urchins. And then there were the continental vegetables, the ratatouille, green beans, all in sauces, oils, salad dressing, and garlic – a novelty to us. And then the fruits: enormous, juicy peaches and nectarines. You couldn't get that in England. My mother would marvel at them. And the prices. Fabulous. What bargains in the markets! And you were allowed to pick the fruits up and squeeze them and handle them, and argue and shout while shopping. All absolutely taboo in Ruislip. And what about all the different cheeses? Goats' cheeses, stinky cheeses, runny cheeses. And the croissants, brioches and baguettes, and the pains au chocolat, all warm and fresh in the mornings. Yes. French children were allowed bread and chocolate for breakfast. And wine with their dinners.

The French knew how to eat. The English did not. My mother could exclaim about the quality, the deliciousness, the freshness and juiciness, the sight, the colour and the value over and over again, on every shopping trip, at every stall, in every supermarket, café, restaurant, snack bar, and nobody minded. The French adored it. They were not embarrassed by praise, enjoyment or robust jokes. Imagine doing that in Ruislip High Street. At home, among the pale, thin-lipped English women, my mother would be seen as a vulgar loudmouth. In Cannes she was an attractive, voluptuous person appreciating things and enjoying herself rather noisily, which to the French was normal, so here my mother came into her own. The heat and the luscious food suited her. She could be herself and still seem normal. Perhaps she should have been born French.

But being Jewish and French was not all fun. It hadn't been fun for our friends the Gerstls, who had survived the death camps, just, unlike many of their relatives, and now lived in Cannes. We stayed with them occasionally, but more often in Mme Zich's small *pension* in the Avenue de Lerins, near to the Gerstls' house, a quiet back street where the ordinary French lived, brightened by purple and magenta bougainvillea, but with no proper pavement, just sandy ground and the odd bit of kerb. But who cared if there wasn't a proper edge between the road and pavement, if the houses didn't match, if there were no traffic lights or strict cross-roads, if I never wore any shoes? Here it was too hot and mellow to care. And luckily for me, the Gerstls had a daughter of my age, Jeanette.

For a treat, my mother would take us both to the Alaska ice-cream parlour. The Gerstls could not afford visits to the Alaska, so for Jeanette, this was a first. Here, she and I entered heaven. A bluey-white pretend ice-cave heaven, with giant icicles hanging from the ceiling and polar bears and penguins painted on the walls, and then, those ice-creams, from the complex melbas, *coupes* and *bombes*, with their dark chocolate or fruit middles, their pralines, peaches, sauces, *sirops*, *crème chantilly*, sprinkled nuts, to the modest two or three scoops or takeaway cornets of rich, exotic flavours a million miles from the pale, slimy Walls Neapolitan of England. Here were ice-cream colours I had never seen before: deep-purple cassis, dark shiny-red *framboise* and *fraise*, lemon, hazelnut and green pistachio – a new, foreign type of nut. We could never go enough. We could never sample every flavour or combination but, licking a cornet one day, Jeanette spoke almost swooning between licks.

'*C'est* lick *la plus belle* lick *glace* lick *que j'ai mangé* lick *dans toute ma vie.*'[43]

My mother was thrilled. This was her favourite ever holiday episode and she repeated and acted it out every time anyone mentioned the Alaska, for the rest of her life. '*C'est* lick *la plus belle . . .*'

[43] This is the best ice-cream I've eaten in my whole life.

My father also loved the French. He turned French upon arrival in Cannes. Being dark-skinned, he already looked rather foreign, and once he had changed into his sandals, khaki or navy shorts, string vest and navy beret, you would have thought he was a real Frenchman, sitting in the local PMU, drinking pastis and reading the runners in the *Nice Matin*. This was his version of heaven – sitting in a French betting shop. He couldn't speak French as well as my mother, but he could gesture and make noises rather well in French and as men are not meant to talk as much as women, this got him through. He also loved the food, the heat, the markets and the casinos and France in general, but most of all he loved the PMU. And in France he loved my mother. He did not sulk, she did not shout. Here there was no office, no manager and staff, no kitchen, no cooking, no rain, no clouds and they were happily married.

Not that Cannes was perfect. There were some areas which perhaps could have been a little more tightly reg-ulated. Out one day on a pedalo with my parents, I sat on one of the front bits with my legs dangling in the clear, blue water, looking down at the sandy parts of the bottom of the sea, jumping off now and again for a swim while they pedalled, when suddenly, something brown came bobbing past my dangling legs. What was it? A sea cucumber come loose? An odd sea creature? No. It was a floating poo from the American army ship anchored off shore. I lifted my legs out of the water. Together we counted 35 more American poos floating by, flushed straight out of their ship's lavatories into the azure water. What a laugh. Here was another advantage to having a mother and father like mine. Thirty-five poos would float past and they would have a laugh. A horrified one of course, but still a laugh. And the laugh would go on, because this was a fabulous story to tell one's friends. It had four top-notch ingredients: danger, horror, thrills and bowels. Perfect. If you couldn't laugh at that, what could you laugh at? And here you could repeat it to everyone loudly. The French didn't mind, and neither did Celia. She had her faults, but she did love a bowel story. We could all, for a brief while, forget that there was probably trouble brewing.

But when you take your child to the South of France, you like to have something to show for it when you get home. My mother liked to have a brown, sun-tanned child to show. What was the point going to the lovely, hot, Mediterranean sea-side, if there was not some visible benefit? So she liked me to sunbathe, preferably on my back with my face in the sun. There is no point coming home with a brown back and a white face. The face is the bit people see, and a brown one looked more attractive, my mother thought, than a white one. Jeanette Gerstl had a lovely brown face, and big brown eyes and beautiful brown curls, like a proper little French girl, and that is what my mother wanted to return home with to Ruislip – a healthy-looking child with a lovely sun-tanned face. But she was out of luck, because I liked my face out of the sun and my back in it. When you are busy making dribbly castles or watching for fish, or playing bar-football, there is no way that you can put your face in the sun, and so I had a French-looking brown back and legs and much of my body, but a white 'Ruislippy' face.

Soon the beach café staff had learned my mother's regular cry, 'Put your face in the sun'. So they all copied her. Ha ha. They saw me pass by; they spotted me at the football.

'Put your face in the sun!' they all cried out, laughing away, siding with my mother.

But I couldn't do it. Because it is uncomfortable and

My father in Cannes, 1955.

boring to just lie with your face in the baking sun, sweat coming out of your head, boiling and roasting, desperate to swim or run about. I could manage just a few minutes before rising up rebelliously and running away, or complaining, or wanting an ice-cream, and probably saving myself from melanoma. But in those days, coming from the cold, fog, snow and asthma of Ruislip, sunbathing was a good thing. We didn't know in those days that it could be another killer.

14: FILTH FROM LONDON

In my class was a group of popular girls, with whom I was friendly, but not really best friends, or properly in their gang. I didn't really want to be, because they did very rude things that I couldn't imagine myself doing – a sort of advanced version of Doctors and Nurses. Danielle Hewitt came in to school one Monday morning, all excited. She was telling them something, but we were all listening on the outskirts, because Danielle's report was so thrilling, in a horrid way. She'd been to a party, gone upstairs to the bedroom with a lot of boys, she'd laid on the bed and they'd taken her blouse and her brassiere off, which was shocking enough, but the worst thing of all, I thought, was that Danielle had liked it. She was not ashamed. As she told this story, she was laughing, and so were her friends, who all wore brassieres and had bosoms.

Bosoms were the last thing I wanted. There was something terrifying about them. They hurt if you banged them. I knew that because the bosom area hurt already if I banged it accidentally on the desk. They would have to be strapped up in brassieres or they wobbled about, they stuck out in a very obvious way, boys stared at them, and usually, once you had brassieres, you had periods as well. I was now nearly 13, neither of these things had yet happened to me and I hoped and prayed that they never would, or at least that the bosoms wouldn't grow for years, and I would always be like Miss Hilary. Rita Henshaw had large pointed bosoms in a sort of double-cone brassiere, the cones ringed with lines of stitching, which rather emphasized the bosoms and made them more pointy. Why would Rita want to do that? Rita also curled her hair into sausages and of course had periods too, as did many of the other girls. And Rita's mother had told her that a girl should not wash while she had her period, because it was bad for you, which meant that Rita was very smelly when she had one. Luckily nobody else was but still the bosoms and periods were a terrifying combination of developments which I dreaded. It led to boys, sex, marriage and having babies. I couldn't imagine the awful meeting of bottoms which sex required. I didn't want to think of it.

Up in the north of England, that sort of development seemed to happen later. Although she was six months older than me, my cousin Olga knew almost nothing of it. I became her tutor, as I came from London, city of vice. When I visited her in Barrow I brought with me the latest ghastly revelations. I was now old enough to travel to Barrow alone on the train. My mother put me aboard at Euston and Uncle or Auntie and Olga met me at Barrow. Changing at Crewe or Rugby was a bit frightening, but as the train got nearer to Barrow, the views improved and it seemed as if I was going on a proper holiday. Between Lancaster and Barrow-in-Furness the train goes across the sea in several places as the coastline goes in and out, past Grange-over-Sands and Arnside and Cark and Cartmel and Ulverston. Miles of flat, empty, dark sand and flat stretches of grass with sheep grazing here and there. It's a rather beautiful journey, especially in the evening with the sun setting in the west out to sea and a streaky sunset beyond the flats. Why were the sands so empty? I asked Olga. Wouldn't they be lovely to run across or paddle beside? No, she said, because they're quicksand. Very dangerous.

Then you arrive at Barrow-in-Furness, like Ruislip but not so busy and with smaller houses. In Barrow I noticed that people tended to stare at me and mock my London accent.

'Oh Aaaahhhntie Betty, oh what laaahhhvely trousers.'

What I should have been saying was 'Antie' and 'luvly', like my 'cusin' did, if I wanted to avoid criticism. But at least there was the seaside up here, at Morecambe or Walney Island, and the lakes.

From London I had brought a new swear word for Olga: fuck – the verb. Or fucking, to be used as an adjective: e.g. 'That woman next door is a fucking stupid cow'. Olga had never heard it.

'Don't ever say it in front of anyone,' I warned her. 'It's terribly, terribly rude. Promise never to say it. And don't say that I've told it you.'

'I won't. Why should I? I promise.'

The next day we were all in the car, Uncle Cyril driving us to Lake Windermere for a picnic, Auntie Betty in the front, me and Olga in the back, and suddenly a rabbit ran right across the road in front of us.

'Look at that fucking rabbit,' shouted Olga, then straightaway she realized what she'd done. Her mouth remained open, gaping. Her face went pink. Uncle Cyril lost his temper and shouted. He had never, ever done that before.

'Don't you come up from London with that filthy language. You bloody little *drek*. If I hear that once more, you'll not come and stay here again. Ever.'

It was a whole hour before he spoke to me again.

Sex bombs, real and pretend. Olga, her friend Larraine, and me
with oranges in Barrow, 1956.

15: GRANDMA'S DECLINE

My Grandma Davidson had been feeling poorly for some time and, as she was feeling generally under the weather and talking about death and planning her funeral, Celia had been up to Barrow to see her several times in the last few months. That was much more often than usual. My mother suspected that she was up to something.

'She's got an ulterior motive,' said my mother, and we all knew what that meant. Auntie Celia used to have two ulterior motives: money and men, but now that she was married to Bill, she only had one – money. My mother was dead certain that Celia was up there making sure that Grandma stuck to her plan of handing over my inheritance. So my father, who had to go up north selling, drove to Barrow and brought Grandma back with him to stay with us for a bit. If Celia wanted to talk to her anymore, she could talk to her at our house, and then we could hear for certain what she was up to.

It was becoming more and more difficult for Grandma to get down to London by herself. It was a long train journey and she was not as fit as she used to be. She reported regularly to my mother over the phone, and my mother passed on the news in instalments. Grandma couldn't walk far without her two sticks, or even with them, her feet were burning, she had pains down her arm, she couldn't sleep well, she couldn't eat much. Nothing tasted so good anymore. When she got up in the morning she looked in the mirror and she looked like hell. The beautifully smooth skin of her youth hung in wrinkles.

'I look *geferlekh*,' she would moan, looking in the mirror. 'Don't grow old.'

A terrible warning. Grey whiskers sprouted from Grandma's chin and around her mouth, which sunk in around her toothless gums, if it was early in the morning, or late at night, or no visitors were expected and she hadn't bothered to put her teeth in. Her thin hair clung to her skull. Ruth the hairdresser would come, and Grandma would cry out tragically, 'What can she do with my three hairs?' But somehow, like magic, Ruth would turn the three hairs into a full and glamorous shape, and Grandma would put a net over it to try and retain its glamour, but if she slept on it for just one night it would be more or less flattened again in the morning, almost as though the hairdresser had never been.

To reach the bathroom, Grandma had to put her hand on the wall. We needed a rail for her to hang on to, and what a palaver to get on to the lavatory. One hand on the bath, one hand on the toilet roll holder, a terrifying drop

on to the seat, and then how to get off again? Lean forwards, cling to the towel rail, haul herself up. Everything
was a struggle.

How long could she go on like this, crawling about,
no use to anyone? She wanted to make plans and tidy
things up. She wanted to be sure she knew where her
money was going, and she had said that she wanted it to
go to me – Chuckles, her favourite and only official
grandchild. She often told me of my cleverness, just as
Grandpa had done. When I was two, I could point to any
flower in the garden and I could name it.

'She's got more brains in her little finger,' repeated
Grandma, over and over again, 'than the rest of the family
put together.'

And such lovely fat cheeks. And what a peach bottom.

'Peach bottom,' Grandma would call from the sofa on
her visits. Even though I was 12 and my bottom was never
seen, she still said it. 'My lovely peach bottom. *Kenenehora*.
Come to Grandma.'

Celia came to visit Grandma at our house. She arrived
late morning, when Grandma was still in bed, so she sat
on the edge of the bed, holding Grandma's thin, papery
hand and looking at her in that sweet, regretful and rather
innocent way that she had, as if the world and our family
were a bit of a risk and here she was just doing her best
to help everyone.

Celia patted her hair. It was swept back into a chignon,

blonde, natural but enhanced, revealing the whole of her moonface. She'd been called Moonface as a child, because her face was smooth and oval, her forehead sloping back, and now her hair was scraped back revealing the moon-shape clearly. Her skin was freckled and tanned from the frequent cruises and holidays. Perhaps it was the time away that helped her to relax. She never seemed to flap or scream or panic like my mother did. Nothing ever made her hurry.

I had been with her when she was not hurrying, when she had needed a lemon for her tea. Down we went to the ground floor in the lift, along the street to a nearby fruit stall. Auntie had walked smoothly about, gazing at the shops on the way, then picking up a lemon on the fruit stall, looking at it carefully, working out whether it was an expensive lemon, beating down the price, enraging the stallholder. But she remained calm and beautiful and put the lemon down again. She could go somewhere else for her lemon. She had time to choose, time to be careful. She had a little think and then took the lemon after all and, holding my hand, took me back to the flat for tea.

There was one very important thing that she would never hurry over – telling anyone what she was going to do with The Money, once she became custodian. Just because she was here, in our house, didn't mean that anyone could get anything out of her. No one could ask her in front of Grandma, who would only say that 'Celia knew what to do with it', and even if you cornered Celia downstairs, you wouldn't get anywhere. Celia would just say it was safe with her, and then she would put on her surprised simpering look and open her eyes wide, as if to say, 'How could you doubt me? How could you think I would fail to look after my own niece's money, or spend even a penny of it on myself?'

And how could my mother say 'Because you're a bloody liar, and you always have been'? She couldn't, and she never did. Why bother? She knew she'd never get a straight answer. So she had to wait. For a very long time. But I wasn't really bothered. Why should I know or care about money, when I was only a child?

From left: Celia, Grandma Davidson and my mother.

16: THE LIFE OF A SUBURBAN HOUSEWIFE

When Grandma had gone home and the holidays were over, my mother needed something to take her mind off her worries — how Grandma was coping with her health, what bloody Celia was planning — and she turned to bridge. Life in Ruislip was not easy for her. My father would be thinking of nothing but The Business, which made him anxious, which made him sulky. He would come home, sit down in the lounge with his back to my mother through the hatch, read the papers and demand silence.

'Switch that off,' said he, about the jolly wireless.

'Stop yakking,' he said to my mother and me and our friends, and he failed to respond to questions properly, replying with a grunt or one word. Which only made my mother ask more questions, just to force another few words out of him.

'Do you want fish or chicken?' asked my mother.

'Chicken.'

'Why not fish? What's wrong with the fish?'

'*Grunt.*'

This is a well-known joke about Jewish women. It shows that even if you do answer one question, she will not be satisfied with your answer. She will wonder if there is more to it. And with reason. She knows that life cannot be that simple. You can't just make your mind up in one, two, three. You should be thinking of the pros and cons, wondering out loud, giving the topic a good going over, which would mean a nice talk about it. The fish has this and that merits, but so has the chicken. You have to weigh it all up before you decide. Not just say 'chicken' baldly like that. It wasn't good enough.

'What do you want? Cake or biscuits? Milk or cocoa? Fish or chicken?'

She didn't want a plain decision. She wanted a little interchange, an acknowledgement that she was there, that she had cooked this fish or chicken, that she had done it beautifully, that it was the best, juiciest fried fish in Ruislip, that she had *schlepped* all the way to town to her favourite fish stall off Berwick Street near my father's Poland Street factory, in search of quality, or that smelly Mr Clanfield had delivered the chicken fresh yesterday and hung about stinking out the kitchen as usual, and without this complex background, which deserved far more than a one-word answer, you would not be having fish or chicken at all.

No wonder my father's sullen answers made my

mother shout all the more and bang about on her kitchen side of the hatch.

'Is that all you can say? Can't you give me a decent bloody answer? I've been standing here cooking all day and you just come home, you sit there . . . *blah, blah . . .*'

Usually nobody saw all this, but this time my cousin Olga and Auntie Betty had come down to London to do a bit of shopping, and were visiting. Even in front of them – guests with whom one was meant to be polite – my father still grunted. This was too much for my mother. A public humiliation in front of Olga and Betty, who were not used to ill-mannered husbands because Uncle Cyril was always polite to visitors and to his wife and daughter. He would never have dreamed of sitting with his back to his family and visitors, grunting rudely.

But would my father speak? Would he come to the table? No he would not. Only '*Grunt*', which is why my mother blew a gasket.

'Your dinner's ready. Are you going to come and bloody eat it?'

'*Grunt.*'

Understandably, on this occasion, the grunting so infuriated my mother that she threw my father's whole dinner at him, past Auntie Betty and Olga, both seated politely on his side of the hatch. Auntie and Olga went pink and quiet and then wham! The dinner went flying through the hatch and showered the living room with fish and chips – home-made of course, and it is no fun making fish and chips in hot weather. Only a fraction of it reached my father.

'Here. Take your sodding dinner,' screamed my mother as she threw it. But it did no good. My father left the room, and we had our dinner without him, with my mother carrying on about what a miserable bastard he was, and that she was ashamed, and that he did this every bloody day, but to do it in front of visitors! That was the bloody limit. What a *drek* he was, all he thought about was his work and his *farkuckteh* factory. First it was the factory, then it was bloody Dennis, then the girls (his employees), then the dog, then me and her, last. Now she could barely eat a mouthful of the dinner, she felt sick. Sick of bloody cooking. She had no appetite.

Lusty ate up most of the fish and chips scattered about, and Olga and I picked up the rest. Auntie Betty made her a gin-and-tonic and tried to perk her up a little.

'I can't throw chips at my husband,' said Auntie. 'We haven't a dog to pick them up.' Ad probably had worries, she tried to reassure my mother (my father was still called Ad – short for Adolf, despite the smart name change to Arthur); he was perhaps working too hard, he always had been an anxious man, she was sure he was sorry, he'd come and have his dinner soon.

'Will he bugger,' moped my mother, exhausted by her outburst. 'Worries my arse. He can *gey in drerd*[44].'

---

[44] Drop dead, lit. go in the earth.

We ate our fish and chips. We all praised them. But this was just a temporary reprieve. My father had stayed upstairs and had no dinner. Nothing was going to change. Because the more you scream at a sulker, the more he sulks, and the more you sulk at a shouter, the more she will shout.

Luckily my mother had bridge to sustain her. If she could make up a bridge four at least once a week she was happy. She had a little event to work towards, she could make a cake with purpose – a marble cake, or stuffed-monkey cake, or cheesecake, or an upside-down plum cake or a strudel – then give it to her friends with tea in a break in the game. They would appreciate it and eat it. She could usually get Elsie, June and Gracie, Kathy's mother, to make up the four.

My mother had mixed feelings about Gracie. Yes, she was very fond of her, but it did rather get up my mother's nose that Gracie always won at bridge. She wasn't very good, she hadn't taken it seriously and practised for years as my mother had, but she was lucky.

'Beginner's luck,' my mother would say sourly, controlling her fury.

But she couldn't really be furious for long, because Gracie was such a cheery, bubbly little person and bridge was only a game, wasn't it? My mother could never have a *broyges*[45] with Gracie, because Gracie could never have

[45] Long-running falling out, life-long row.

kept it up. So they remained friends. But my mother did not mix socially with Pamela's mother, the Irish *kurve*, and not just because she couldn't play bridge. She knew Pamela's mother was up to no good, but she didn't know all of the no good she was up to, or what she was doing to Pamela. None of us guessed. Not me, not even Kathy or Gracie, and they lived just a few doors down from her house on the opposite side of the road and sometimes even chatted to her, which was more than my mother ever did, but Gracie still never guessed what was going on. No one could see any signs.

Gracie did, after all, have her own problems. Sometimes she couldn't make the bridge foursome. My mother knew why. She told me when I was a little older. It was because Gracie had been drinking. And why had she been drinking? Because of her husband. No wonder. The *schtunk*. Couldn't keep his hands off anyone. He'd even tried it on with her – my mother, his own wife's friend, if you don't mind, driving her back home one night in his car from a dinner and dance at the Orchard Hotel – the most glamorous place to go in Ruislip, where they served cocktails with red cherries and little brightly coloured Chinese umbrellas.

'How about it?' said Gordon, with his hand going up my mother's leg.

Naturally she had slapped his hand away and given him a mouthful. What a bloody cheek, with his wife's best friend, and did he think she even fancied him? My father at least was tall and handsome, but Gordon was a little short-arse with his red face. The *schtik drek*. He never tried that again. Here was a husband a hundred times worse than my father. And that was what Gracie had to put up with. It was beginning to grind her down and she found she didn't really have the energy to get up off the sofa and out of the house, even if it was to go just up the road to bridge at our house. Which all annoyed my mother, even though Gracie was one of her best friends, because if you pull out of a bridge game at short notice, it is difficult to find a replacement, which ruined my mother's vital weekly treat.

There was one good thing about Gracie being at home on the sofa so much of the time, as far as I was concerned. Sometimes, when my mother was in more of a temper than usual, I could go to Kathy's house, and if she was out, I could sit next to Gracie on the sofa and chat, while she had a little drink, which had a rather odd smell. She was never cross, nor did she ever shout. And she was much smaller than my mother, even with her clip-clop high heels. Lucky Kathy. Her mother seemed happy to me, but my mother knew that she wasn't.

She often remarked upon that embroidered waistcoat Gordon wore. It was turning Gracie into a *shikerer*[46]. It certainly wasn't Gracie who had embroidered the waistcoat for him, said my mother, then she clamped her mouth

---

[46] Heavy drinker, alcoholic.

shut, loyally refusing to say more. So who was it? The
clamped look showed that it was someone who had no
right at all to be embroidering for a married man. Perhaps
another *kurve* sort of woman, like Mrs Saunders. There
were obviously a few of them about in Ruislip, but no one,
except my mother, on occasions, actually said who. You
couldn't always tell a *kurve* from a normal woman here,
whereas in Cannes you could see them out and about,
walking boldly along the Croisette – the sea-front prom-
enade – deeply tanned, in tight skirts, low necks, high heels
and sometimes with a little dog in a jewelled collar.

'Look at that one,' said my father one balmy evening
as we walked back along the Croisette to Mme Zich's

Tea on the lawn in Ruislip. My mother, her friend Sophie Parker
and my father, 1956.

bed and breakfast establishment. 'I tell you, that one's a fellow.'

'Can't be,' said my mother. 'Look at that bust.'

'But look at those hands,' said my father. 'Look at the size of them.'

What had they been talking about? Why would a man, dressed as a woman *kurve,* be walking along the sea-front? It couldn't be anything that dreadful, because my parents were not upset by it. Spotting these *kurve* persons put them into a cheery mood. It perked up an evening stroll. 'Look at that one,' they would say. And 'how about that one!' Large hands were a give-away. But how could they be sure? Not all men had large hands. Gordon the waist-coat wearer's hands were small and pink, for example. But he lived in Ruislip, where things were different and *kurves* did not make people cheery.

17: THE OUTCAST AND HER DOG

Summer holidays again. Everyone was going away: Pamela to Ireland with her mother, Jacqueline to Pevensey Bay with her family, Kathy to stay with her auntie in Scotland. That left me by myself and Pamela's father, Albert, all alone in his big house and garden, with nothing to do but look after the bantams. There was no longer any need for him to make mouse palaces. We had all rather grown out of mouse breeding. Albert was left with plenty of time to worry about what his wife was getting up to all those miles away.

'Albert must be going mad,' my mother said to Gracie, who kept her up to date on the state of Pamela's parents, 'if he doesn't know what Cleonie's playing at and she won't come home.'

'You're right,' said Gracie. 'I saw him this morning. She promised she'd be back last week, she's still not back and poor Albert said he's tried to ring her and he can't get an answer. Nobody will tell him what's going on.'

'I could tell him,' said my mother, in a sinister tone.

'He should only know what she does. *Nebekh*[47]. He doesn't deserve it. He's mad about her, the cow. The bloody old fool. And she *schleps* poor Pamela all over the place with her.'

'Where?'

'Where d'you think?'

'Surely not. How d'you know that?'

'Ruth told me. You want to know anything, ask Ruth. She knows everything, and Maureen, one of her girls, told her, because Maureen always does Mrs Bradley's hair, and Mrs Bradley's daughter works at the grocer's for Mr Hardwick, she's on the till. She's seen Cleonie Saunders going in there with Pamela. She knew perfectly well what Cleonie was up to . . .'

'No! What? In the shop? How should she know? She's only guessing.'

'I'm telling you, she knows. It's after the shop's shut, and then Pamela sits in the shop and waiting room, and they disappear.'

'Where? What d'you mean?'

'I don't know where. How should I know? Somewhere. The stock-room? And they leave poor Pamela sitting there. She reads her comics or something.'

'Clarice, I don't believe it. What a terrible thing. What would she do that for?'

'Because then she's got an alibi, hasn't she? She's been

[47] Poor, unfortunate person.

out with her daughter. What can you do when you're out with your daughter? Poor Albert. It would never enter his head.'

'Terrible. And I thought it was just men, Clarice. Didn't you? What woman would do a thing like that?'

'Cleonie Saunders would.'

What would Mrs Saunders do? Pamela hadn't said anything about her mother and Mr Hardwick to me. Pamela had wanted to go to Ireland, because over there her uncle had horses, and she could ride and ride and ride on her own. She was mad keen to go to Ireland. It was heaven because in Ruislip you couldn't ride very fast. You first of all had to walk or trot a bit all the way along the high street, then down St Martin's Approach, then along past Paula Cattermole's house, into the woods, where you still couldn't even canter, until you got to the Common, and then you could have about five minutes cantering if you were lucky and you had to come all the way back again. That was your ride. But in Ireland, Pamela could gallop everywhere. For free.

Her mother didn't care, just so long as Pamela kept out of her way, which she did, for as long as she possibly could. So what was the matter with that? Sounded all right to me. I would have liked my mother to tell me to keep out of the way, but she never did. Until this summer, when she suddenly decided that I could go on holiday by myself. Perhaps she was sick of me hanging around with no one to play with and nagging for more rides or stuck indoors playing the piano. When one is on edge, someone practising the piano does not help. Yes, my mother adored *The Legend of the Glass Mountain*, by Nino Rota, but those arpeggios were difficult and I had to play them slowly, over and over and over again. Same with the crashing chords.

'It's giving me the screaming abdabs,' shouted my mother, busting. 'Your tea's ready.'

But Ruislip riding was expensive, and there wasn't much else I could do on my own. Ten weeks of summer holidays is a long time, and my mother was doing rather a lot of shouting. Most things made her shout: Cissy – '*shout shout miese meshuneh*[48] on her', stinking Mr Clanfield – '*fercuckteh* this, *farschtunkener* that', my father – *shout* – because he'd forgotten to bring a belt home that she needed, or to tell Dennis off, *farshtopteh kop*.[49] Why did she bother to ask him anything? He never remembered. He could *gey kakken*. And perhaps he could come home early for once in a lifetime, like bloody Dennis did.

I came home one day and my mother opened the front door. I put one foot into the hall, and off she went. *Shout, shout, shout*, about nothing at all. I'd heard that said: 'Before she'd/he'd even put her/his foot in the door', and now it had happened to me. One foot in, and already something was wrong.

[48] To wish lots of trouble on someone, lit. a strange death or a tragic end.
[49] Stuffed-up head. Thick.

Things seemed to be getting on top of my mother, perhaps because she and my father were planning to go on holiday with Celia and Bill to Israel. Why spend two whole weeks with Celia? We all knew that two hours with Cissy was almost more than any of us could endure. Why two weeks?

'She takes my *kishkes*[50] out!' my mother would cry out after just a phone call, but she was determined on this holiday, because she hoped she might get a straight answer out of Celia if Bill was there. It had become her life's quest. To get a straight answer out of Cissy. Surely, in a whole fortnight, she'd be able to.

'In a pig's ear,' said my father. 'You'll be lucky.'

But my mother still wanted to go to Israel and have some lovely hot sun, even if she would also get aggravation, and would probably not get her straight answer. So they were going anyway, to stay at the Red Rock Hotel in Eilat, and meanwhile what about me?

That's when my mother came up with her clever idea. I would go on a riding holiday to High Corners – a small hotel in the New Forest which we had visited together several times before, with Kathy and both our mothers, where it would just be riding, riding, riding. Even my father had been riding there. Not only did he adore horses, for riding and gambling purposes, but it also gave him the opportunity to wear another type of hat, with

[50] Intestines, guts.

complete riding outfit. He had ridden a camel dressed in appropriate Arab outfit, an elephant dressed in Big White Hunter outfit, and now he could do the English gentleman horse outfit. And for some reason both he and my mother liked the people who ran High Corners. These were the people who would look after me on my holiday. My mother had vetted them carefully: a married couple, Roger and Jane, and the wife's sister, Di, who was in charge of the horse-riding.

It was unusual for me and my parents to be keen on the same people. They had their friends, I had mine. There was very little crossover, except perhaps for Miss Hilary and Kathy's mother Gracie, but we all liked Roger, Jane and Di. Perhaps because they were country farm people. They didn't mind a bit of shouting or loudness, or jokes, or robust remarks. The country was somewhere between Ruislip and France, where my mother could feel comfortable. They liked her and my father. There were no markets, or azure sea or golden beaches or fabulous ice-creams, but there was shouting and crap – with horses, dogs and ducks you cannot avoid it – and lovely big, home-made country dinners, fresh air, heavenly scenery. My parents could not fault these people, and they trusted them absolutely with my welfare. They trusted them so much that they allowed me to take Lusty, which meant that they could go away to Israel with Celia and Bill, and not worry about either of us.

As for me, I was in heaven. I particularly adored Di.

She was a sort of informal version of Miss Hilary and everything I aspired to be. A brilliant rider, casually dressed in shirt and jodhpurs, but no waistcoat and tie; never wore a frock, hair rather wild, no Brylcreem but no official curls, and, just like Miss Hilary, she knew all about animals. Perhaps I couldn't have managed to stick to Miss Hilary's very particular outfits, and look exactly like a man, but I could probably copy Di without causing alarm. My loathing of frocks and dolls had already worried the family for years and put my mother under pressure. Dolls and frocks had been bought by my aunties, my father's sisters, curls were encouraged, invitations to ballroom dance classes had been issued, and my mother had to stop the flow. She knew that I would reject them, the aunties would be offended and I would be regarded as odd. In the aunties' world, girls were like those two at the wedding, who loved dressing up in frocks, and my mother wanted a girl like that, but she was out of luck.

'Just give her a cut and shampoo,' she had told her friend Ruth the hairdresser. 'No curls.' And she left me there, but the minute she was out of sight, Ruth defied her.

'Take no notice of this plain-Jane-and-no-nonsense business,' she said behind me to the assistant. 'Do her a nice set.' And the assistant did. My mother returned to a curly-headed, piss-faced child.

'Jesus Christ,' exclaimed my mother. 'What have you done to her?'

'We've made her look very pretty,' said Ruth, unashamed. 'Haven't we Mish?'

No answer.

'She'll get home, she'll like it. You wait.'

'Oh will she?' said my mother. 'I bloody hope you're right.' She screwed her face up as if a vile smell was hanging about just under her nose, paid the bill and drove me home. It was a five-minute car journey and during that time I successfully clawed out all the horrid curls with my bare hands, weeping with fury.

Strangely, my mother was rather proud. I had proved her right.

'She thinks she knows my daughter better than I do,' she told her other friends triumphantly over the weeks to come. 'I said no curls, so she gives her curls, and look what happens. Perhaps next time she'll do what I tell her.'

But here at High Corners, there was absolutely no risk of anyone disobeying my mother, or of any curls for me. There were no hairdressers for miles around. No one here wanted or needed them. On this, my first independent holiday, I had a bedroom in the staff bit of the hotel and didn't even have to wear a frock for dinner, even though I would be having my meals in the proper dining room, with another family and their son – a boy of my age. Because there were limits to what a girl of 13 could do alone. Staff ate later, and I could not sit by myself in the kitchen for meal-times.

I would, however, be allowed to look after my dog, Lusty, by myself – a rather tough thing to do – tough in the way that boys do things. For a start I had to make the dog's dinner in the hotel kitchen, which meant cutting up slabs of raw horse meat into chunks on a big wooden board with a sharp knife, and mixing it with cabbage and scrunchy biscuit or Shredded Wheat. This was a thrilling task, because my mother would never have allowed it. Perhaps she would have let me do it under close supervision, but she could never have borne to leave me alone with a big knife. But now she was hundreds of miles away, knew nothing of the big knife and nothing about the thrilling, galloping rides through the forest, past dangerous wild boars, with Lusty often running alongside the horses, also at risk. What if he had been kicked by flying hooves, gored by passing boars? What if I had fallen off and broken my legs or arms or neck? She didn't know, so she didn't mind, so Lusty and I had freedom for the first time ever.

This was a first experience for me of the terrors of responsibility. We'd be off on a ride, tearing through the forest, and suddenly Lusty would disappear. Where was he? Gored? Lost? Dead? It was terrifying, because I couldn't see Lusty all the time on these rides. I had to ride on, swept along with the other riders, and could only pray that my dog would return.

'Lusty's gone.'

'He'll turn up. He knows where we are.'

How did they know what he knew? How could they be so sure? This was a town dog. How would he know his way around a forest? I had never come across this before – a grown-up who wasn't worried about a disappearing dependent, who just assumed that my dog would come back, was safe, hadn't run off after boars. So I had to stay on the horse, keep up, and pretend I believed them. But what if a horse kicked him? When he was alongside, he was often too close, running right next to the horses' feet. A metal hoof could seriously damage his squashy face.

It never did. These grown-ups were always right. Lusty always found us, came back, stayed alive and he and the horses never collided. They seemed to know what they were doing. But I could never be sure, so the rides were always scary.

It wasn't all terror-rides on this holiday. There were other safer places to play: a squash court, and a small, home-made swimming pool at the far end of the lawn, dug out by hand in an oval shape and lined with white concrete. It wasn't very big, but it was big enough for a little swim after boiling hot riding or stinky mucking out. And I only rode once a day, then it was fiddling about with the horses, grooming, breathing down their velvety noses like that woman Barbara Woodhouse, which they seemed to like. And there were the ducks, Muscovy ducks who had just had ducklings. Lovely little fluffy yellow ducklings. If only I could take two home I could perhaps have a modest duck colony myself, and sell duck eggs. This was my plan. Surely our garden was big enough. The shed could be a duck home, a small bath could be dug into the ground in the vegetable area. I saw a whole new future taking shape. Farming. Even if it wouldn't have all the advantages of the country – boars, forests, and deer wandering about the garden.

Waking up early one morning at High Corners to take Lusty for a walk, I looked out of my ground floor window across the lawn and there was a deer, just standing looking. Nothing moved at all. Magic, just for a few moments.

Oddly enough, the more serious horrors came from unexpected places. The first trouble came from the squash court, where I played daily with the boy whose table I shared. I happened to have the same T-shirt as him – thin blue-and-white striped – and the same jeans. What a coincidence. We could have been brother and sister, until the squash got out of hand, because I won too much. Soon the squash court wasn't so much fun. It was a fight, with me winning, and the boy became more and more sulky and furious. Occasionally I lost, and he cheered up a bit, but then I won again and he sulked. We stopped laughing and talking, we just played in a fury, both red in the face, while Lusty waited outside, until I got out. And then I won once too often.

'Why d'you always have to win? You bloody Jew,'

shouted the boy, threw his racket on the floor and ran away.

What? I had never been called such a thing before. What did that have to do with squash? What a horrible boy. What a horrid thing to say. I came out of the squash court and there was Lusty, sitting waiting. So I sat down next to him and had a short cry. But what should I do next? I couldn't play with that boy anymore. Obviously not. If he didn't like Jews and thought I was a bloody one, then obviously I could not sit at his table for breakfast, lunch and dinner. So that night I told the hotel people that I wanted to eat my dinner in the kitchen.

'Why? What's the matter?'

I couldn't tell them why. What if I did? Then the boy would get into trouble and then he'd hate me even more. But luckily no one screamed and shouted or demanded an answer, as my mother would have done. So I was allowed to eat my dinner alone in the kitchen with the dog. Perfect.

But I could only do this for a few days, because there was a plan for me to sit with some newly arrived children. This was another set up. These two girls' parents were Celia's friends, and so vaguely my mother's friends, and Celia had said they were very nice girls, so who was my mother to argue? She had to take Celia's word for it. We were under Celia's command again. The invisible Threat worked in all sorts of ways. I had to play with the two nice girls. And my mother also benefited from it, because it meant that during their stay I would be doubly supervised. The girls' parents would see how I was getting on, and send an emergency telegram to the Red Rock if anything dangerous had happened. A mother could never have too much reassurance, and even then she couldn't really relax until she was home, so she rang High Corners the minute she got home to England.

My mother was right to worry, because things didn't run as smoothly as she would have liked. For a start these girls had a Scottie dog with them who did not like Lusty. When your dog sides with you when you're in trouble, as I had been with the Squash Boy, then anyone or anything who dislikes your dog is your enemy, and these girls didn't appreciate Lusty. They thought him ugly.

'Er, what a funny-looking dog. Its face is all squashed up.'

'Has it walked into a wall?' They both laughed together in a little gang of two. And they wore smart kilts and jumpers. In a stable yard. How stupid. So what if my mother had planned that I would play with them? I didn't like them. Or their silly dog, which was next to them, in its silly plaid collar, snarling at Lusty. Then suddenly it attacked. It flew at Lusty and bit him in the side. And what did those girls do? They just laughed. So I gave one of them a huge shove, and she fell over, then she cried, then she ran to tell her parents, because she'd grazed her knee. How pathetic.

No friends left. Who cares? I hadn't chosen them. I still had my dog, which always helps when one is an outcast. This was a bit like the Hartley's peas competition all over again. I was in trouble for nothing. Other people behaved badly and got away with it: the Squash Boy, the vicious Scottie and the giggling sisters didn't even get a whisper of a telling off, but I got strange looks.

'What an odd child,' thought the grown-ups. 'She falls out with everyone, she won't tell us why, then she pushes that nice girl over, she stays in the kitchen. There must be something wrong with her. Her mother should never have let her come here alone.' I could tell from the looks that that was probably what they were thinking.

Next morning the dog was in trouble. A lump was growing on his side over the Scottie bite. Luckily the next day my mother was arriving to collect me with her friend Jean Riley, a nurse, the very nurse who had been my mother's midwife when I arrived, and they had stayed friends. So not only was my mother coming, but she was bringing a medical person. Lusty and I would be saved. And just in the nick of time. The lump was growing bigger and Lusty looked rather glum.

It was a bit of luck for me that the Squash Boy and his family had left the day before my mother's arrival, which meant I could tell her about him in detail. And he was *goyim*, which did him no favours as far as my mother was concerned.

'The little *mamser*,' said my mother, heating up. 'Did

you hear that, Jean? They only get that sort of thing from their parents.' And to me, 'I hope you bloody told them. Did you?'

'No.'

'Why not? I suppose the little *drek* got away with it, did he? What a disgrace.'

'Terrible,' agreed Jean. 'Never mind. Take no notice of that sort of person. They're not worth it. They're ignorant.'

'I'd have given him a mouthful if I'd been here,' said my mother in a righteous fury.

She liked to speak her mind. She didn't mind having a shout at people who were clearly in the wrong. Who cared if everyone was staring because she was having a shout? If anyone behaved badly then they deserved a *brokh*[51] and she would give them one. But annoyingly she didn't give one to the Scottie girls, because their parents were still there, were friends of Celia's, and were Jewish, and although I had complained about them and their horrid dog, I felt that my mother did not give them what they deserved. And things were not so clear cut. I had, after all, pushed one over. Only because she deserved it, but my mother, disappointingly, seemed to side with them a little. They wore skirts and pretty clothes, which was what she had always wished for in a daughter, and it blinded her to their faults.

'What's wrong with them? They seem very nice girls to me. I don't know what's the matter with you. All

51 Curse.

right, you couldn't play with that other *drek*, but what's the matter with them? *Blah blah blah.*'

But it was handy, in a way, that I had had difficulties, because that meant that I deserved a reward. And the reward was two darling little yellow, fluffy Muscovy ducklings that we took home to London in a box. Meanwhile Lusty's suffering became clear in the car. By then the bite had swollen up into a monster lump. What luck that we had a nurse with us. Jean sat next to Lusty and squeezed pus out of his lump as we drove along. Now that we were far away from the girls and their parents, my mother was free to be outraged.

Miss Hilary the vet, my heroine, with Lusty in the garden.
Ruislip 1953.

'Bloody cheek, Jean. What were they doing leaving those girls with a vicious dog? They had no right to do that.'

'You're right, Clarice. That was a nasty bite. Dear me. I need a hanky.' Squeeze, squeeze. 'Don't look, Clarice. Oh dear,' squeeze. 'Good job we got here.'

'Good job you got here, you mean. The little stinkpot.'

Sometimes, my mother's outrage played in my favour. She had said yes to the two ducklings, perhaps because this time the anger stopped her from carefully considering what it might be like to have two ducks in a London garden.

18: SUB-STANDARD HUSBANDS

Blanche visited a lot during the summer. During the day, when my father was at work and if the weather was fine, she and my mother would sit on the lawn on blue canvas relaxa-chairs chatting and drinking Martini or Dubonnet, with lemonade, ice and lemon. From my shed, half-way down the garden, or from the duck enclosure next to it, or from the shady lounge, with its French windows wide open, I could eavesdrop if I felt like it, while I was playing jacks or five-stones on the carpet. Or I could drown them out with the piano. Best for drowning out was *The Glass Mountain* – a safe piece to play because my parents adored it. They were rather proud of my playing and never tired of the music. They sometimes got a bit sick of Bartók's *Hungarian Dances*, but they never sickened of *The Glass Mountain*. It had everything that my parents loved: dramatic, crashing chords, huge, rolling arpeggios and a grand and luscious tune which tore at your heart-strings. But it did mean that I missed chunks of my mother's conversation with Blanche.

They seemed able to sit out in the sun for ages, even if the weather was boiling, because they both wanted to be brown. They were both fairly brown already, but they both needed to top it up which they did by sitting in the sun whenever they could and covering themselves in dark brown, greasy Ambre Solaire sun-tan oil, because with a sun-tan they both felt healthier and more attractive. With a sun-tan you looked as if you had been somewhere exotic, and not just been stuck in Ruislip. The scent of Ambre Solaire drifted across the lawn, reminding us all of Cannes. A heavenly smell. It looked rather lovely out there on the lawn, but they were not happy. The sun and the garden were not enough. It only looked like enough. Blanche desperately wanted a more exciting life.

'You're so lucky, Clarice. You don't realize.'

'What's so lucky? I'm stuck here, day in, day out. He's at his bloody factory, and do you know what, Blanche? He comes home and he doesn't even notice what I look like.'

'He must do. He's such a charming man, of course he notices.'

'Charming, my arse. I left my curlers in all day last week, I didn't even realize, then he comes home, I remembered they're still in, I still had my pinny on, and do you think he noticed? Did he bugger.'

'Oh I can't believe it, Clarice. He's so much more talkative than Stanley. Stanley barely says a word to me all day. I wish I could meet someone handsome and exciting who'd just come along and take me away. I could start again. A new life.'

'Are you mad, Blanche? At least Stanley is a gentleman. You should hear Ad when you're not around. D'you think he talks to me the way he talks to you? No he doesn't. All I get is a grunt or a *grepse*[52]. Charming? Do me a favour. Only one charming man comes to see me, and that's Mr Chapman. Now that is what I call charming. He has manners.'

Mr Chapman was the estate agent. He visited because my father wanted to move his works out to Ruislip. For how long could he keep driving up and down Western Avenue? The traffic was shocking, it was getting worse, he was worn out with it so he needed to work locally. Perhaps then he wouldn't be so bloody exhausted, said my mother, and perhaps he'd get home at a reasonable hour. And property out here would be cheaper. My mother could have a look at a few places with Mr Chapman, and if she saw anything she thought was good, she could tell my father, then he'd come and look at it. He didn't have time to go round looking at all the *drek* estate agents showed you first.

Luckily Mr Chapman was really a very nice man. Clean, smart, interesting, funny. He wore a waistcoat and a check shirt and hat. He seemed to cheer my mother up. When Mr Chapman turned up she was never in a

[52] Belch.

temper, and if she knew he was coming she would often make a cake: chocolate and vanilla swirl sponge, upside-down plum cake, or pear and almond flan, covered in apricot glaze, or apple strudel in a Robert Carrier pastry, very light and made with icing sugar, and sometimes even a stuffed monkey, which was a bit of a perform-ance – the same strudel pastry, but stuffed with all sorts of dried and crystallised fruit and nuts and ginger. I rec-ognized, even as a child, that my mother's cakes were of a very high standard. So it wasn't surprising that Mr Chapman often dropped in if he was in the area, and he also found properties my mother could look at while I was at school.

But she didn't tell Blanche about Mr Chapman's visit last week, or about the premises they'd been to see. Why not, if Mr Chapman was so charming? Mr Chapman would bring his sandwiches that his wife had made for his lunch, and while he and my mother were out search-ing for factories, they would sometimes stop for a picnic and share them. Mr Chapman couldn't eat them all himself and why waste food? My mother often told me that food always tastes nicer if someone else makes it. So that was very nice of Mr Chapman to share his sand-wiches.

So he kept looking for factories, and while he was at it, he sometimes showed my mother the odd house, because my mother was interested in houses and interi-ors, being a bit artistic. She had had our house decorated rather boldly. We had red seats in the kitchen, red Formica work-surfaces, purple and turquoise striped wallpaper on the hatch wall, wall lights with twirly gold brackets and apricot coloured shades, whereas Blanche's house was rather drab inside. There were no particular colours.

On went my mother and Blanche, comparing and contrasting: Mr Chapman, Blanche's husband, stinky Mr Clanfield, with his chicken-shit-spattered brown corduroy trousers and his great enormous stomach sticking out. However did Mrs Clanfield put up with him? Horace the coalman – who also had manners, according to my mother, and was a gentleman, even if he was a coalman and covered in soot – and men in general, particularly my father, about whom my mother was right as usual. Blanche didn't know the half of it. Although her husband was probably worse. I'd only seen him a couple of times, he was always reading the paper, and all he'd said was 'Good afternoon/morning', whatever it was, and he looked very old and dull, like Blanche's home decor. At least my father had his hat collection and, when he was not sulking, often wore his hats: a fez, a keffiyeh, a sailor's hat, a Sherlock Holmes hat, a French beret, a Russian fur hat in the winter and, for a laugh, and when he was in a particularly cheery mood, the donkey's ears.

'I need a new belt,' said Blanche. 'This one's beginning to look a little shabby.'

'Don't buy a belt, Blanche. Are you mad? Why didn't you ask me for belts? We've got belts up to here. I'll take you to the factory, you can choose belts. For Christ's sake don't buy any more belts.'

'Oh no, Clarice, I couldn't . . .'

So the next time my mother went up to town, she took Blanche to see the factory, where she left her with my father, to have a tour and choose some belts, because my mother had other things to do. She wanted to buy fish and fruit and vegetables from Berwick Street market, which was just round the corner and my mother loved markets. They reminded her of France, although they were nothing like as good. For a start you couldn't as easily pick the fruit up and squeeze it as you could in France, although you could more or less choose your own things and have a shout. And what did my mother want to go round the factory for? She'd seen the factory, she was sick of the factory. Always the factory, the factory. She'd got belts. Why did she want to hang about while Blanche sodded around looking at belts?

Meanwhile, my ducks had grown up. They were not as beautiful as they had been as ducklings. Although some of their feathers were a handsome dark green, they had developed dark pinky-red lumpy bits round their bills, which were not attractive, but on the other hand I had trained them rather cleverly to accompany me down the garden path. I would lift a stone or slab and spiders, centipedes and other creepy crawlies would jump out but the ducks would snap them up and save me. I had called them Dickens and Jones and loved them, but my mother was going off them a bit. The bigger they grew, the more they poo-ed and the less she liked them. She had not really taken on my dream of a duck farm and duck-egg business, which I was in the process of setting up, in a modest way, in the garden.

And then I had to leave them in her charge while I went for a short holiday to Pevensey Bay with Jacqueline and her family. When I returned the ducks were gone, given to Mr Clanfield, the chicken farmer. I was furious with my mother. What a horrible, cruel thing to do – to give my pets away without my permission. He had hundreds of ducks, she said, and they would be happier there. I could go and see them at Clanfield's if I wanted to. She took me there when she next went to buy eggs and a chicken, and there, as far as the eye could see, were chickens and ducks. Hundreds and thousands of ducks, and somewhere among them, my very own Dickens and Jones. I thought I saw them in the distance.

How could she have done that? And why? But she was unrepentant. The ducks had shat once too often in the wrong place. She'd come in through the French windows in the piano room without realizing that she'd stepped in duck poo, and then trodden it all across the pale green carpet, and that had been it. Goodbye ducks.

Did she think that was a good enough excuse? Just

because she didn't look where she was going or notice what she was treading in, my ducks had to be banished and my plans for a duck-egg farm wrecked. Could she have done anything worse? Yes, but luckily I didn't find out until I was 21.

Here is the true story. My ducks did not have a pleasant life at Mr Clanfield's poultry farm. They were murdered by him almost the minute they got there and then a terrible thing happened: my parents ate them. But even that wasn't the worst possible thing. There was another grotesque horror to come. Did my parents enjoy their evil dinner? No they did not, because the ducks were a bit too tough, and one of them was full of eggs. Eggs. My planned eggs. This was a blow to me, even at 21. Thank heavens I never knew at the time.

19: THE NOSE

My new friend Lynne Harrison was the rudest girl in our school. I had never met such a rude girl. Not only did she know absolutely filthy, disgusting words which I had never even heard before, but she used them to describe our teachers. To appreciate how shocking this was, you first need to know what these teachers were like.

They had a teacher look, most of them, and wore tweed suits, sensible walking shoes, thick, woolly or lisle stockings (some of the younger, more modern ones wore nylons) and pastel-coloured blouses, sometimes with a little embroidery round the collar, in the same colour as the blouse. These were the clothes that Miss Harold our headmistress wore, setting the code for the rest of the staff, and many of them followed her example to the letter, occasionally wearing a less formal cardigan, or twin set, rather than a jacket, and many of them, like Miss Titmuss, the Jew shaker, had a shelf-bosom – a solid bank of bosom with barely a central divide.

Hairstyles were, in the main, fairly rigid. The hair was

moulded into helmets, or buns, or stiff sausage curls, or
grey waves, firm as metal, or a smooth top cap area over
the skull, with a ruff of frizzy curls around the bottom. In
those days, perms and sets began in largish curls, which
soon turned to frizz, especially after a wash, unless one
put them into curlers night after night. But it was Miss
Ashley's hair that we marvelled at. Tall and thin, with a
long horse-face, she parted her hair strictly to one side,
it lay smoothly against her head until it got to about ear
level, and after that it was rolled into identical grey
sausages, a row of three down each side, with four at the
back, down to neck level. If Miss Ashley were to come
and stand beside you and lean over your desk to glare at
your work, however frightened you were you had to try
and look down the inside of those curls. You had to get
the angle right so that you could look straight down a
curl, because there, inside, holding each one in place was
a yellow pipe cleaner. We mocked her pipe-cleaner curls
because we all hated her because she was so strict and
cruel. Run one step along the corridor, speak one word
before you made it to the playground, and she would
have you.

One sunny day, when it was time for morning break,
the lawn was green outside, the sky blue, the weather
balmy and I felt suddenly happy and wanted to get outdoors quickly, I jumped down the three steps into the
garden. I did not walk, as I was supposed to do. But bad
luck, Miss Horrid Ashley saw me.

'Detention,' she snapped, with a cruel smirk. 'Back you go, and then you may come out of the door properly. Walking.' The next day I got a half-hour's Latin detention. An unfair punishment.

So when rude Lynne Harrison made up a filthy name for Miss Ashley, we became best friends. And we made up names for all of them: for the spiteful, round-faced French mistress, whose pale yellow jumper cuffs were grubby, and still she had had the nerve to call me a slut because one of my sandals was undone; a c-word for Miss Cadman, who waited outside the classroom doors, red-turkey-faced, waiting for us to open them for her, who couldn't teach Latin for toffee; and an f-word for Miss Foxton, who poisoned geography forever. The filthiest words for the most frightening teachers. But there weren't really many of those. Some we admired, some we almost loved, and so going to school wasn't too bad.

Then one day, I was walking along the road to school, nearly at the gate, and Lynne Harrison drove past in the car with her father, and he leaned out of the car window and shouted at me, 'Hallo Conky.' He must have thought this was funny, because he laughed. What did he mean? I asked Lynne Harrison in the cloakrooms.

'What does conky mean?'

'It means you've got a long nose. A conk is a nose.'

Had I? I didn't know that. I worried about it all day and when I got home I went up to my mother's bedroom and looked in the mirror, because she had a mirror with

extensions which showed your face from the side. Mr
Harrison was right. My nose was enormous. What's
more, it had a bobble on the end. And I couldn't help but
notice that my actual head was very small and I looked a
bit like Mr Turnip on the telly, who was a scarecrow with
a small, round head and wispy hair. And a long nose. I
realized, for the first time, that from the side I looked
ugly, and I didn't want anyone to notice.

From then on I worried about my nose, and always
tried, when possible, to sit in a corner seat on the tube so

Me, the nose and Lusty, 1956.

that no one could see it from the side. But I did not tell my mother what Mr Harrison had said. It would have only caused more trouble, because my mother might easily have tarred Lynne with the same brush. For a start, the Harrisons were Catholic – a low-level sort of Christian with poor hygiene, in my mother's opinion, so they were not off to a good start – and then to be calling me rude names on top of that would be bound to throw her into a fury, and there would be a *brokh* on Mr Harrison, and a risk that Lynne would be banned from the house, and I would never, ever hear the end of it, so although Mr Harrison was a pig and deserved his *brokh*, I kept it a secret.

20: THE ROAD TO RUIN

My mother often seemed to be increasingly irritated by Gracie, although she felt sorry for her at the same time. She was cross about the dirty cooker, the unreliable attendance at bridge games, and the drinking.

'Gracie's drinking too much,' she told my father one evening. 'I went to see her yesterday and I'm telling you, she was already *shicker* at eleven o'clock in the morning. Eleven o'clock! Look what bloody Gordon is doing to her. It's his fault. I don't know why she puts up with him and his *kurve*.'

My father grunted as usual. This particular *kurve* seemed not to interest him as much as the French ones in Cannes had done. Here in Ruislip it was made clear that *kurves* brought only misery. And perhaps my mother was infuriated not just with Gordon and his *kurve*, but with my father refusing to support her view or even express an opinion. What was the point her trying to talk to my father?

'I may as well talk to the bloody wall,' she shouted.

But the Wall took no notice. And who else could she

talk to? She didn't like to tell all her bridge friends about Gracie's drinking, so she went on telling my father, which gave her an outlet, but not a good enough one, and she was still annoyed, which made her sound as if she was annoyed with Gracie. But she wasn't. Only worried.

I gathered, from overhearing my mother talk to the Wall, that Gracie had been drinking more and more lately. She'd begun to drink more to help her through all the parties her husband took her to, with all his friends from work. She felt she couldn't keep up with them. Standing about, drinking, chatting. About what? What did she know about Foreign Office business? They were all so smartly dressed and that woman was always around. She'd made Gordon that hand-embroidered waistcoat, which he often wore, then people would say, 'What a marvellous waistcoat! Where did you get that?' and he'd say, 'Somebody made it for me.'

'Who? Your wife?'

'No. She hasn't got the patience. Ha ha.'

So naturally, in that situation, Gracie would need another drink. And then he'd send her home in a cab and stay out all night. Presumably with that bitch who'd made the waistcoat. Gracie knew, my mother knew, everybody knew, and Gracie would feel humiliated, insignificant and stupid, a cast-off, so she'd just sit in a corner and have another drink, until in the end she stopped going. Why bother? Gordon didn't care.

Occasionally he would insist on a party at their home,

which meant Gracie had to be hostess. My parents would go, and so would I, being Kathy's friend.

'*Kuk im on*,'[53] my mother would whisper conspiratorially to the Wall at one of these events. 'He's doing it again. *Gib a kuk*. He's got his hands on that woman's *tokhes*. The *alter kakker*.[54] *Kuk*.'

This is where the Yiddish came in particularly useful. Nobody knew what my mother was talking about. There were no other Jews at these parties. Meanwhile, in the crowded front room of Kathy's house, Gordon could slyly pinch bottoms without being noticed, but my mother spotted him. As well as a super-sensitive nose, she had eyes like a hawk, especially when she was suspicious.

'Hawk-eye,' my father would say proudly, when he was in a chattier mood.

But if Gordon thought he could get away with that sort of thing when my mother was around, then he was wrong. And it wasn't just her who noticed. I noticed as well. I never told Kathy about it, because you can't really tell your friend that her father is always touching bottoms. It isn't a nice thing to do, and she might be ashamed, and the year before, he had even pinched my bottom. So now I too was on the look-out, for two reasons: one, to keep out of his way and ensure he never caught me again, and two, to see who else he was pinching.

---

[53] Look at him.
[54] Lecher, lit. old shitter.

And another odd thing I noticed was that nobody ever complained or said anything. Perhaps, like me, they were all embarrassed, but they were grown-ups. Surely they could have stopped it? But they didn't. None of the women whose bottoms he stroked or pinched told him off, or even looked cross. And nor did Gracie seem to notice. But I knew that she did really, because I heard her tell my mother.

'Do you think I'm bothered?' she asked my mother. 'She can have him as far as I'm concerned. She's welcome. She's doing me a favour. I've had enough of it to last me a lifetime.'

I knew what 'it' meant by now. Danielle Hewitt and her friends were always talking about 'it', Miss Matthews had told us about 'it'. 'It' sounded really horrid. I didn't like to think about 'it' if possible, so I could see why Gracie was sick of 'it'. Hopefully I would never, ever have to do 'it' myself. I could hardly understand why it was allowed. If playing Doctors and Nurses was naughty and bottoms could hardly be talked about, then how come that sort of thing was permissible? And even more puzzling, how come my mother and Mrs Walmesley seemed to want their husbands to do it? To me, Gracie was the sensible one. I heard her describe the sort of life she would prefer: 'a nice man to take you out to a lovely meal now and again, a few jokes, a dance, and that would be it. None of that, thank you.'

*

Meanwhile, Gracie's dog, Gaddy, was spending more and more time lying outside on the pavement, and seemed to be getting thinner. I felt very worried about her. But my mother seemed to have hardened her heart where Gaddy was concerned. Gracie was her main worry. Gaddy was just a by-product. But it seemed to me that Gaddy had had a difficult life, full of rejection.

My mother had turned against her soon after she gave birth to four puppies. Only two survived, Wootzie and Lusty. Wootzie (short for 'Woots a matter then?') went to live with Auntie Millie, who adored and pampered him. Lusty nearly died of gastroenteritis, but did his mother care? No, she did not. She ignored him in his time of need, which is what dogs do if they think their puppies have had it, but my mother never forgave her. To her, a mother – any sort of mother, even a dog mother – should never, ever, even under the most difficult of circumstances, refuse to look after a sick child. Lusty survived and for a couple of years he and Gaddy lived happily together with us, occasionally racing round and round the garden in mad circles, and then suddenly Gaddy was given to Celia.

Why give an innocent dog to Celia, who lived in a flat in town? I was only nine at the time, so I never questioned it, but soon Gaddy was back again, rescued from Celia, who never took her for walkies or played with her, and then wondered why she crapped on the carpet. Then Gaddy was sent down the road to Kathy's house. My mother could still not forgive the poor dog for neglecting her son. But luckily Gracie and Kathy loved her, and her rotten life of rejection seemed to have perked up, until now, when even Gracie was in no fit state to love her. Gracie stayed indoors on the sofa, while Gaddy lay outside on the pavement.

21: THE COFFEE BAR

Soon my mother would have little time for bridge games or sitting on the sunny lawn in relaxa-chairs, or picnics with Mr Chapman, or worrying about Gracie, or chatting to Miss Hilary or Mr Clanfield or Horace. Or even me, because the factory removal was on hold. My parents had a new and thrilling plan: to open a coffee bar. That meant that this year, for the first time in my experience, my mother had a job.

It was 1956, coffee bars were the new thing, and my mother was opening one. A couple of years ago Gina Lollobrigida had opened the Moka coffee bar in Frith Street, just a couple of streets away from my father's factory, with thrilling new Gaggia Italian coffee-making machines. The Mediterranean had come to Soho, and La Lollo had been only round the corner. There was something else that united my parents and cheered them up, rather like the *kurves* of Cannes had done – La Lollo's bosoms. Italy was, after all, next to France. You could do it in a day trip. You drove along the coast to

Menton, a lovely drive, across the border and into Alassio, with its wide sandy beaches, big waves and fabulous ice-creams, and women like La Lollo all over the place. And now my mother could recreate all that in Soho.

At last she was in business. On the ground floor of my father's factory in Poland Street. Why have a belt showroom, when one could have a coffee bar? The showroom could go upstairs in the little office next to the factory. Belts were ordinary, but coffee bars were all the rage, and my mother's, called La Ronde – reflecting her love of France – was one of the first. She had brought a touch of Cannes to London.

It is hard work setting up a coffee bar, especially as my mother was baking her own cakes. She did her fabulous strudel, cheesecake, chocolate marble cake, and lemon meringue pie, and sometimes, once the coffee bar was up and running, Celia would come along and sit languidly on one of the high coffee-bar stools at the end of the counter for free coffee and cake, smiling occasionally in a rather coquettish way at male customers, because she needed a little outing now and again. Uncle Bill's work kept him busy and Celia was often alone during the day. What was she meant to do with herself? She couldn't stay in all day and there were not many places she could go alone. It wasn't much fun going out to lunch by herself, but the coffee bar was one place that she could visit, and it was just a few steps from Berwick Street market, where the fruit and veg were a *metsieh*[55], so she could also do her shopping there.

'Give me a hand Celia, can't you?' my mother would occasionally ask. 'Get up off your *tokhes* and do something, for Christ's sake.'

'But what shall I do, Clarice?' asked Celia, looking helpless and bendy as usual.

'Clear some tables,' snapped my mother, but rather half-heartedly, because she knew it was pointless. It would take more energy than it was worth to get Celia to do anything, other than sit and simper.

And what was I meant to do while my mother was so busy? I couldn't be left alone in the house, I quite plainly could not rely on neighbours – look what had happened at the Andrews'. I couldn't hang about a coffee bar, Celia was no help as a child minder, even when she was on the premises, and I couldn't play about the nearby streets in town as I could in Ruislip, because Soho was a dangerous place. It was full of traffic, and *kurves,* and with *kurves* one usually finds badly behaved men, and having driven and walked around Soho with my parents when visiting the factory, I had seen the narrow streets, and gambling places and little clubs with rude pictures of women in the windows and dark stairways with sparkly tinsel in the doorway, which my mother didn't like to talk about and nor did I want to

[55] Bargain.

know about in detail. Or think about. Clearly this was
not a suitable place for a girl.

And then my mother came up with the answer. She
would have an au pair. Preferably French. Then there'd
be someone in when I got home, I could practice talking French, so could my father – my mother did not
need to practise – and my mother would be able to stay
up in town and not worry.

My mother found Juliette, a friend from Cannes.
Juliette was not your average au pair. She was not a young
girl, but a woman in her forties with a grown-up daughter left behind in Cannes, but she was perfect, because a)
she was French, b) her cleaning and cooking and tidiness
standards, like all the French, were tremendously high,
but best of all, c) she had the most terrible sailor
boyfriend, with whom she had frightful rows. He had
even, on several occasions when he was really drunk and
furious with Juliette, put a poo in an envelope through
her letterbox. She was escaping him, which gave her and
my mother something thrilling to talk about – ghastly
men. My mother and she would compare and contrast
Bertrand the sailor with my father, and recount in detail
their misdemeanours. Both men were like the girl with
the curl. When they were good they were very, very
good – both mad on boats, both wore French sailor outfits: the navy beret, string vest and khaki shorts which my
father so loved, both were cheery and amusing (I knew
because we'd all been out for a picnic in Bertrand's fishing

boat), both knew how to enjoy themselves, both were handsome, both loved the betting shop – which had its merits and its disadvantages; but when they were bad, they were very, very bad. My father with his horrible sulking, and Bertrand with his drunkenness and shit-posting. I thought the sulking much worse than the posting, but to my mother and Juliette, it was a tie. Both men, to them, were equally insufferable. But magically, with Juliette around, my father's sulking evaporated, perhaps because my mother's mood was so much more cheery. Not only did she now have a career, but she had darling Juliette around to constantly yak and have endless laughs with.

Juliette (left), my mother and Bertrand on his boat, Cannes, 1955.

Meanwhile, my mother also had the coffee-bar menus to work out, the new staff to interview and select, the workmen and decor to supervise, because she knew, as with me and my father, that if she did not supervise properly, people were bound to make a mess of things. Opening a coffee bar was a huge responsibility, and cost an arm and a leg, my mother said, and unlike my father, she was not prepared to have some lazy bastard like Dennis not doing his or her share, but still she was in heaven. For the last few weeks of the summer term, while I was at school, she'd been there preparing. She and my father and Juliette (who needed to learn English) had been singing around the house.

'Hold my haaaand, I'm a scrubber in Poland Street.' Instead of a *Stranger in Paradise*. They'd been singing it while cleaning away up there. They sang it at home to each other, through the hatch. My father, the Wall, had come back to life.

22: THE VERY RUDE MAN

After school I often met Pamela at the station, and we would walk up Windmill Hill together and then stay talking at the top by the roundabout before we went home. My road went off to the right, Pamela's road went off to the left. We were slower in the summer and talked for longer, and from the top of the hill, looking away from the station and High Street, we had a rather good view down to the woods towards the lido, which is where we would have preferred to be going.

Anyway, I wasn't looking that way. I had my back to the woods and was looking down the other side of the hill, back towards the station, and Pamela was facing me, when suddenly, I noticed a man coming up the hill behind her. He had on a rather shapeless brown hat, with the hat bit in a dome shape and the brim rather wavy, and he had a large, pink thumb sticking out of the front of his raincoat. That's what I thought in the first few seconds, but then I realized it was not a thumb, because the man's hands were at his sides. It had to be a penis. I just knew it, although I'd never seen such a thing before. I gave a little scream, and pushed Pamela to alert her.

'Look, look at that man. Look.'

'What?'

'Look. His thing!'

'What thing?'

'You know.'

'Err! Where?'

But Pamela didn't see anything, because the man had come up behind her, and by the time he passed by and came into her view, he had his back to us, then he went off, round the roundabout and back down the hill, towards Ruislip Manor station.

Along came Mrs Geeley, a neighbour, on her bicycle. I told her what had happened.

'Go home and call the police!' cried Mrs Geeley, looking a bit ruffled.

So we both ran to my house and told my mother.

'Phooey!' she shouted. 'Bloody disgusting,' and rang the police at once.

This was a rude and terrible thing for me to have seen. Men's bottoms were not something that were even talked about in our house. No wonder, if the police were to be called and a man possibly arrested, just for showing a particular front bit of his bottom. Although the bowel part was under fairly constant supervision and discussion, when it came to bottoms doing other things, especially men's, then no one would talk about it. There was a bit of a clash here. There were obviously strong links between the two sorts of bottom, they were more or less in the same place, weren't they? Right next to each other, but in my life they were light years apart. One was a normal everyday function, the other was filth fantasy from another planet, which is probably why my mother strode quickly past the shops in Soho because she knew, and I guessed, that there were horrible bottom things going on in there.

Not until about 13 years later, when I had read *Portnoy's Complaint*, did I realize that my mother's attitude to bottoms was not a general one. And it would put me into rather a quandary. The average mother, I would find, did not enquire about the state of her child's bowels daily. If she was a Christian, it was unlikely that she would ever enquire at all. But from what I could gather from my mother, the bottom must be washed and its functions and productions noted every day, but it must never be touched other than for cleansing purposes, and only via a flannel, never with a bare hand, meaning your own. The thought of anyone else's bare hand going anywhere near it was too terrible to even contemplate. From what I could gather, anything to do with bottoms other than digestion and washing must be strictly ignored, which meant that you had to think about it and not think about it simultaneously and frequently. This would be even more difficult for me when, and if, boyfriends ever came along. But for now, it was a subject best avoided, especially when it applied to a man.

The police soon arrived. My mother had been standing on a kitchen chair in the hall attempting to fit a new bulb into the light fitting. So as she opened the front door to the policemen – there were two in plain clothes – she pointed it out to them.

'Could you help me, please?' she asked what looked like the chief policeman. He had a pink face and blond wavy hair which he had parted on the left and tried to flatten sideways. 'I can't get this bulb in.' The chair was still in position.

'Madam,' said he crossly, 'I am carrying out an investigation.'

And he left my mother standing by the chair under the useless light fitting. She tried to follow us into the living room, but was banned. And bad luck, this was the piano room. She couldn't even listen through the hatch. This lounge was a haven of privacy in which the policemen wanted to interview me and Pamela alone.

'What was the man doing?' asked the policeman. Pamela and I sat on square pouf sections of the brown herringbone-patterned sofa, and the policemen remained standing. The chief one directed his questions at me. Impossible. For a start, I didn't really know what the man was doing. He was smiling and walking along and his thing was showing, but I couldn't say all that to the policeman, and I certainly couldn't say the word penis at all,

never mind out loud to a strange man. Did I even know
it? I'd never heard it used, no person I had ever known
had ever said it and my mother called it something else, a
horrid squashy Yiddish word, '*shmeckle*',[56] which I could
not bring myself to say either, because it was only used by
adults for rude jokes. Not even the policeman could say
penis. He said 'it'. This seemed to be a difficult area for
him too, which hampered his enquiry. He was getting
nowhere and tried to be more specific.

'Was he fiddling with it?' he asked. His pink face was
going red. The other policeman, standing a few feet
behind him, said nothing. There was no sound, except
from Pamela, who I could hear behind me, out of sight,
making small spluttery noises. I knew she was shaking
because I could hear the sounds of the pouf moving
slightly beneath her.

'Mmm.'

That was all I could say, while shaking my head to
mean no, because if I'd opened my mouth to speak, then
I would have laughed just like Pamela, so I had to keep
it clamped shut. And anyway, I couldn't describe what
the man was doing. It had all been so quick, and what did
fiddling mean? He could have been fiddling, but only
slowly. I didn't remember much movement.

The policeman went redder. He was desperate for a bit
of information. He gave as many clues as he possibly

[56] Penis.

could, each one more daring than the last. The next one took all his courage.

'Was it sticking out?' he asked, his cheeks going purply red. It got him nowhere.

'Mmm.' I pulled a face and nodded, to suggest 'Yes, sort of'.

Because what did he mean by 'sticking out'? How far? I felt I hadn't really helped the policeman much. He didn't seem to understand my face, but he still needed to warn us. Something had to come out of this investigation, even if it was just some advice to help out two girls and prepare them for their next rude encounter, should they have one.

'That's when you want to be careful,' said he. 'When it's sticking out. Then call to the nearest passer-by, "Grab that man!"'

'Mmm.' I couldn't say more, because by now I wanted to laugh so much that I was sweating trying not to.

Then luckily, the policemen went away and my mother burst in.

'What did they say? What happened? Where've they gone?' but Pamela and I were rolling on the floor, laughing, screaming, doing policeman impressions. Especially 'Was it sticking out?'

'Yech!' said my mother. 'Disgraceful. I hope they bloody catch the *ferschtunkener drek*. What a thing to do to two young girls. What sort man does that? Yech!'

But my mother was unusually flustered. She was not

straightforward cross, as she had been over the sugar mouse, or even over Celia Moonface.

'It's no laughing matter,' she said, hurried off to the kitchen and left us laughing.

We couldn't stop. We laughed on and on, reciting the policeman's warning, until, about ten minutes later, there was a fierce banging on the door. Lusty barked, my mother rushed to answer it.

'Who the hell is that?'

It was the policemen back again, very excited. They had caught the man!

'We may have found the gentleman, Madam, and we need your daughter and her friend to come with us at once in the car and identify him.'

'Gentleman?' said my mother. 'Is that what you call him? Where are you taking them? I'd like to know . . .'

But the policemen wouldn't answer. They had no time. This was a top-speed police operation, and we were hurried out into the police car, still laughing. My mother was left with her mouth open.

What excitement. We sped along in the police car, away from my mother, to identify a criminal, and as we went, the chief policeman gave rapid instructions.

'Now this is what we want you to do, girls. We're going to bring this man out of the shop and you're to say yes or no. That's all. Is it the man you saw or not?'

The policemen were now decisive and excited. Zoom! Down the road to the little parade of shops, where an innocent man was bundled out of the barber's. Definitely the wrong man. He was far too small.

'It's not him,' I said. 'The other man was taller.'

A big disappointment for the policemen. They had us in the car, they were poised for an arrest and they couldn't give up now.

'We'll just drive around and see if you can spot him,' said the chief policeman. 'They often stay in the area.' And then a couple of streets further on, 'Ah! There he is!'

He had spotted a suspicious-looking man in a raincoat and a navy beret. It was the Rabbi Solomon trudging along.

'That's him!' shouted the chief policeman, sure as anything. The police flung open the car doors, all jumping out and ready to arrest the rabbi. Panic. I yelled for them to stop.

'No! No! It's not him!'

'How d'you know?'

'Please. No. It's a different hat.'

But one cannot stop a policeman once he has the bit between his teeth.

'They often change their hats,' snapped the chief policeman.

He was half-out of the car, about to run and seemed to have set his heart on this arrest. Within seconds they would be across the road and grabbing the rabbi, and for some odd reason I still didn't want to tell them it was him. Perhaps because he did look rather shabby and I felt a bit ashamed of him. A rabbi should not even look remotely like a rude man who would do such a disgusting thing in the street. He should not look suspicious. He should not be wearing a horrid old mac. But I had to own up and tell them. I had to admit that he was our rabbi. Quickly. I had to save him from disgrace.

'It's the Rabbi!'

What disappointment for the policemen. They never caught the penis man. But it was their own fault. How stupid they were, Pamela and I thought, because we'd told them that the man was walking and probably fiddling all round the roundabout and back the way he had come, down the hill towards Ruislip Manor Station, and what did the police do? They went to Ruislip Station instead, before coming back to collect us at my house. Idiots.

23: TWO DEATHS AND A
CLOSE SHAVE

How thrilling the coffee bar had seemed when my mother started it, but that's the trouble with a new life. It looks exciting, and then once you're doing it, all sorts of annoying little things happen which take the gilt off the gingerbread. For a start, the assistant cook/washer-up Nora had BO. What was my mother to do about it? She couldn't just say 'You stink'. My mother always spoke her mind, but with BO it was different. In all other respects Nora was perfectly all right. She was a hard worker, she was friendly, she was punctual and most important of all, she did not take liberties, but she was stinking out the kitchen. There was my mother baking fragrant cakes and deliciously aromatic pasta sauces and meat-balls, and there was Nora smelling of stale Heinz onion soup. Yech.

'You're going to have to tell her,' said my father, not because he ever had to put up with the stink, but my mother had told him, and me and all her friends, a lot about Nora smelling. Some days it wasn't too bad, but some days it was terrible.

'I've never smelled anything like it!' said my mother. 'Phooey. You can't imagine. I can't bloody stand it. It's all right for you. Perhaps you'd like to tell her?'

'Why should I tell her? You hired her, you tell her.'

So my mother did, but not in the usual way, because my mother may have been outspoken, but she was not an unkind person. She did not want to publicly shame Nora, nor did she want to look her in the face and say 'You smell', so she thought up a clever plan. She bought an Odorono and put it in Nora's overall pocket, and Nora must have used it effectively, because my mother soon stopped complaining of the stink, but instead began boasting of her methods.

'She must have got the hint,' my mother told everyone.

It wasn't just the staff who caused problems. There were the customers as well. They'd have one coffee and sit for hours.

'I can't get rid of them,' my mother would complain. 'How am I meant to get rid of them? I can't tell them to bugger off.'

'Tell them you need the table. You've got customers waiting.'

'You think that'll get rid of them do you?' said my mother in a mocking way. 'They'll get up and go just like that, will they?'

'Yes,' said my father. 'Just like that,' and put on his red Tommy Cooper fez.

'Silly bugger,' said my mother.

This was to be the least of my mother's worries. Later that year, my grandma died of stomach cancer. I remember nothing of it. My parents went up to Barrow for the funeral, leaving me behind with Juliette, because Jewish children do not have to go to funerals. Death was one thing my mother successfully protected me from. I hardly noticed it. I can't remember what I felt, or seeing what my mother felt.

I had hardly noticed my other grandma's death either. Shortly after the wedding, my father had received news of it. Someone phoned to tell him. From the top of the stairs I could see him, sitting with his back to me on a chair next to the telephone table in the hall. Suddenly he bent his head over and made an odd sobbing, crying noise. So he must have loved her a bit.

I did of course know about the main problem that my Grandma Davidson's death had caused. Celia now had the money. My money. Ten thousand pounds, which was quite a lot in those days. This was a horrible worry for my mother. It was as if the money was afloat in space and drifting farther and farther away. Grandma had been a bit of an anchor. With her alive, there was always a chance that she might reclaim it, or reconsider her foolish decision. Now that hope was gone.

*

Summer came round again, but how could my mother leave the coffee bar? She didn't dare leave her employees to get on with it by themselves. And what about the cooking? No one could bake cakes to a high enough standard, and by now my mother was famed for her cheesecake and strudel. Customers came especially to eat them. She could perhaps take a couple of weeks off at the most, but that was it. She couldn't possibly go to Cannes for a month as usual. So she sent me ahead with my Uncle Cyril, Auntie Betty and Cousin Olga. They were also mad about Cannes. We would all drive down there, and my mother would join us later.

But she never turned up. Why not? Uncle Cyril told us that she was in hospital – just for a little operation – but would be all right and would try to come to Cannes if she was better in time. He did not tell us that she'd suddenly collapsed with a brain haemorrhage and had just about escaped death by a whisker, and might easily still die. It can't have been easy for my uncle to have his sister dying, and Olga and I carrying on and squabbling in our usual way, because he loved my mother. She was his big sister and had always adored and looked after him. She had been like a second mother to him and now here he was, hundreds of miles away from her, looking after me and having to pretend to be cheery.

Meanwhile, Olga and I had other dramas going on. We didn't really notice what Cyril was doing or feeling. Perhaps he just made a good job of covering it up. As

Olga was 15 and I was nearly 15, we were allowed to go, attended by Mme Zich's grown-up daughter as chaperone, to the night club, Whisky à Gogo, just down the road from our *pension*. It was initially thrilling – going to a night club very late in the warm evening, where the lighting was dim and cocktails were served, but it was rather disappointing after a couple of visits, because Olga and I had imagined ourselves jiving with handsome French boys. Instead we found ourselves dancing slowly and clutched rather tightly by unattractive French men, usually short ones. And the music wasn't our favourite sort. In England we had Little Richard, the Everly Brothers and Buddy Holly, but here the music was French, which was entirely different. It was slower and we thought it rather sloppy. One couldn't really bop about to it. The first time we put the slimy music and short men down to bad luck. But then it happened again, and again, and Whisky à Gogo lost its charm.

What disappointment, because we had dressed up especially, in our circular skirts, which whirled out in a complete circle when you spun round jiving. I had two such skirts: one black and covered in a martini-label pattern, the other bright blue, decorated with two red and turquoise pretend purses, out of which tumbled gold coins, all sewn on to the skirt. But I was deprived of the chance to swirl around in it. No one at Whisky à Gogo ever saw the purses and coins properly. They remained partially hidden in the blue folds as I shuffled about, clutched by the short Frenchmen, who often smelled of garlic. And as I was taller than Olga, I suffered more than she did, because the men nearly came up to her face, but they only came up to my chest, so I felt particularly silly dancing with them. Why did they ask me to dance? Could they not see there was a height problem? Why didn't they feel silly too?

And then one day on the Bijou Plage, something terrible happened. Olga and I were lying about sunbathing, by ourselves, when this young French nanny that we knew came up to us. She was in charge of two little children. Would we mind just looking after the children for half an hour while she went for her swim? She'd been having lessons and needed to practice. We said yes, we played dribbly castles down by the water's edge for a while with the children, then we took them back to our towels for a sit down, and suddenly there was a big fuss and shouting on the beach. Two men ran very fast into the water. Everyone stared at them. They pulled somebody out of the shallow water near to the shore – a woman, and they half-dragged, half-carried her up to the sand, and lay her on her back and pushed at her chest and pounded at her. It was the nanny, with her head sideways, her blonde hair wet and stuck to her head, with white slimy froth pouring out of her mouth, while the men kept pushing at her wet body very hard with their hands. And the top of her swimsuit had come down, which was all very embarrassing. They must have been hurting her, but she just lay there limp and flobby, like a big wet doll, being pounded by the men. I didn't really want to look.

Olga reminded me of this horror decades later, but I had no memory of it. I'd cleverly managed to blot it out. Then as soon as she told me I saw the whole thing again. However did the nanny manage to drown? She was only swimming in very shallow water, but apparently the water got into her mask and she couldn't breathe. And afterwards, said Olga, we were interviewed for the local paper, because we'd been looking after the children. I can't remember a thing about that.

My father in his fez, 1940s.

24: A HOLE IN THE HEAD

When I returned home to Ruislip, my mother was in hospital. I went to visit her. She was sitting up able to talk, but had a bald head with bandages round it. They had shaved her hair off, sawed out a triangle of skull, mended the haemorrhage, and sewn her head up again, with the skull-triangle missing. For the rest of her life my mother was frightened of this missing triangle, and so was I. She reminded us of it whenever she had a headache or there was any sort of threat to the nearly exposed brain underneath it. Any loud noise could go straight through it. And what if she banged it? Then what? Whatever had banged it would probably also go straight through. It always seemed dangerous to us, that she should have such a feeble bit of head, underneath which the poor brain wasn't properly protected.

Luckily, by the time I saw my mother she was on the road to recovery. She had only made it by the skin of her teeth, because when she first woke up, she told us all, she'd been in a horrid, miserable ward, where all the other patients were lying about like dead bodies, motion-less lumps under blankets, and if she'd stayed there, she definitely would have pegged out too, so she begged them to move her somewhere more cheery, and they did. To this present ward, with people who were more alive and able to move about, a sunny aspect, and loads of flowers all over the place, and she had perked up.

But it was months before she could come home. And who was going to look after me? I wasn't quite 15, my father had to keep going to work, then to the hospital in the evenings. He didn't have time to do cooking and cleaning and all the rest of my mother's tasks. So he hired a sort of nanny/housekeeper, Joan, a dumpy woman with a suet pudding complexion, flat, round face and little cur-ranty eyes. I didn't like her very much. If only Juliette had still been here, but she'd had to go home months ago. My father perhaps wasn't as good at choosing people as my mother was.

School started, and on Friday 13 September, I was 15. Friday the Thirteenth. Bad luck day. Worst birthday of my life, when I got my first period and asthma. And I wasn't prepared for the first period. Lucky me, that my horrid periods were so late starting, the last in the school. I had almost begun to believe that they never would. Good. But here they were at last, at the worst possible time. I asked Joan for a sanitary towel. She had some but wouldn't give me one. She needed them. Now what? I couldn't ask my father. I was too poorly to go out. I asked Joan again and again. Eventually she relented, but by then my asthma was worse. I lay in bed wheezing noisily.

When my father came home from work he sat on the edge of my bed and stroked my forehead. There wasn't much else he could do. I had my Piriton, I did my diaphragmatic breathing exercises. I had had this type of asthma attack time and time again. It usually lasted two or three weeks and eventually faded away. But as it was my birthday, Kathy and Jacqueline came round to visit with presents, while my father went off to the hospital to see my mother. But my friends didn't stay long. They came into the bedroom, said hallo, heard the terrible loud wheezing, which they hadn't heard before, dumped the presents and ran off, all the way to the doctor, and told her that I was about to die. That's what it had sounded like to them. Then they came back with instructions from the doctor that I should get up, have a cup of tea, watch the telly and take two special pills that she'd given them, now that she realized I was upset because my mother was in hospital.

Get up? I thought that rather a cheek. Here I was, sounding close to death, and the doctor's idea of a cure was that I get up and watch telly. But I did, and my friends had bought me a cake, which I didn't really like, but I thought I ought to eat it as they'd been kind enough to get it and to try and look after me, even if the doctor didn't seem to think me worth an ambulance or even a visit. I drank the tea, ate most of the cake, took the pills, and hey presto, within minutes, I was cured. My worst ever bout of asthma gone, like magic, and I never, ever had it badly again.

Eventually, after four or five months, my mother came home. She had had a couple of glamorous turbans made by her milliner, and once she was home she made a few more herself, because although her hair had grown back, it was rather patchy, and she still felt nervous about the missing triangle. At least the turban offered it a little more protection.

But that was the end of the coffee bar. My father sold the Poland Street premises and moved into a small factory in South Ruislip, and the bits of coffee-bar interior were sold to another coffee-bar owner, who reassembled them in premises somewhere along the Edgware Road. Now and again we would drive by and my mother would point them out, a little nostalgically, but not too much. The coffee bar had become all-consuming and tremendously hard work, so perhaps she wasn't all that upset at having to give it up. And when she felt properly better, the next year, she found another little job.

My mother was rather pleased to have my father in his factory just down the road. He could come home for lunch, she could pop in with her friends for belts and bags, and she could keep an eye on things. And when he opened a small shop round the corner selling

his produce – suede and leather goods: bags, belts, waistcoats, skirts, my mother did a couple of days a week
there as saleslady. She knew how to do this. She'd
worked in her mother's dress shop as a young woman,
and in a baker's shop in Petticoat Lane before she married my father, so she was good at it, if rather more
forthright than your average shop-assistant. If someone
tried on something that looked ghastly, then my mother
felt obliged to tell them the truth. As usual, she could
not lie. She was not the sort to send some poor woman
out of the shop looking an idiot, just to make a sale. But
still she did rather well. Only one thing upset her. My
father had yet again appointed a *drek* as his factory manager, Dave Martins.

You'd have thought, after Dennis, that my father might
this time have listened to my mother's advice, or at least
let her in on the interview procedure. Clearly he needed
guidance when appointing staff. He had not done too
well over Joan either, but luckily she'd gone soon after my
mother returned from hospital. Now here he was, sailing
off and employing someone else my mother distrusted.
And worse still, not only did my father employ Dave
Martins, but he also employed his son, Trevor Martins,
who my mother immediately identified as a *potz* and
good-for-nothing.

Again, sadly, she was to be proved right, but it would
be years before my father found out just what a thieving
bastard Dave Martins was. Because my father was fond of

Dave. Unlike Dennis, who thought himself rather swizzy, Dave was a straightforward, working-class, secondary-modern-educated English man. To my father, Dave came from humble beginnings and deserved a bit of a leg-up. This is what my father felt, because he was secretly a socialist. It wasn't really a secret, but he never said much about it, just like he never said much about anything, and if you weren't on the look-out, you would never guess his philosophy, or that he even had one. In years to come he would pretend to admire Margaret Thatcher, and plaster his lavatory walls with colour photographs of her (my parents each had their own favourite lavatory and always made sure that there were two lavatories in every one of our homes) because he knew it was bound to annoy me, being a rabid lefty, and so I never realized the depths of his socialism until he was almost dead.

Had I paid attention, I should have been able to work it out. He was always on the side of the downtrodden. Visiting my mother's relatives in South Africa in the late thirties he helped a coloured person who had been bitten by a dog and collapsed in the street. No one else would help this man – the whites wouldn't help him because he wasn't white, even though it was their dog which had rushed out of the house and bitten the man's leg in an unprovoked attack; and the blacks wouldn't help him because he wasn't black. He was half-and-half, so my father helped. My mother was always rather proud of this action, which she often reported, and now, twenty years later, here he was, at it again. He appointed a black secretary at his Ruislip factory. She was perfect for the job: clever, charming, efficient and beautiful, but there was one thing my father hadn't foreseen – the reaction of the rest of his staff.

They did not want a black person in their midst. They felt very strongly about it. They were all women from Ruislip (where one rarely spotted a black person out and about), my father called them 'The Girls', and so far he had managed to charm them, as he charmed most women. And he was fond of The Girls. His factory was, until this appointment, a happy, harmonious workplace. But The Girls were buggered if they would have a nigger working in it. They came to his office and complained en masse, but still my father stuck to his guns. He tried to talk them round, but they didn't give a toss that she was charming, clever and perfect. Why should they? She was black, and the cleverer she was, the worse that made things, because if there was anything worse than having to work with a nigger, it was having to work with a clever nigger in a position of superiority.

So there was a bit of a stand-off, and my father tried his very best to keep his new secretary, but in the end he had to give in, because the girls were threatening to strike, and of course it wasn't very nice for the secretary to be shunned and glared at every time she left the safety of my father's office. He was very ashamed to have to sack her, my mother told me, but she was a *schwartzeh*. What did he expect from those ignorant *beytsim*[57]? She'd warned him, of course, that they would never put up with a *schwartzeh*, but as usual, he wouldn't listen.

And now my father was refusing to listen again, and pandering to Dave Martins. He paid Dave a good wage and lent him our car in which to go on holiday, infuriating my mother. What else could my father do? The Martins were going camping. How else were they to transport all their equipment?

But he had clearly taken a step too far in employing Trevor. It was just Trevor's bad luck to be spotted driving about in my father's car by my mother, when he should have been at work. She spotted him parking and nipping into the betting shop, which proved it definitely wasn't a work-related errand, and she immediately reported back to my father. But did he sack Trevor? No he did not. He just told him not to do it again. My mother was in a boiling fury. She cursed the Martins. A double-breasted *miese meshuneh* on the whole lot of them. Here was my father allowing himself to be *kakked* on all over again, as he had done with Dennis. But even she could never have guessed exactly how wicked the Martins were.

Meanwhile she had enough on her plate dealing with the shop. She liked working there, because she was in total

[57] Working-class Christians. Pejorative. Lit. testicles (in our house this applied to male or female).

charge: she chose the staff, she selected the stock, she
made the rules, and best of all, it got her out of the house
and among the public, which gave her opportunity to yak
to new people, which is what she badly needed, in view
of my father's sulking and Gracie going off the rails and
some of her other best friends rather getting on her
nerves. So the shop was fresh air for my mother. But it
also proved, as if we didn't know already, that some
people tend to go barmy living in Ruislip.

There were probably barmy people everywhere, but
now that I was 15 I had begun to suspect that there
were more than average in Ruislip, perhaps because
there was nothing much else to do. Ruislip had just one
cinema, and the lido and woods, riding and pets, which
had been perfect when I was younger, but what was
there here for me now? Everything closed on Sundays,
hardly anything moved, there was barely any noise, and
nothing, nothing to do, so that one sometimes wanted
desperately to go wild in some way or other, or scream.
My mother often did. Life in Ruislip didn't seem to be
much fun for grown-ups either. Just look at Gracie,
stuck indoors drinking, and Mrs Saunders being a *kurve*,
and all those men in the High Street doing that sort of
thing with her, and as if that wasn't mad enough already,
into my mother's shop one day came someone even
madder.

There wasn't a proper changing room in the shop, just
a curtained-off area behind the counter where women

could try on skirts and waistcoats. A lady customer wanted to try on some leather skirts.

'Of course I will,' said my mother.

'But if you look, you mustn't laugh,' said the woman.

'Why should I laugh?' asked my mother. 'I won't laugh.'

The woman tried her skirts on and called my mother. But my mother must not look if she was going to laugh. She promised not to. All right, she could look. But she mustn't laugh. Well she wouldn't look. Yes she must look, but not laugh. This went on and on, and my mother was getting a bit sick of it by the time the woman allowed her to look. My mother looked. The woman had tried a white leather skirt.

'Very nice. That's a good fit. What about the other one?'

The woman took the first skirt off. But whatever was she wearing underneath it? A fur triangle strapped to the front of her bottom. What a shock for my mother, even after all the you can/you can't look/laugh business.

'What's that in aid of?' asked my mother in her usual forthright way, trying very hard not to laugh.

'My husband likes me to wear it while I'm going round Sainsbury's,' said the woman. My mother didn't say much. She didn't quite know what to say, but naturally she was *platzing*[58] for a laugh, and only managed not to by keeping her mouth more or less shut, which was the technique I had used when being questioned by the policeman. Then the minute the woman had gone – she bought the white leather skirt, which she'd tried on first – my mother straightaway rang my father and screamed with laughter. She could not believe what she'd seen. And she'd thought my father was a bad enough husband. What sort of a husband asked his wife to do that? In Sainsbury's, *nokh*[59]? And what sort of a *drek* was that woman to do it?

'I know what I'd have told him,' said my mother, disgusted. 'Phooey!'

Mother in her shop, 1957.

[58] Busting.
[59] Even. Emphatic.

25: VULGAR WORLD

I began to think, at about this time, that my parents were much too rude and vulgar. I did not wish to know what husbands and wives did, and if I did have to know, then I would rather have known in a more refined and subtle way. I did not want to hear my parents laughing loudly and crudely at things to do with sex and bottoms, or using Yiddish words beginning with '*schm ...*' which to me sounded distasteful and squelchy. And also I thought my parents perhaps rather too irreverent. They were not serious enough about being Jewish. They ate bacon and eggs and shellfish. They did not pray properly. My mother prayed in occasional snatches and my father never prayed at all. They told vulgar jokes. They often farted loudly and then laughed, and they shouted. It was a dreadful embarrassment going out with them in public. No one else's parents, as far as I could see, behaved like that.

I did not want to copy them. I wanted to feel clean and polite, and to raise myself above the noise, rudeness and vulgarity, the Yiddish jokes and the Latin American ballroom dancing, and be rather more sophisticated. So I turned to God. Seriously. If I was going to be Jewish, then I might as well do it properly, I thought, and take Modern Hebrew for my GCE. Why not? I had come top at Sunday morning *kheder*[60] classes, why not take a proper, higher grade exam? I started going to the synagogue on Saturday mornings, saying my prayers, and believing in God, which meant sticking to all the Jewish dietary laws, according to His instructions.

This was not easy, living with such slapdash parents. How was I to eat only kosher meat, drained of blood, no milk after meat for two hours, no milk before meat for twenty minutes, no fish without scales and fins, no animals who do not eat grass and have cloven hooves, no birds of prey or scavengers in a household which ignored all these rules? It would have been difficult enough to give up my favourite foods, even with parental support, but without help, my task was monumental. It meant no shellfish, no pork, no lovely scrunchy bacon, no ham sandwiches, no puddings with cream, no skate, no crevettes in Cannes, no moules marinières.

Still, I felt it was worth it. And hard as it was avoiding all this sinful food at home, with my mother cooking it all in defiance of His will, it was even harder at school. At least my mother provided a tasty alternative. But at

---

[60] Jewish version of Sunday school, where children learn religious studies and how to read prayers in Hebrew.

school, sticking to His regulations was almost impossible. The only alternative to banned meats was a lump of cheddar with my potatoes and vegetables. But I carried on being fearfully strict with myself. Clearly there had to be an absolute ban on pork. And of course I couldn't have the gravy, which was pork juice. I could eat beef or lamb, but that meant I couldn't have custard or any milk puddings afterwards. Then worse still, I realized that none of the meat was kosher, it was all *treyf* [61], and I shouldn't have been eating any of it, and so I was forced into vegetarianism, which was not an option I would have chosen freely. The only school vegetarian was Janet Anderson, who had greasy hair, terrible spots and bad breath with a sickly, carroty smell. Would I end up like her?

My whole life had become a struggle, not helped by my mother, the temptress, making delicious but forbidden foods and even sabotaging my religious observances. On *Yom Kippur* [62], when I was trying my best to stick to the obligatory 24-hour fast, I came home from my devotions absolutely famished at the twenty-third hour. Only one hour to go and I would have done it. A fantastic achievement. But as soon as I got in, my mother offered me a slice of delicious, freshly baked stuffed-monkey cake. It was too much for me. I gave in. I ate it.

---

[61] Non-kosher meat.
[62] Day of Atonement. Most important day in the Jewish religious calendar, when Jews atone for their sins. It is like all the Catholics' weekly confessions rolled into one.

For some time I blamed my mother for my failure, but
the truth was that I was already beginning to have my
doubts about religion. I had noticed, during the long
hours I had spent at the synagogue through *Kol Nidrei* [63]
and *Yom Kippur*, that I seemed to be the only seriously
pious child in Ruislip. The rest were outside *shul*, [64] loi-
tering on the pavement for much of the time, chewing
gum and telling rude jokes. At such a time and in such a
place! I was bitterly disappointed. There seemed to be
nowhere clean on earth. Everyone was vulgar. What was
the point in my attending synagogue, if all the other
young persons there were only pretending to behave
themselves? And during prayers the women at the back
would not stop talking throughout the service, even
though it was meant to be the most tragic and serious day
in the Jewish calendar, and so it began to seem to me that
perhaps I was heading in the wrong direction, spiritually.

Unfortunately, at the most intense stage of my religious
period, I had insisted that my mother book me on a religious holiday to Bnei Akivah camp in Wales. Olga would
come with me. By the time I started to go off the whole
idea, it was too late to cancel, and anyway, perhaps it
would provide a last-ditch chance to show that being
seriously religious was a good idea. But that would be

[63] The evening before the Day of Atonement, when prayers for the dead
take place.
[64] Synagogue.

next summer. I didn't need to think about it until then. How bad could it be? It was only a fortnight's camping holiday.

Meanwhile, the school carols this year were so spectacular that the BBC had been begging to record them. But the school wouldn't allow it. I rather admired this principled stance. It was confirmation of the Christians' purity, strict moral code and abhorrence of things commercial and common. But I was still excluded from these exquisite carols, so I batted on with my religious mania and studies. I had to. Not only was I committed to the holiday camp, but the Hebrew GCE was looming and I had to continue with my lessons with the Rabbi Solomon. But bad luck for me, he was a hopeless teacher. He of course knew nothing of the time that I had saved him from ignominy by preventing his arrest, so he couldn't be grateful. He whizzed through the lessons, *gabbly gabbly gabbly*, glaring down at the page, and he never smiled or chatted. I barely knew what he was talking about, and when I did dare to ask, I couldn't understand the answer, and so by the time I reached the stage at which the vowels were omitted, I was completely lost and floundering. What is the point of a language without the vowels written in? How was I expected to guess what they were? These lessons, like my mother's stuffed-monkey cake and the collection of rude youth outside *shul*, were only confirming my worst suspicions – that I had made a huge mistake.

26: A GERMAN IN THE HOUSE

None of my friends had made my mistake. They had all found something else more interesting and apparently much more rewarding. Boys. Considering that Ruislip was so dull in many ways, it did have a varied selection of boys. Because Ruislip had an American base, which meant that as well as the usual array of boys: the rude ones outside *shul*, the Teddy Boys (who came mainly from Uxbridge, four stations along), the familiar neighbourhood boys, the ordinary boys from the grammar school and the dangerous boys from the secondary modern, we also had the American Dependent boys, whose parents worked at the USAF base, South Ruislip, HQ of the US Third Air Force. It was like a little self-contained town, with its own hospital, cinema, bank, Boy Scout troop, chapel, shops, bar and liquor store. Conductors on the 158 bus, which passed by, would often call out 'Texas' as they reached the base stop.

The base was also a plus for my parents, as they had somehow made friends with an American couple – Mike and Wanda Barnes, who supplied them with American bourbon whisky, my father's favourite drink. The Barneses were a glamorous pair, sun-tanned, attractive, cheery, and they laughed and talked loudly, rather like the French, and perked my parents up in the same way, so all in all, the base seemed to bring sunshine to Ruislip. And a thrilling new brand of boys.

We often bumped into the American boys at the lido. It was easy. We could sit on the lawns by the café having an ice-cream, or go out in a rowing boat, and there were bound to be some, sitting or rowing about, and Jacqueline and Shirley would somehow start chatting to them. They were bolder and keener to do so than I was, me being what was called a 'late developer' in all sorts of ways, and they thought the Americans superior to Ruislip boys. For a start, they looked different. They did not have quiffs and Brylcreem, they did not wear slacks, shirts and ties and lace-ups and look greasy, they did not wear school uniforms. They wore blue jeans, sneakers, a wide range of T-shirts (we only seemed to get plain or stripy ones) and white bobby-socks, and had flat-top haircuts – a tall crew-cut which was flat on the top. If they bent over and you looked straight at the top of their heads, you could more or less see their skulls, so I wasn't particularly keen on this style, and thought the bobby-socks rather soppy, but Jacqueline and Shirley thought them magic. And as it was Jacqueline's birthday, she was allowed to invite a couple of these boys to her party.

Shirley fell in love with one of them immediately. He had a flat-top, blue jeans, a big red T-shirt and Buddy Holly glasses. And a German name. Eberhardt. There was only one thing wrong with this boy as far as I was concerned. I knew that the name Eberhardt would not go down well at my house. As far as I knew, a German had never entered our home, and never would, if my mother had anything to do with it, because the Germans, as everybody knew, hated the Jews and liked to murder them.

Sure enough, when Shirley brought him round, there was trouble. Out of the front windows I saw them coming along our road, Shirley in front, already somehow looking like a proud wife in a rather grown-up matching salmon-pink skirt and blouse. I let them in and directed them into the piano lounge and away from my mother. I had already let slip what his name was, and my mother knew it was German.

'Peh,' she said when she heard it. 'Bloody, stinking Germans.'

It didn't make any difference to her that he wasn't a real German. He was American. There was no chance on earth that he was a Nazi murderer but to my mother the German name was enough. She refused to offer Shirley and Frankie Eberhardt a scrap of food, pulled a horrible face when I went to answer the door, and stayed in the kitchen. She did not wish to be introduced.

This was very unusual for my mother. Usually she

would want to inspect anybody's new boyfriend and stuff
them with food, like any visitor. And yak at them, and
butt in to our conversations and be a frightful embarrassment to me, but a German sent her into silent exile
in the kitchen. From which the German was banned. I
had to beg her for a glass of orange juice for my friends,
because otherwise, what would Shirley think? She was
used to the usual food stuffing when she came to my
house, now suddenly everything was different. So I had
to pretend my mother wasn't very well, and get the
orange juice myself, and even then I was only allowed to
give them a weak orange squash. My mother allowed the
drink, because although having a German in the house
was intolerable, she still could not bring herself to be
completely inhospitable, because that would bring her
down to the Andrews' level, which she couldn't have
borne. I kept my visitors, with their pissy orange squash,
in the piano lounge, and then we went off to the woods
with the dog.

I personally preferred English boys. Jacqueline and I
had made friends with two local ones, with motorbikes.
Not Jewish, but still miles better than a German. And
they suited me, because they had motorbike helmets on
which I painted some rather striking flame patterns. I was
beginning to fancy the idea of becoming an artist. Or a
vet. The boys, so far, were not priority. I still had art, animals and God to think about and sensed that boys were
a dangerous area, which I would rather not enter. But

Jacqueline and Shirley went rushing in. Pamela was in less of a hurry and Kathy and I not in a hurry at all.

To me the boys were not all that exciting. Until I went, with Jacqueline, to the Odeon Hammersmith to see Buddy Holly and the Crickets. This was one thing I could thank Auntie Celia for. Uncle Bill was manager of all the Odeon and Gaumont cinemas and theatres in London, and he could get free tickets to anything. And he gave them to me: for Frankie Vaughan, for Wyatt Earp, who came on stage on his horse and, best of all, for Buddy Holly and the Crickets.

Unlike Celia, he wanted little in return for his favours — no lifts to France, no company at the Carvery, the Curzon Club, the gaming tables, the shops, the greengrocer's stall, no hanging about waiting, no cooking, no pandering. Just respectable clothes and manners, and the free tickets would come our way, for whatever we asked. Sometimes, when we arrived, Uncle would be standing with another theatre manager, both like penguins in evening suits: black bow ties, jackets with tails, white shirts, shiny, flattened hair, shiny bald heads, Uncle's large stomach sticking out, and we would say hallo and smile nicely, and then, with any luck, Uncle would get us autographs and take us backstage to meet the stars.

And our tickets were always either in, or close to, the front row, which brought us very close to Buddy and the Crickets — live, right there in front of us, making such a loud, new and wonderful sound, as Buddy did his strange and thrilling dance across the stage with his guitar, almost hopping on one leg, to the thumping great rhythm and the huge waves of screaming from hundreds of girls. Screaming and screaming, nearly all through the songs, but specifically at certain points. I knew where these screaming points were. I could feel the exact place in which I ought to scream, but somehow I just couldn't do it. Jacqueline could. She screamed and screamed and almost fainted. All around me were hot, yelling girls, who cared about nothing in the world but Buddy, or one or other of the Crickets, which seemed to free them up to cry and sometimes even faint and swoon, they were just so overcome with the excitement, rock and roll, noise and heat and sudden and entirely novel screaming opportunities. Light years away from Ruislip.

Meanwhile, the ordinary world seemed suddenly full of boys, if you cared to go out and look for them. Jacqueline was particularly keen on them, and she was in a better position to find them than the rest of us, because she had left school straight after her O Levels, a year earlier than the rest of us because she had an August birthday, and gone to work in Harrods as a sales assistant. It was a tough life. She had to wear black and was never allowed to sit down. Even if there was nothing to do, she had to keep standing and pretend to be doing something. But what did she care? She was out of Ruislip and up in town. What thrills. And she had her own wages and if she wanted to she could go out after work, to Soho, epicentre of vice and excitement, where the selection of boys and men was breathtaking and included exotic foreigners: French, Italian, Spanish, African, and all she had to do to find them was to walk into a coffee bar. Her favourite was the Heaven and Hell, next door to The 2I's in Old Compton Street.

This was right in the middle of that dangerous area through which my mother had escorted me when she had her own coffee bar, and in which I was never allowed alone, because the whole place was awash with prostitutes and sin, strip-clubs, brothels, rude pictures, red lights, sparkly curtains, wicked men, criminals and sex. Now here was Jacqueline nipping along there after work as if it were Ruislip High Street. Naturally she asked me to join her. I could come straight from school and meet her after work, and she would take me along.

For some odd reason, my mother allowed this outing. She perhaps thought, when I told her I would be visiting a coffee bar, that it would be like hers had been: well lit, serving delicious pastries and coffee from a Gaggia machine, with respectable clients and business persons going in for a cappuccino and snack. And that is what I also imagined. I was not prepared for the Heaven and Hell.

The upstairs wasn't bad. It was painted blue, with white clouds, like heaven, but I didn't notice any pastries, and we didn't stay in this bit, because Jacqueline preferred the Hell part, which was downstairs, painted black with red flames and dim lighting, and choc-full of men. They were men rather than boys. Through the darkness and smoke, I could vaguely make out their shapes. But where was Jacqueline? I called her name and heard a muffled reply. There she was in a pile of men, wound round one of them, kissing him. Erk. What was I meant to do? I was still in my school uniform, but to look more in keeping with a coffee bar had taken off my black velour hat and stuffed it in my satchel. I still looked rather out of place. But good. Suddenly I didn't want to fit in. Whatever was Jacqueline doing? She refused to detach herself. I didn't realize for a while that she was taking part in a kissing competition. She therefore could not break away from the man to explain. That would have ended the kiss and ruined her chances of winning. Eventually one of the men told me. The ghastly kiss seemed to go on for ever, while I stood there, leaning against a pillar.

For once I was deeply grateful for my uniform. I knew that it was not attractive to men. Somehow even I sensed that men did not like knee-length grey socks, long, calf-length dark greeny-blue shapeless tunics, and pale greeny-blue round-necked blouses, all covered with a long dark mac, which matched the tunic, and which I sensibly kept on. And I replaced the hat, for extra safety, and waited for the kissing to stop, so that we could go home. At last it stopped, but bad luck for me, Jacqueline did not want to leave the man she had been kissing. He and his friends, who all looked rather dark, Mediterranean and grown up, wanted us to go to a party. I knew that my mother, and Jacqueline's mother, would never have allowed this, but they weren't here. They didn't know, and Jacqueline was mad keen to go off with these strange men to their party. Nothing would stop her. I couldn't, but should I go too? I absolutely didn't want to, but how could I let Jacqueline go on her own? What if something dreadful happened to her, alone with these men? I would get into worse trouble. So I had to go with her, squashed into a car with three strange, rather large men, talking a foreign language, to Heaven knows where, and in a thick pea-soup fog, which had descended over London while we'd been in Hell.

Where were we going in this car? I couldn't see the street names, and Jacqueline wasn't looking, because she was kissing again. So I tried to look out for signs – stations, shops, but everything was blotted out by fog. And our car was going quite fast – another danger, as other cars loomed up in the greyness. Whatever would my mother think? What sort of ghastly trouble would we get into? At last we reached the party destination. But it wasn't a party. It was a flat, and in the flat was a sunken bath and another foreign man, dressed only in a vest and no trousers or knickers at all.

How pleased I was that I still had my hat on and satchel. And as the rude man appeared at the other side of the room, I could tell at once that his knickers were missing, but managed to focus straightaway on the middle distance, which meant that I couldn't actually see the terrifying details of the front of his bottom. It had blurred over. Luckily he soon left the room, and I could allow myself to refocus, but I remained standing, with a sullen expression.

'I have to go home,' I said. 'My mother will be cross.'

'Ring her and tell her you're with friends,' said one of the men. 'Tell her you're staying the night.'

'She won't believe me.' What fools these men were to think my mother such a pushover. At once I realized the value of not being able to lie to my mother. These men were no match for her. But where was Jacqueline? She was collapsed on a sofa with a man, writhing and kissing again. Yuk. So I maintained my sullen pose, repeatedly telling her that we had to go home, and at last Jacqueline detached herself and we escaped. The men didn't argue much. I felt, rather proudly, that my uniform and sulky-faced, nagging method had defeated them. I was more trouble than I was worth, and had saved Jacqueline from God knows what, and together we found our way through the fog to a Metropolitan line station and home. I had a feeling that all this excessive kissing would lead to danger, so I warned Jacqueline in the train on the way home, but she wouldn't listen, of course, and sadly, I would be proved right. Just like my mother.

Luckily there were boys in Barrow that Olga and I met who weren't half so dangerous. One came to visit me in

London. I rather liked him. He was a hundred times better than the foreigners in the Heaven and Hell and wanted to marry me. He had blond hair and was very handsome, I thought, just like Eddie Cochran. He was older than me and famous in Barrow for his wild behaviour – getting drunk, climbing up drainpipes, working for the union and having lots of girlfriends. What an exciting boyfriend. Auntie Betty was rather worried when she heard that I was going out with him, so I told her he was very polite to me and never got drunk, which seemed to stop her panicking. But his spelling was very poor and when he arrived in Ruislip, he weed in the bidet, thinking it was a strange new sort of men's lavatory, and I knew that he wasn't the boy for me. I didn't tell my mother about the bidet. She would have laughed and told the world. Nor did I tell her about the men with the sunken bath.

27: REBELS

In a way it was no wonder that Jacqueline was going off the rails. I thought Ruislip and our schools should take a bit of the blame. Hers was just as strict as mine, she'd left because she was pretty sick of it, and then she found herself under another terrifically strict regime working as a salesgirl at Harrods, so when at last she was free to have some unsupervised fun, she understandably went a bit mad. Our parents may have had their own dull things to do: play bridge, go to the Orchard for dinner and dance, go to Latin American ballroom dancing or stay in cooking and eating, but what was there for us? One cinema. And the woods and lido, which one couldn't really visit in the evenings. What were we free to do? Next to nothing. And school was almost a prison.

When we were little, the school rules were just annoying but had to be obeyed. We didn't question their validity. But the older we grew, the more infuriating and pointless they seemed, so we began to want to defy them. By the time we were 15 we felt almost obliged to do so.

How petty these rules were, how ridiculous. They made us want to burst out and be wild. We rebelled in our own particular ways. Going out with boys was a fairly popular form of rebellion, and once she had escaped, Jacqueline had merely taken it to extremes. We all did it in milder ways.

At school we threw tennis balls over the walls at the handsome passing tradesmen, builders and the milkman, we sat on the front steps in sunny breaks, where we were clearly visible from the street, and rolled up our shirt sleeves, exposing our arms to passing boys, and, as far as we could, we altered our horrid school uniforms. The velour and panama hats could be creased at the back and so made to look almost jaunty, skirts could be shortened, by rolling the waistbands over and over and on the way home on the trains and buses, hats could even be taken off and gum chewed. There was a risk that we might be spotted by a tell-tale prefect, but we were prepared to take it.

Once the O Levels were over, we had felt able to increase the level of rebellion. My leaving and going to art school was my master stroke. I needed to pay the school back for ruining my life and plans. I had wanted to take art and history O Levels but the school had insisted I take physics with chemistry and geography instead, all of which I hated. And it meant not only giving up the subjects that I loved, but also my favourite teachers, Miss Evans the art teacher and Miss Holland the history teacher. Instead I had Miss Foxton, the cruel geography teacher, with her tweed suits, stout, highly polished clomping shoes, white, iron-waved, short cropped hair and her leather-brown outdoor complexion, probably from striding across deserts and rough terrain, and up steep mountains, particularly those with the closest contour lines, so that her holidays would be harsh. Endurance tests, like our lessons. Nothing less than absolute silence and deference would do in her classes, and perfect handwriting, neatness and accuracy. What a horrible subject to study. And I had to do it because history didn't fit with science – another grim, joyless, almost incomprehensible subject in which I had not the weeniest bit of interest, but at least with a more pleasant, fairer teacher.

To get my own back I had taken drastic action. I dressed incorrectly for early morning tennis. This wasn't a compulsory games lesson. It was voluntary. It was meant to be fun, so instead of the uniform grey skirt-shorts which had to be no more than three inches above the knee when you knelt down, and the pale blue-green Aertex shirt, I wore one of my father's big, white shirts, and some very short blue shorts underneath, which were hidden by the billowing long white shirt.

I was only a little way through my game when Miss Parker, PE and swimming teacher, tall and strict, with another weather-beaten tan, white bun and perfect posture, came striding up to the courts in a terrible bate and made me stop playing at once.

'Whatever are you wearing? And where are your shorts?'

But I wasn't scared anymore. I was leaving at the end of term, forever. I'd done my exams, even my swimming exams. I had a silver Award of Merit, which meant that horrid Miss Parker had no right to be rude to me, so I replied rather cockily that my shorts were under my shirt.

'Tuck your shirt in,' snapped Miss Parker, disgusted. But the big shirt wouldn't fit.

'I can't.'

'Because your shorts are far too tight.' Miss Parker glared as if at a shameless whore. She could barely bring herself to look at such a huge area of exposed leg, but it was her own fault. If she'd allowed me to keep the shirt hanging out, more leg would have been covered. She stood glaring until every bit of shirt had been crammed into the short shorts, and then strode ahead like a brave ramrod, trying with her perfect posture to create a physical and moral distance between herself and the tall, thin, long-legged slut behind her.

What a laugh. Lynne Harrison and I and our chums were thrilled by my short shorts story, now that we were all leaving. Ha ha to those old bitches who had bossed us about for seven years. It was nearly over. We were almost free. The tellings-off almost delighted us. I got another one as soon as I got to my classroom.

'This morning I was sitting in the staff-room,' said Miss Woods, my form teacher. 'I looked out of the window and what did I see?' Pause. She glared at me. 'Michele Hanson playing tennis in an indescribable garment. What was it?'

'A shirt.' Muffled laughter. We were all old enough to laugh now. The end was in sight.

And on the very last day, on our way home, we threw our horrid hats away – into trees and, most daring of all, hurled them into the swimming pool. Mine was wedged into the traffic lights. It had been my final act of defiance. It wasn't much compared to kissing competitions in the Heaven and Hell, but it was the best I could do. Along with the tiny shorts.

Jacqueline and me, front garden path, 1960.

28: SHORT SHORTS

I suspected that I had done badly in my Modern Hebrew GCE. I could just about manage some of the Hebrew into English translation, but when it came to the English into Hebrew, I hadn't a clue. But by the time my results arrived, Olga and I were in Wales, at Bnei Akivah, a Jewish holiday camp.

We had loathed it straightaway. It was our first real contact with *frummers*,[65] and I saw at once that my recent efforts at strict religious observance had been utterly feeble compared to the rigours of real religion, as practiced in the Bnei Akivah camp. Even though we were camping, stacks of rules had to be observed: two lots of crockery, cutlery and washing-up equipment must be used − one lot for *milkhik*[66]*,* one lot for *fleishik.*[67] Nor could we go to any cafés in the local town, even for a

---

[65] Strictly religious Jews.
[66] Dairy products and fish.
[67] Meat products.

coffee, in case the crockery we used there had been washed up in the same water that had been used to wash crockery which may have touched bacon or other forms of pig. Nor could we buy ice-creams, because, as everybody knew, Wall's ice-cream was made with pig fat, or whale fat, both on the list of forbidden food-stuffs. Outside the camp there was peril at every turn, because normal Wales was full of *treyf*, so we were more or less imprisoned in the camp, away from temptation.

For some there was another form of temptation in the camp: sex. But the rules on that seemed rather confused, depending on which sort of boys you listened to. The very religious boys were pale-faced, crotchety and wore long trousers and white, short-sleeved shirts, at all times (*kippah*[68]), and their *tzitsis*[69] dangling, and glared fiercely at girls in shorts and short sleeves, which included me, because I had, of course, taken my very short shorts which had so upset Miss Parker, and wore them almost daily. But on the other hand, the not so very religious boys were doing things to some of the girls which Olga and I could hardly bear to think about. Neither category of boys appealed to us. One lot abhorred anything to do with sex, the other lot were forever trying to do it. To Olga, the goings-on in tents were far more

[68] Hebrew word for skull cap, lit. dome, known as 'yarmulke' in Yiddish.
[69] Fringes. 'The Lord said "thou shalt wear fringes upon the corners of your garments."'

shocking than they were to me. I was her main source of knowledge in this area, and without me she would have continued to think that one could have a baby from kissing someone. What an idiot. This was what came of living in Barrow.

But Becky Costa enraged us both equally. Becky, who went to my school and had rather large, pointy bosoms, had the cheek to tell me that I was not at all sexually attractive. Sexually attractive was top of the list of all things in the world that I did not want to be in this situation. I did not want to do any of the things that being sexually attractive might involve, with any of the boys in this camp – the soft and waxy-looking religious ones, or the darker, hairier and more muscly not so religious ones. Both types compared unfavourably with the Ruislip motorbike or American Dependent boys. As far as Olga and I were concerned, the thought of any physical involvement with any of these creatures was absolutely out of the question.

But it was still deeply upsetting that Becky Costa had decreed that I was unattractive in this particular way. Never mind the 'sexually', the 'unattractive' itself was hurtful. I already had The Nose to contend with, now my whole person wasn't good enough. Who was she to decide? What did she mean? And what did this whole camp mean? On the one hand I was not allowed to use a pig-tainted coffee cup, but on the other hand I was unofficially allowed, if only I was Sexually Attractive, to do heaven knows what with these awful boys. What was worse? The slightest, glancing contact with pig fat, or all sorts of contact with boys?

Olga and I escaped to the nearby village, phoned our parents and begged to be allowed home, but they wouldn't have it. They had paid for this *meshugene*[70] camp, we had wanted to go, now we could stay there. So we had to stick it out, singing songs round the campfire, doing Israeli dances in circles, washing up in two different kitchen areas, and going on exhausting and terrifying mountain walks in the pitch dark, laden with soldier-type equipment, because this camp was preparing us all for call-up into the Israeli Army, although we didn't know that when we applied.

And then, on Friday afternoon the post arrived at camp. It included my GCE results, but they were in an envelope. Friday evening was the Jewish sabbath. No one may work on the sabbath. Tearing paper counts as work. I was absolutely not allowed to tear open my envelope. I could not even have it, in case I was tempted.

This religion rubbish was getting sillier and sillier. I was losing all patience with it. I had heard barmy stories before but could barely believe them. Now I believed every word. The worst had been the one from my friend Yvonne Schneider at school.

Her little sister had invited a deeply religious friend to tea. On a Friday evening. The Sabbath. The friend had gone upstairs to the lavatory, but never came back.

[70] Mad.

Yvonne's sister waited for ages. Whatever could her friend be doing? Eventually she went upstairs and called to her friend from outside the lavatory. Was she all right? Had she fainted? Was she ill? She was fine, but she was stuck because she couldn't tear the paper, so she couldn't wipe her bottom, so she couldn't leave the lavatory. In her own home, the lavatory paper would have been already divided into sections, so that tearing on the Sabbath was unnecessary, but things in Yvonne's house were comparatively lax, so the little sister had to go in and tear it for her. Stupid. But also contradictory. How come one Jew couldn't tear the paper, but another could do it for her?

And even if one had a *shabbes goy*, why should that person be slaving away tearing paper and switching lights on and off (which is the same as lighting fires and so counts as work), on the Sabbath? Did God not care about anybody else? Did he really care about my envelope? Was he watching? Did he not have better things to do? Was he there at all? And if he was, could he not at least provide clear and sensible instruction as to what was and wasn't allowed? Obviously not, and if this is where my religious mania would take me, then I had had enough of it. Just like that. The camp finished it off, like an overdose. I felt that I had struggled painfully, and fairly pointlessly, up a steep slope, and was now whizzing down the other side at top speed without any difficulty at all.

Eventually someone took pity on me and smuggled my envelope into the tent. I ripped it open. Only 21 per cent

for Modern Hebrew. A dreadful failure. But who cared?
Not me. I'd passed everything else, and I didn't need
Hebrew at art school. I felt rather disobedient, as I had
towards the end of school, because as well as the envelope
ripping, Olga and I had been secretly flouting the rules,
smuggling in cakes from cafés and Christian biscuits, and
hiding them in our sleeping bags. And we continued to
defiantly wear shorts. In this way, we managed to survive
Bnei Akivah, which had cured me of religion forever.

My mother was thrilled by this development. Not my
religious turnaround, which I did not discuss with her,
but the stories of the mad *frumkeyt*[71] which we told, and
of course the change in my diet back to normal, which
meant she could once again stuff me with fabulous stews
and roast dinners and puddings covered in cream.

I did visit the local Jewish youth club once more, because
I felt a bit of a traitor. After all, not all Jewish youth were
like the Bnei Akivah variety. And many of the local club's
members were fairly liberal. So I took Jacqueline, because
there was a selection of boys there which she had not yet
investigated. But it was a bitter disappointment. No one
spoke to us. They stared, but they didn't speak, except for
the odd hallo. All the boys played ping-pong and all the
girls sat in chairs around the edge of the room in frocks,
whispering and laughing now and again. Jacqueline and I,

[71] Strictly religious goings-on.

influenced by the Americans and Buddy Holly, were wearing calf-length, pedal-pusher trousers. Why were there no girls playing ping-pong? Or at least mixed doubles? This seemed unfair and rather old-fashioned to us. We did, after all, have experience of motorbike riding, helmet painting, kissing competitions, dangerous foreigners, boat-rowing on the lido and generally mixing, and sharing activities, with boys. We couldn't go backwards to just sitting, watching and waiting for them to allow us to do things.

And I sensed disapproval in their stares. Perhaps what they were whispering was, 'What has she dragged in here? Has she brought a *shikse*? She has sullied our club. How dare she do that? Does she have no Jewish friends? Is she a bit peculiar? Is her friend common?' Whisper, whisper.

Anyway, that's what I thought they were thinking. When Jacqueline had taken me to her Christian youth club, in the days before she started to go wild in Soho, people spoke to me as if I were normal. I had been included with no questions asked and no whispering. But here my own people were shaming me. They did not make my friend welcome. They were not interested in who or what she was, because they could tell straightaway that she wasn't Jewish. There weren't many Jews in Ruislip, and they knew all of them, at least by sight, and anyway, you could tell a Christian a mile off. They were just different. Everything was a giveaway. Not just what they looked like, but the way they talked, moved, behaved, dressed. I knew they could tell, because I could tell too. Not infallibly, but nearly always. And so could my parents. '*Unsere*,[72]' they would mutter approvingly to each other when they spotted other Jews in public, as if we were a secret society.

First the mad *frummers* at Bnei Akivah, now I had come up against this, which was rather a worry, because if this was how Jews behaved, then other people were never going to like us. We didn't like them, they didn't like us. Ridiculous. Who could bothered with all this? I would never go to that youth club again.

Olga and me at the Bnei Akivah camp, Wales, 1959.

[72] Ours.

29: PAMELA HAS HAD ENOUGH

Pamela was also planning to go to art school. I would be going to Ealing, she would go to Harrow. To me she looked rather artistic already, with her long, straight dark hair and black tights. Her mother seemed somehow even more unpleasant and was still able, just about, to make Pamela do as she was told, and was using Pamela as a cover for the horrible things that she was doing. For years Pamela had told her father fibs because her mother had ordered her to, and she was getting sick of it. She felt terrible deceiving him, because she loved her father. He was a kind man. He would have done anything to make Pamela happy. Remember the mouse palaces? He didn't seem to have anything to do with the harsh regime imposed on Pamela. It had always been her mother saying she couldn't go out. When the *kurve* was away, Pamela could do what she liked. But when her mother was around, did her father know Pamela was locked in the cellar? Did he have any say in the matter? Because he never dared contradict the *kurve* and was besotted with her. But my mother and I knew nothing about the cellar. We only knew what Mrs Saunders was up to with those men in the High Street.

'The bloody old fool,' said my mother. 'If he only knew.'

But he didn't. He hadn't a clue what the *kurve* was up to. And Pamela felt worse and worse deceiving him. She was sick of being dragged round by her mother and made to hang about while she disappeared, sometimes for hours, with different men. Mr X the baker, Mr Y in the carpet shop, who had a storehouse that nobody knew about. Mr Z who came down from Leeds on business and stayed in a hotel. My mother and the rest of Ruislip, except for Albert, somehow seemed to know that Mrs Saunders was having a go at most of the High Street traders. Pamela had spent countless, never-ending evenings and weekend afternoons in hotel lobbies, in deserted reception areas, in empty offices, while the *kurve* did God knows what, and then she had to come home and lie and say they'd been visiting her mother's women friends for tea, or cinema, or cards, or just a chat.

'I need a nice chat with someone,' said her mother venomously to Albert with Pamela standing behind her. 'I can't have a nice chat to you, can I? You're a fine one for a chat, I must say. You've got nothing much to say, have you?' Then she flounced off upstairs for a relaxing, perfumed bath while Albert and Pamela made the dinner.

And then she did it once too often. Pamela was now

old enough to understand the dreadfulness of what her mother was doing, and she couldn't keep the secret in anymore, so she told her father. What did she think would happen? That he would say 'thank you very much', throw her mother out, she could go back to Ireland where she came from – and apparently where her name was also mud, according to my mother – and then Pamela and her dad would live happily together and perhaps Albert would even find a nice new wife who loved him and Pamela would never have to fib to him again?

But she didn't really think. She just blurted, because she was beginning to hate her mother. How could anyone love such a woman? She couldn't imagine, so she didn't realize that Albert did love her, and that his world would come tumbling down, and he would just crumple up and sit crying for days, begging his wife to stay. He forgave her everything, if she would only promise never to leave him. She could do what she liked – go out, go to Ireland for holidays – he wouldn't mind. She was his life. He couldn't live without her. He still loved her with all his heart.

The person he was now cross with was Pamela. He had loved her so much, but she had ruined their lives. Now neither of Pamela's parents loved her. She couldn't wait to leave home, and now that she was going to art school, she started to plan her escape. Surely she could get a part-time job, as a waitress or something, and share a flat with friends. Isn't that what students did? Because she couldn't stick it at home for three more years, until she'd got her NDD. She knew she'd never last that long, without even Albert to turn to. She needed him more than ever, because now that she had become very beautiful indeed – a cross between Cleopatra and Juliette Greco – her mother had grown even more spiteful. My suspicions that she had become nastier were right. Just as Pamela was about to go out, her mother would rip her black tights so that she couldn't go. It was Pamela's Cleopatra eye make-up that upset her. She thought Pamela looked like a prostitute.

'You're not going anywhere, you little slut,' the *Kurve* would shout. 'What d'you think you look like? A tart, that's what.'

But Pamela was going. She knew she was on her own now without Albert to defend her. Not that he'd ever been able to defend her much anyway, but now he wouldn't even try. She kept all this a secret from Kathy and me at the time, and never, ever told anyone, until it was far too late. Who can blame her? She'd given up on telling people what was really going on. Look what had happened when she told Albert the truth.

30: ART SCHOOL

In my class at art school there were ten boys and three girls, including me. Ten boys. It is an odd feeling sitting next to loads of boys, if, like me, you have only ever sat in classes of girls in uniform. And these boys seemed far more sophisticated than any boys I had so far come across. A couple had acne, but it didn't seem to matter. They were pretty handsome and arty-looking to me. None of them wore nylon shirts or used Brylcreem, like the boys I had known.

Sometimes these boys sat rather close, as if that was a normal, ordinary thing to do. It wasn't like sitting on the back of a boy's motorbike, or next to one in a rowing boat at the lido. Now I found myself sandwiched between boys, on a bench or stools, close together, touching boys, as if that were just routine. The whole side of my left leg would perhaps be touching Mark Dix, but he didn't seem to notice. And my right shoulder might be simultaneously pressed against Laurie Baldwin, but he didn't notice at all. Sometimes we all sat together in the dark, watching a film or a slide show.

What was I to do here? I couldn't shrink from the boys, because a) I didn't want to and b) what would they have thought if I had? Would they be offended? But nor did I want to get closer to or lean on the boys, because what might they have thought of that? Was I leaning on purpose? Did I mean something by it? So I had to stay exactly in the position I found myself in, rather tense and frozen, neither increasing nor decreasing the closeness to, or pressure on, the adjacent boy, hoping that I gave an impression of nonchalance, just as they did. And they were very friendly, as if I were one of them – just another student of whatever gender, because they were used to girls in class. All their lives they had sat next to girls, because they had nearly all come from secondary modern schools. They were the terrifying hordes from my childhood, grown up, and no longer terrifying, even though their language was very rude, they often said 'fuck', as if it were an everyday word, and they smoked. My mother would have thought many of them 'common' and of course they were all *goyim*. These were the children that she believed had been brought up on fish paste sandwiches and lard cooking, whose parents didn't feed them properly and were fairly slapdash about bodily hygiene, but they exceeded her expectations. To me they looked adequately fed and clean, and they seemed a cheery and sophisticated lot. Compared to Haberdasher's Aske's girls' school, this school was thrilling and modern.

It was another world and I was the odd one out. Because for a start, I hadn't got the clothes right. I had tried to dress appropriately, in what I thought was an art student outfit. It being autumn when we started, I wore an extra-large, crew-neck, purple jumper, down to just above my knees, which my mother had knitted. I thought purple was probably the right sort of colour, but I went a bit wrong with the skirt. It was grey and permanently pleated. A big mistake. It was frump rather than trend, but how was I to know on the first day?

I had to learn quickly from looking at the other girls, in the corridors, canteens and other classes. I noticed that, along with the purples, ochres, dark browns and blues that seemed to be all the rage, especially for tights, on warmer days, dresses made of Indian striped bedspread material, all bright and subtle at the same time, were popular. Miraculous. Even the teachers wore striped ties in Indian silk, and pale linen jackets with brightly coloured linings, which they occasionally swirled, or hung on one finger over their shoulders, linings flashing smartly.

That was another huge change from my old school. These teachers were nearly all men, often young and handsome men, men who smoked and drank. One was found drunk in the bath in the sculpture room, another did heaven knows what in the still-life cupboard with a female teacher, some even did awful things with female students. To one of these men teachers, everything was a phallic symbol. Walk into Derek's classroom with a big roll of paper or card under your arm and you were done for.

And of course the boy students went out with the girl students. It was sex, sex, sex everywhere. But I somehow did not and could not join in. Anyway, nobody seemed to want me to join in. Why not? Was I weird? Was I sexually unattractive, just like Becky Costa had said at Bnei Akivah camp? Was it my nose? Or just the clothes?

There was another class in our year, but like my class in reverse – only three or four boys and all the rest girls. But what frightening girls – so cool, so sophisticated and artistic, so attractive, so bitchy, and one particularly sulky-looking girl, Ann, who often wore rust corduroy trousers. She would hardly answer me, and if she did, she spoke with a sneer, as if I were pointless. What was the matter with her? What a fierce little face. What a grump. Most beautiful of all was Gloria. She had that same Shirley Butterworth complexion that I had envied at school – creamy English skin with a slight but becoming blush, a perfectly shaped face and nose, huge blue eyes and a mole positioned in exactly the right spot high on her cheek. And her figure, of course, was perfect, so that anything she wore looked stunning – any old bit of cloth that she might throw over herself, and then she would glide along, leaving in her wake a trail of gaping men and boys. There was no point even trying to look anything like Gloria and her classmates, so I chose a contrasting style – beatnik. Dark and shapeless.

But one day a week I had to mix with most of these girls. On that day we all did our chosen craft, all day, in a craft room. I had chosen textile design. So had they, and so had Ann. There were no boys in textiles. Boys were nearly all across the corridor in etching or lithography, or perhaps pottery. So the textile room was girls only, full of gossiping, whispering, cattiness and jokes. Even our teacher was a woman. She introduced us to cream cheese with raisins, which she spread delicately on wafers and ate for her lunch, and she shared only with those who deserved it. What sophistication. She often shared snacks with Lesley, whose designs she admired, and who was a sort of queen among pupils, rather as Danielle Hewitt had been queen of our class at school, because she had a quality that none of the rest of us had. Danielle knew all about sex. But Lesley was superior in almost everything – her designs were the best, her jokes were the funniest and bitchiest, her tastes the most sophisticated, her stripes the broadest and Swedish, her boyfriend, the most handsome and grown-up. I know because Lesley once invited me to her house for dinner. There was the charming, tall, blond boyfriend, and Lesley had made potato salad with green grapes in it. Grapes in a potato salad! More sophistication. Even my mother had never made that. It all confirmed Lesley's position as Queen of the Textile Room.

Lesley would often sprawl boldly across one of the slightly padded printing tables, her ochre or purple legs splayed about, being spiteful but very amusing. How could I not laugh? Lesley was ever so witty, often about lesser persons, like the girls in fashion, who we thought were not real artists – too commercial and nearly all fluffies, and then afterwards, when I'd laughed like mad at one of Lesley's merciless stories, I was tainted. I had joined in on the massacre and laughed heartlessly at some other pathetic person's expense, who'd probably done something horribly un-cool, but wasn't there to defend herself. And I had encouraged Lesley, by laughing and appreciating her, because the last thing I wanted was to be on the other side, with the squares. Although perhaps I was. I never really made friends with any of these smart girls, and heaven knows what Lesley said about me when I wasn't there, even though I never wore my permanently pleated skirt again after the first day.

Luckily there was one girl in textiles who I dared speak to – Laraine, because not only did she come from Ruislip, and rode horses, but her hair was frizzy. With that hair she could never look cool. It would never be turned into a straight, gleaming bob like the other girls'; it would always be dull frizz. It was African hair, but in a dull mousy brown. Sometimes Laraine would wander past Lesley and look at her work and try and speak to her, because she thought Lesley's designs were really good, her work was very inventive and she was more or less top of the class, but Lesley would only ever say 'Fuckoff' to Laraine, in one word. Or 'pissoff'. Laraine didn't seem bothered, she just took it in her stride, and to me she seemed both cool and approachable at once, so I asked her what was the matter with that girl Ann, with the rust trousers. What should I say to her, the next time she was sarcastic and horrid?

'Tell her to go back to her candles,' said Laraine.

What? I didn't say 'what' to Laraine. I said 'OK', because I hadn't a clue what the candles business meant. Clearly it meant something particular, which I ought to know about, but I didn't like to ask what. What should this horrid girl, Ann, be doing with her candles? Could it be something horribly rude?

I knew next to nothing. But at least I could look as if I knew everything, with my black, beatnik outfits, and I grew my hair longer and straighter. This all upset my mother and father dreadfully. I was aiming for the Juliette Greco sort of look – but to them I no longer looked like a proper girl. And my mother hated black. To her black was the colour of death. And in her opinion, it did nothing for my complexion. She preferred nice, bright colours – tangerine and apricot, turquoise, gold, red, royal blue – or, if anything did have to be brown, then she liked it to be a bright brown, a rust or a tan, then next to a bit of turquoise, it would be fine. She mourned the jolly girls' skirts that I used to wear, the starched petticoats, the smartly fitting jumpers, the twin-sets, the nylons and dainty shoes. She yearned for curls and lipstick and glamour, but there wasn't the tiniest hint of it. It had all gone. I spurned it. Worse still, I sneered at it. Twin-sets? Ha ha ha.

Even worse, my mother had to face the world, and the world disapproved. She had to brave the whole family, who had never seen such terrible clothes. They expressed their opinions. This distressed my mother much more than my father.

My parents expressed their opinion as well, but they were allowed. I was their daughter. If they thought I wasn't making the most of myself, or had made my head look pointy with a centre-parting, or looked a *drek* in my shapeless jumpers, or looked washed-out in black, or would never meet a nice boy looking like that, they could say so. My father could call me 'coconut-bonce', my mother could say I looked *geferlekh* and beg me, as she had begged Miss Hilary, to have a blow-wave, but if anyone else were to criticize, then my mother would fight to the death and attack them in my defence like a lioness.

'Bloody cheek,' she would say of this or that auntie or uncle. 'Do they know what a *lobus*[73] their so-and-so is? Have they seen how *ongepotchket*[74] so-and-so looks? She's got no dress sense.'

'I should care. Pfah!' said my father, meaning that he shouldn't care and that was the least of his worries.

---

[73] Stupid, lumpen, clumsy person.
[74] Overdressed, excessively and unaesthetically decorated, overly baroque.

In his opinion they were all bloody idiots. What was my mother driving herself mad for? He didn't like to join in a fight unless it was absolutely necessary. He had enough on his plate.

His sister Annie was very cautious with her criticism. It was hardly a criticism, and if you rejected the stuffy mores and style of Ruislip and our relatives, as I did, it was almost a compliment.

'She's very unusual,' Annie said to my mother, with a stress on the second u, and a rather apologetic simper, as if it were all a bit modern and beyond her. My mother and father fell in love with this phrase. It was one of their favourites. They often looked at me in my art-school clothes, put their heads to one side as Annie had done, and said to each other, 'She looks very unuuuusual, doesn't she?'

'Oh yes. Very unuuusual. Ha, ha, ha.'

But Uncle Charlie went a step too far.

'Have you seen what your daughter looks like?' he asked, as if he had a bad smell under his nose.

'Yes I have, thank you very much,' said my mother in a voice of such barely repressed fury and menace that he dared say no more. But neither did she. Mummy just came straight home and erupted. What a bloody *ferschotpterkop* the man was. She had no idea why Leah put up with him. How could she bear it? Look at their television. Hadn't my father seen it? Hughie Green's face was green. His eyes were red.

'The contrast was wrong, and you told him,' she roared. 'You told him to adjust the contrast and what did he do? He said it was fine, and to leave it alone. Fine? A bright bloody green face! That's all right. No one can tell him what to damn well do, but he thinks he can tell us. He has no bloody right – *blah blah, scream, scream . . .*'

But my father would not join in. He wouldn't argue, nor would he pretend to agree. In 23 years of marriage he had still not realized that a shouter like my mother needs a response to stop her shouting. All he needed to say was 'Yes, you are quite right. What a bloody idiot', and my mother would have felt she had an ally, which would have calmed her, but he would not. He would only say his usual, 'Do me a favour.'

My mother was probably particularly upset by Uncle's remark, because a month or so before he said it, I had given up wearing shoes. Travelling on the 49 bus one morning with my new friend Maurice, from Ealing Broadway station to school, the conductress spotted my bare and filthy feet, glared at them and told me off.

'That's disgusting,' said she, with her nose wrinkled up. 'You should be ashamed of yourself. You want to put some shoes on. You've got no right to be walking around like that.'

'Mind your own business,' said Maurice.

'It's my business on my bus. You talk to me like that and you can get off.'

We got off it one stop early. Stupid conductress. I had

a sensible reason for my bare feet. My feet were enormous – size nine-and-a-half, and I'd like to have seen her or anyone else find smart shoes in that size for girls. Girls' shoes went up to size eight at the most. Why drive myself mad shopping for practically non-existent shoes? I had quite enough problems coping with The Nose and my pin-head and what seemed to me a staggeringly ugly profile, and this had been confirmed by the boys in my class.

Not that they were rude or said anything about it, but whenever the model failed to turn up, they would pick me as stand-in. As they were serious artists they did not approve of making someone look attractive. The model was a tool for them to use, through which they might demonstrate their particular invention and genius, not a girl who was worried about her nose and lacking in confidence. The odder my nose, the better they liked it, and so they would often draw me from the side, exaggerating the nose and hair. Laurie Baldwin was particularly keen on these profiles. Not only did he go to town on the nose, but he made the ears stick out of the weedy hair like huge, misshapen flaps, in a bold charcoal sketch, around which all the rest of the boys gathered for a laugh.

Why bother with glamour in this situation? I stuck even more fiercely to my beatnik look, and beatniks wore no shoes, which reinforced my decision to go everywhere with bare feet. This terrified my mother. God knows what sort of *drek* and germs I was treading in, never mind the possibility of broken glass, but luckily for me, there was a family precedent. My grandma had often gone barefoot. Probably only in the house, but it helped a little. It would be four years until Sandie Shaw came along with her bare feet, which proved me a pioneer of a trend, but in the meantime, my mother was anxious and rather embarrassed, and she could have done without Uncle Charlie's observations, thank you very much, rubbing it all in.

Anyway, what did my aunties and uncles know of 'unusual'? What a narrow-minded lot they were, living in Ruislip. At art school we were far more worldly. They had one cinema in the High Street, where *South Pacific* was favourite and *Spartacus* was daring, but we went further afield for altogether more thrilling and baffling cinema. We had *Hiroshima Mon Amour* and *Les Quatre Cent Coups*. My parents would have lasted five minutes in there. Their unusual was our normal.

Just take our life models, for a start. They were all sorts: queers, blacks, bohemians, and all naked. Uncle Charlie would have had a heart attack, stuck out in Ruislip in the dark ages. We had Quentin Crisp, the pouf, who I never drew, but saw walking about in a tightly fitting pink and grey striped jumper, with his hair curly and blue. He looked straight ahead and his posture was excellent and confident, and I bet he couldn't have cared less what his uncles and aunties thought. Then we had Ritchie Riley, much taller, black and muscly, who posed in leopard skin, and another model who we weren't keen on, because he wore a loose, black, satiny thing and smelled horrid, so that we all sat as near the door as we could, until our donkey seats were nearly out in the corridor, away from the smell, then there was Greta, who wouldn't pose without her beads.

'I feel naked without them,' she would say.

And one day Laraine came a bit late into class and found the model going up and down a ladder. It took her a while to work out what was going on. He was meant to be drawn moving, in the style of Marcel Duchamp. This was all now part of our everyday life. Fancy being upset by ordinary long jumpers and bare feet? What a fuss about nothing.

Ravers, 1960.

31: DEBBIE KATZ'S SHOCKING NEWS

Shocking news. Debbie Katz, who was in my class at school, and always naughty during prayers, is having a baby. Worse still, Debbie is Jewish and the father is a *yok*. And Debbie is only just 17. She had left school with me and was also just starting an exciting new life at another art school. But now she was leaving almost the minute she got there, because of the baby. Terrible. How did this happen?

Debbie explains that as there is so little to do in Pinner (which is next to Ruislip but even more boring), and what there is to do costs money and neither she nor Tony (the *yok*) had any, the only thing they could do was go for walks in the woods, where they eventually got bored just wandering around holding hands and snogging, and ended up doing It. I couldn't really blame them. And they were, after all, In Love. But as I thought their behaviour fairly reasonable and understandable, I assumed, foolishly, that my mother would too, and so I made the gigantic mistake of telling her.

Here I was, after 16 years of experience and learning what I should and should not tell, and I go and tell her such a thing. It was bad enough telling her that Debbie was having a baby, which I couldn't really avoid, because it was obvious and the Katzs went to Ruislip *shul*, so she was going to find out anyway, but why did I go and tell her how Debbie had got herself into this situation? Perhaps because it was such a shocking event, so naturally my mother questioned me closely. I couldn't pretend I knew nothing about it. I couldn't lie, but probably, on that occasion, I should have done.

It was the word 'bored' that my mother latched on to. For some reason she thought it a huge joke. She had asked me why they had done it, I had told her, and then she repeated the reason loudly and sarcastically. 'They were bored were they? They were bored! Bored, *nebekh*. Excuse me!' And then she laughed and told my father the minute he got home, and he also liked the word 'bored' and joined in the chorus.

'Very nice,' said he, with a mocking laugh. 'Is that what you call it? I wouldn't mind being *bored*,' he said to my mother. 'How do you fancy being *bored*?'

And that's how they carried on. For the rest of my life, and her life, Debbie would be the girl who got 'bored', and with a *yok*. Which turned the joke rather sour. Debbie had only been to my house occasionally, and I never dared ask her again, but I did go and visit her at her house, where she lived with her baby, once it had arrived.

Her parents had given her the largest bedroom, so that it could be a sort of living room/bedsitter for her and the baby. Was she banished up there, out of the way, or was it a privilege because she was now a grown-up? I wasn't quite sure. The Katzs didn't shout and scream, so you couldn't quite tell whether they were furious or not. Of course Debbie used the kitchen and bathroom and rest of the house normally, but she could now invite her friends up to her room to visit, and there was her baby, crawling on the carpet. Then she lay down on the carpet and the little baby crawled over her, and although she was only my age, she seemed to know what to do with it. She knew how to play with it, feed it, change its nappy and give it a bath, and while she did all these things, she still laughed and joked like she had at school while the Christians were in prayers, because she still wasn't frightened of anything.

So having the baby didn't seem to be difficult. What was difficult was Debbie's separation from Tony. Her parents were not keen on her marrying a *yok*, even though it was his baby too, and she'd promised not to see him, but they couldn't keep her a prisoner, could they? So she secretly saw him whenever she took the baby to the park. There would be no art school for her. No career. And no Tony, until he got a job, then Debbie was going to run away and marry him, because his mum and dad didn't mind. So what was the matter with her mum and dad? They were being ridiculous, weren't they?

Yes. Just like my grandma.

32: WHAT THE MARTINS DID

Sometimes during half-terms or holidays I worked in my father's factory, for pocket money and, as I was now an artist, my father wanted my opinion on style. He thought that I would know what was up to date. What was the latest trend? I should know, being artistic, so I could tell him, couldn't I? I designed some wide, suede belts, decorated with coloured suede patterns stuck to them: flowers, leaves, clouds, simple country scenes, rather like Fuzzy Felt, but more subtle, and I spent the days in the factory stamping holes and rivets into belts, fixing buckles on, cutting out and sticking on the bits of suede pattern. It wasn't difficult. You just had to be careful to keep your fingers out of the way of the hole-puncher and riveter.

I liked the ladies who worked there. They were all friendly and jolly, but Dave Martins, the manager, didn't seem too pleased to have me there. He occasionally threw things at me that I was meant to catch – some webbing, a piece of leather, a bobbin, a packet of rivets – but he would cleverly aim them a bit short, so that they landed on the floor and I had to bend down and pick whatever it was up in front of him. Did he like the boss's daughter stooping before him? Did he perhaps not want me to get above myself? He always looked cheery. Extra cheery when I was picking things up, but there was a strange edge to his cheeriness.

And soon we knew why. It didn't suit him to have me around, because he was up to no good. Why would he want a possible spy on site who would naturally report anything she spotted to his boss? Is that why I'd been put there? No it wasn't. Because my father was an innocent. He trusted Dave Martins absolutely. He didn't know that Dave had his own secret business going on, like a parasite feeding off my father's business and draining its blood.

As well as the 'girls' who worked in the factory, my father had outworkers. More 'girls' who did piece-work at home, sewing up the suede and leather clothes that my mother sold in the shop. It was part of Dave's job to deliver materials and collect the finished products from them. Who would notice, he had thought, if he just took a few extra bits of leather and suede to the girls, and had them make up some extra pieces which he could then sell himself, and keep the cash? A lovely little sideline and some extra cash for the 'girls' who were in on it. And for his wife, who was in on it, too. Every single person connected to the factory knew about it, even if they weren't part of it, except for my father. He never guessed. Because he was not suspicious. And I never guessed.

Not everyone in the factory approved of what Dave was doing, but they didn't dare say anything, and the longer it went on, the less they dared say anything, because surely then my father would want to know why they hadn't told him before, and they would be tarred with the same brush as Dave. How would they be able to prove they weren't also a part of the swindle?

But there was one person who found it unbearable: John, my father's general assistant and sort of deputy-manager. He was very fond of my father and had been feeling more and more dreadful about deceiving him as Dave's succubus business went on. Eventually he could bear it no longer, and told my father.

It came as a crushing blow. Here was someone who my father had trusted absolutely, had been generous towards, had thought of as a friend, had worked with for years and had paid generously – more generously than he needed to have done. And all along this man had been cheating and making a fool of him. My father had always thought of himself as an astute businessman who knew the ways of the world, and now he found himself to have been taken for a fool, made a monkey of, and it didn't help that once again my mother had been proved right. More right than ever before. But even she was shocked at the depths of Dave's deceit. Yes she had always thought him a lazy bastard and *shnorer*,[75] who took advantage of my father's good nature, but she had never imagined that he was an actual crook. She could not even berate my poor father. The whole business had so cast him down that my mother knew that she must refrain from any more criticism, and anyway, she was on his side. In her heart, she usually was, but her screaming often concealed her sympathy.

This time, she directed her venom solely at the Martins. Because she too had been duped by them. She had been rather fond of Dave's wife Marion. Even to my mother, she seemed like a pleasant, honest, hardworking woman. But of course she'd been in on it too. My mother wanted to go roaring round to the Martins' house and give them all a bloody mouthful.

'A *meise meshuneh* on the lot of them,' she said bitterly. '*Khazerei*.[76] Let them *gey in drerd*.'

But cursing them did no good. I can't remember whether my father went to the police. He probably reported Dave, but didn't really pursue things. He didn't have the stomach for it. And sadly, it would not be the last time that my father was ripped off on a grand scale by someone he trusted. He had made an error of judgment, and he would make more, as my grandma had feared,

---

[75] Sponger, parasite 'but always with brass and resourcefulness in getting money from others as though it were his right'. Kogos.
[76] Pig swill. Anything rotten.

putting his business temporarily at risk, but not because he had done anything wrong. He hadn't gambled his money away, he hadn't for one moment stopped working like a slave, and he carried on doing so. His business survived and did rather well. It would probably have done better without the various crooks who ripped him off, but it still kept us in a large Ruislip house and on holidays on the Riviera. It wasn't his fault if the world was full of wickedness. When I was older he wrote me a warning letter.

'Beware of rogues and scoundrels, who will always surround you', it said sensibly.

After Dave, he needed someone else to quickly take over as manager. Really, in his heart, he hoped that one day I would take over the business that he loved. His other baby that he had nurtured and struggled over and brought up from nothing to a whole factory with clientele all over the country and in the smartest shops: John Lewis, Selfridges, Harrods. He wanted to pass it on to me, the only child he had and the only person he trusted. And there were promising signs. I had already had one brain-wave: a webbing belt with a nickel clasp and little zip pocket in it that you could put your money in at school. My father made them in every colour of school uniform and they sold like hot-cakes. So he perhaps had high hopes for me and the future of his business, but I was too young, so in the meantime he chose the next best thing for his manager – another Jew. *Unsere.*

Joe Posner was a taxi driver, but he wasn't doing that well, and he was sick to death of driving round town at all hours, having late nights, sitting in stinking traffic day after day. He'd been thinking of giving it up and trying something else for some time. And he was an old friend, a neighbour. Joe and his wife Eva often played bridge with my parents. They went to the same *shul*. Even my mother had faith in Joe. He and his wife were her friends. Here, at last, was someone who my father thought he could trust. Surely.

Me, my father and Lusty in the garden.

33: LESLEY GOES TOO FAR

We had a heavy schedule at art school: half-days of clay modelling, still life, life drawing, architecture, calligraphy, museum study, drawing from the cast, general education, a whole day painting, and another whole day of our chosen craft – a whole day in the bitchy textile room. It had enormous glass windows all down one side through which the sun blazed and, even in the spring, could turn the room into a bake-house. All along the window side were our big, sloping desks, at which we sat on tall stools, often lulled into a warm stupor, which sapped our energy and creativity. We needed diversion, something arresting, to perk us up.

It was usually Lesley who brought us to life again with her jokes. But one day she went too far. She had been given a sensitive, personal letter to pass on by Daisy Johnson, a rather naive girl who should have known never to trust Lesley with such a task.

I knew Daisy was an innocent, because she knew even less than I did about the world. I was sitting at my desk, on one of those warm days, rather stuck with my half-drop repeat, when Daisy came up to my board and drew a small diagram. It was an elongated U with a line across it about half-way down. She was not sure whether she had actually done 'it' properly with her boyfriend Ginge, and whether or not she was still a virgin.

'It went in that far,' explained Daisy, pointing to the line across her diagram. 'What do you think?'

What did I think? Me? Why ask me? The one person in the whole art school who had never done it and knew absolutely nothing about it? It just shows what a bad judge of character Daisy was, although I was rather flattered to think that a) she thought I would know, and b) that she had put her trust in me. But I panicked a little having such a rude drawing on my board. People might think I had done it.

'Rub it off,' I hissed at Daisy rather meanly. 'Quick. I don't know. How should I know?'

I thought Daisy ought to have easily been able to tell if that had happened. Surely there'd have been a sudden and horrible pain, or blood everywhere. So perhaps she hadn't done it properly, but I didn't really want to discuss it. It was like advanced Doctors and Nurses, and again I wasn't keen to join in. I just wanted that diagram off my board as quickly as possible, so I was no help to her at all.

And another difficult thing about being friends with Daisy was that her clothes were all wrong. Even I could tell. Her favourite skirt was a just-above-the-knee wrap-around in big black and white checks — crude! — with a purple wool fringe around the edges. A purple fringe? Frightful, but she didn't notice all the sneering. She wasn't even ashamed that her mother had helped her choose the check skirt. Did I like it?

'Yes, it's very nice.' What else could I say?

Then she leaves a personal, private letter with Lesley. And although Lesley had absolutely promised on her life not to open it, what did she do? She opened it the minute Daisy was gone, and from her usual position on the central printing table, she read it out to us, her acolytes, as we egged her on from our high stools. It was only brief.

'Dear Ginge,' Lesley read, with her chin pulled in and her mouth pursed, so that she looked and sounded amusingly common. 'Sorry it had to be like this. Let's put it down to experience. Love, Scruff.'

How we all screamed with laughter, and repeated each phrase with our chins pulled in, as Lesley had done. What guilt I felt afterwards. Especially as Daisy thought I was her friend. But even though Ann wasn't particularly Daisy's friend, this episode was too much for her. She decided to give up textiles, and instead, for her craft day, to do lithography, across the corridor with only boys, which suited her better. But before she went, we had somehow made friends. I luckily never had to mention candles, but I had admired one of her jumpers, and she had told me the source — M&S, and advised size 44, which broke the ice, and we both liked to carry large straw gondola baskets.

As she and I no longer spent craft day together, we met at lunchtimes. I loved lunchtimes. They were another complete and thrilling change from school lunches or meals at home, because we could go to Sid's Café, in a little street that ran along the side of the art school. In fact we could see it from the textile room windows – who was going in and out, and when. But it wasn't the people we went for. It was the food. Best of all, the toast and jam, or toast and dripping. A novelty food for me. Something I would never get at home, because toast and dripping was what the poorest of *goyim* ate. To my mother it was slum food. The nearest she got to it was rye-bread with chicken schmaltz, but we wouldn't just eat that. Any form of fat, even chicken fat, was not enough of a topping on its own. The bread and schmaltz would have chopped chicken liver on top – a proper snack. So the toast and dripping was a novelty for me, not just the dripping, but the toast as well, because it was thick, sliced, white bread toast – another form of poor *goyim drek* food to my mother. Even the jam came into the same category. It wasn't home-made, or even a good quality shop jam. It was bright red common jam, which I had never tasted, or even seen, before. Three novelty food-stuffs, with big white mugs of tea, consumed while sitting next to workmen, labourers and lorry-drivers. My absolute favourite lunch of all time.

Sid himself wore a white overall and had smooth, black hair and by the time I turned up, he was long accustomed to art students. He treated everyone in the same way: workmen, the dazzlingly beautiful Gloria, the weird students in black, the groovily dressed boys. His face never expressed the slightest glimmer of shock, disapproval or mockery. And the workmen were the same. Those who were not regulars occasionally sniggered, but they soon became accustomed to us. Funny-looking art students? What funny-looking art students? We barely registered, so we were able to relax in Sid's Café, but I knew that I should not describe the place or menu to my mother. I never did. She thought I spent my pocket money in the canteen.

If Ann and I had any lunchtime over, or didn't go to Sid's, we would buy sandwiches or takeaway snacks, find an empty classroom and, to amuse ourselves, sing like Constance Shacklock: *Rule Britannia*; *Come into the Garden, Maud*; *Nymphs and Shepherds* – anything in that style, contralto, and a particular favourite was *Velia*. 'Velia, oh Velia, the witch of the wood.' What fun we had. Our friendship was cemented by this singing, which no one seemed to know about, until Bill Brooker, the life painting and general painting teacher, heard us and looked in, had a quick sneer and shut the door again.

What did we care? Mr Brooker was our least favourite teacher. He thought himself so clever and suave. And anyway he had favourites, which a teacher is never meant to do: Phillip and Maurice – boys, notice – to whom he devoted most of his time, beckoning them into a small side room to paint under his close supervision, as if the rest of us were a waste of his time. But he did pay attention to Gloria, who rather admired him.

Serioiusly artistic, 1960.

34: MY FATHER, THE FORNICATOR

If my mother had thought that woman buying skirts in
the shop was hiding a shocking secret, it was nothing on
the terrible secret that would emerge in the summer of
1960. I came home from art school one lovely, hot,
sunny afternoon, and found my mother sitting on the
lawn on her relaxa-chair with a blotchy face, dabbing
her eyes with a hanky and trying not to cry. Usually
this sort of weather perked her up. Whatever was the
matter?

'Blanche Walmesley,' blubbed my mother.

What about Blanche Walmesley? Blanche had always
got a little on my mother's nerves. Always looking perfect, turning up and sitting around for ages, never very
happy, a bit wet and not exactly Brain of Britain, but
pleasant enough for a neighbour. I couldn't imagine her
doing anything terrible enough to make my mother cry.
What could it be?

My mother told me the whole shocking story. She was
busting to tell someone and, now that I was no longer a

schoolgirl, but a student and much more sophisticated and worldly, she could perhaps more easily tell me. What an odd thing, though, my mother confiding in me, her child, about something so grown-up.

Blanche had come round just after lunch, they'd been sitting on the lawn, as usual, having a drink, and then Blanche had started crying. What was the matter? Blanche was distraught. She told my mother that she'd met a marvellous man. The man of her dreams. He was madly in love with her. She was madly in love with him. He wanted her to leave her husband and go and live with him and she didn't know what to do. He was so handsome and so wonderful. He was so considerate, such a gentleman, so funny. Just perfect. The sort of man she'd always dreamed of. And all this time, Blanche was crying her eyes out.

'What are you crying for Blanche?' asked my mother, baffled. 'This is what you've always wanted. To meet somebody wonderful and clear off. Your daughter's old enough. She'll manage. You've been sick of Eric for years, haven't you? He never touches you. What are you waiting for? You ought to be happy.'

'I am,' said Blanche, wailing away. 'But I can't. I just can't.' Wail, wail.

'For Christ's sake Blanche,' said my mother. 'Why not? What's stopping you? Who is this man?'

Then Blanche wailed even more desperately. She couldn't say. She didn't dare.

'Why not? Do I know him?'

More crying. Blanche could barely speak at all.

'Well do I? Who is he?'

But Blanche wouldn't say. My mother guessed that it was someone she knew, but who? She kept on asking, trying to cheer Blanche up, encouraging her to leave her husband. Who was this man?

At last Blanche told her.

'It's your husband.'

Imagine my poor mother's shock. She didn't quite know what to say.

'What d'you mean, it's my husband?'

But now Blanche had confessed, the floodgates opened and out poured the details. My father was going to divide up all our furniture, take half of it and run off to set up home with Blanche. My mother couldn't believe it. Naturally she questioned Blanche. Because when would my father have had the time for all this? He was always working.

I agreed with my mother. It was a load of rubbish. I didn't believe it for a minute, because a) he never would have had the time, and b) more important, he didn't like Blanche. She got on his nerves. I'd hear him say it, in a rather coarse way. 'Get rid of her will you? She gets on my tits.'

'Look how he always buggers off upstairs when she's here,' I pointed out to my mother. Blanche must have made it all up.

But Blanche had proof. She'd told my mother everything. She could describe the inside of the factories. Both of them. She knew what times he'd come home, she knew the days he'd been late home from work. That's when they'd been seeing each other. By now my poor mother was weeping again. She believed Blanche's story. How else did Blanche know about the factories? It must be true.

'Because she's been with you. You took her there for belts,' I reminded my mother. 'You took her up to Poland Street, then you took her to South Ruislip. You showed her your shop, you took her round to the Ruislip factory for more belts, and you left her there.'

Yes, my mother remembered. But what about the times he comes home? How does Blanche know that?

Because she can see from her front window. She lives three doors away. She's probably on the look-out, I told my mother. She's bonkers. I really believed that. I knew in my heart that Blanche was making it all up. And eventually my mother nearly believed me, which was quite something, because this was the first time ever that I had known better than my mother and managed to calm her down. That was a bit of break-through.

Obviously Blanche wasn't the poor, harmless creature my mother had thought she was. She was a scheming, wicked fibber. Or raving mad. But my mother was still not absolutely sure that it was all lies. Blanche was, after all, very attractive and always made the most of herself, whereas my mother was not always dressed up to the nines like Blanche. And Blanche was also polite and charming. She did not shout and scream and throw fish and chips about, as my mother did. Perhaps my mother was aware of her own bad temper. But why not be bad tempered, when your husband was always working and paid you no attention.? Or was he working? Perhaps he was paying bloody Blanche all the attention that she herself wasn't getting. My mother wasn't completely convinced by my argument.

I kept out of the way when my father came home, because my mother naturally interrogated him immediately. Was it true? No of course it wasn't. My father was browned off. There he was, an innocent man, working hard, minding his own business, and along comes a *meshugene* cow trying to wreck his private life. As if he didn't have enough problems at work. He gets home exhausted, and finds that another bloody maniac has been sitting scheming in his own kitchen. He marched straight down the road to talk to Mr Walmesley and find out what was going on.

My mother told me all the details the next day. Mr Walmesley had accused my father of 'fornicating' with his wife. How shocking. But my father denied everything, and went on denying it until poor Mr Walmesley collapsed across the kitchen table, with his head on his arms, moaning, 'Oh God! She's done it again.'

That's why the Walmesleys had come to our road in

Ruislip. They'd been escaping from another enraged husband who Mrs Walmesley had been planning to elope with, taking the furniture. Proof of my father's innocence. He was not a fornicator. Mrs Walmesley had made it all up. She was a raving lunatic. What a relief for my mother.

With my father, 1961.

35: FRONT BOTTOMS

My father still often worked quite late. If he wasn't slaving away at the Ruislip factory, he might be up in town visiting suppliers or buyers, which was handy if he did this on the nights I also worked late at art school. We had such a packed timetable that our lessons did not fit into a normal school week, but spread into the evenings, until 9 o'clock at night. Then my father could drive by – because he could easily come home via Ealing Broadway – and pick me up, together with some of my new friends, who lived in the same direction: Laraine because she too lived in Ruislip, and also Maurice, from my class, who lived in Eastcote, right next to Ruislip.

My mother no longer needed to worry about Mrs Walmesley, but she still had me to worry about, and the last thing she wanted was me not coming home until after 10 at night. Anything could have happened. Just because your child is older and at college, that doesn't mean that you need no longer worry about her. If anything, the worry increases. My clothes were already *geferlekh*, I looked liked nobody's business, thought my mother, so God knows what other terrible influences there could be in that bloody art school, because everyone knew that art schools were full of drugs and sex, and if my father could at least pick me up on late nights and stop me wandering about the streets, then that was one peril averted.

There was no need for my mother to worry. I was quite safe. I had nothing to do with sex and drugs, but I couldn't reassure her, because I couldn't really discuss things like that with my mother. Erk. For a start, I could never have told her about Maurice's special paintings. He showed them to me one day when I went round to his house. He painted them and kept them in a shed in his garden.

'Come and have a look, Meechel,' said Maurice, and opened the shed door.

It was stuffed with large canvasses, blazing with mainly reds and purples. It took me a few moments to work out what they were, because it wasn't an area that I was particularly familiar with. Then I realized. Women's front bottoms. Maurice would have said 'cunts', but I wouldn't have dared. And straightaway I had the same thought that I'd had over Linda Bates's and Paula Cattermole's Doctors and Nurses games. They were in a dangerous position, much too close to his mother. What if she were to discover them? What horror. Whatever would she do? Scream? Faint? Disown him? Because even I thought this a worrying subject to paint. And so huge and brightly coloured.

I had only once looked at my own bottom – I couldn't even bear to name the front bit properly – when I was 15 and alone in the bathroom. It gave me the most terrible fright. What a horrid mess and weird shapes. Why did it not match properly on both sides? Was it meant to be like that? Was it normal? Or cancerous growths? And whatever it was, how awful it looked. Yuk. I stayed in the bathroom for ages, sitting on the floor crying, and never, ever looked again, until much later in my life, so it came as a terrific shock to me to find that this was Maurice's chosen subject for painting. At least he wasn't doing these paintings in class. And if I got a bit of a shock, whatever would his poor mother think? Because she was a normal, Ruislip-Eastcote person, and often wore a pinny.

Perhaps my mother was right to worry. Sex and bottoms did seem to crop up rather frequently at art school. The only ones I liked were the huge women's bums that Ann made in Mr Thomas's clay modelling classes. Everyone admired Ann's models of nude women with enormous bums, even the boys. What a fantastic shape they were, even though the bums were massive and much too big for the rest of the woman. Annoyingly, the only person who didn't like them was Mr Thomas. Ann would carefully build up the clay bums, but if she left the room, for tea-break, or even for a few minutes to go to the lavatory, she'd come back and find that Mr Thomas had sliced off a large chunk of buttock. Infuriating. So she just piled it back on again, and he sliced it back off, and modelling lessons were an endless battle for her, which she more or less won in the end, perhaps with not quite as big bums as she had wanted, but still impressive.

But the really dreadful sex episode came from Mr Brooker. He thought we needed a broader education, needed to be more cultured, and luckily for him, *Lady Chatterley's Lover* had just been published. I found a copy stuck down the side of the seat on the 49 bus one morning on my way in to school. What an uproar there had been about this book.

So Mr Brooker – he liked us to call him Bill – decided to read it out to us in class, and he read it in dialect, particularly the words 'fuck' and 'cunt', as if they were nothing untoward. Just ordinary words to him, like 'tea' and 'sandwich'. He had chosen the sex passages, so that he could read out 'fuck' and 'cunt' as often as possible, and to go along with the reading, he gave us a little lecture about sex.

'Sex is an art,' said Bill, in a knowing way, with his head tilted back slightly and his nose in the air. 'It takes practice.'

How nauseating, Ann and I thought, and also we noticed that Bill had upset William, the only square boy in the school. William, unlike the other boys, did wear nylon shirts, ordinary ties and grey trousers, parted his blond hair on one side and combed it flat. During the winter he nearly always wore his mac, done up and belted, and he didn't speak much, but when Bill read out *Lady Chatterley's Lover*, William went very pink in the face. Clearly it upset him. Why couldn't Bill see that? Or perhaps he didn't care, because he just ploughed on and on with his reading, putting William through hell. And making us sick. Obviously he didn't realize how sophisticated we were. The fool.

36: THE BOAT DREAM

Now that Joe Posner was manager and the factory in safe hands, and Blanche's accusations had been proved to be fibs, my mother decided that she could risk a short holiday, and she bloody needed one. Cannes was a bit of a *schlep* for just a week, so she decided on Cornwall, and fell in love with it. Why not have a cottage there? She'd found the perfect one in a heavenly little village called Porthallow, and she could easily nip down there for a few days at any time of year, and just go to Cannes in the summer. If she even needed to. What was wrong with Cornwall? The food was fabulous – cream teas, fresh vegetables, lovely pasties and, best of all, loads of fish and sea-food, straight out of the sea. She and my father could go down to the beach in the morning and buy fish from the fishermen. You could never get such fabulous fresh fish in London: crabs, lobsters, everything. And better still, you could even go out with the fishermen in their boats, which was heaven for my father, because if there was one thing he loved doing, almost more than sitting in the betting shop or working like a maniac, it was going out in boats.

All his life he had wanted a boat. Down in Cannes he would wander about the harbour looking longingly at the yachts and fishing boats, and working out which one he'd like best, and had planned for years, with his brother Phil, that one day they would buy one between them – a modest yacht – and sail to the South of France, and just as they were getting seriously into the planning, Phil died. Suddenly, of a heart attack, while he was skiing in Switzerland.

Phil was the big brother who had protected my father on their way up Camden Road to Holloway Boys' School – a dangerous journey for two little Jews. The *goyim* would try to beat them up, but it is not as easy to beat up two brothers as one lone boy, and my father and Phil were luckily not all that little. Then Phil grew up to be a doctor – the cleverest child in the family. The most cultured. On one of his visits he gave me three classical music LPs: *The Planets*, Rachmaninov's *Piano Concerto No. 2*, and Bach's *Double Violin Concerto*. I didn't listen to them much at the time, because I also had Buddy Holly, Elvis and the Everly Brothers LPs, which I much preferred.

None of this impressed my mother. She had never been keen on Phil. As far as she was concerned, Phil was the one who always got my father into trouble. If my father got drunk, it was usually Phil's fault. He only got drunk when Phil was around. And then one day they both came home to our house late and very drunk indeed, and my father was horribly sick. Well someone was sick, and Phil said it was my father, then he buggered off in the morning, and left my father to take the blame, but somehow my mother found out, with some very cunning and persistent questioning, that it was Phil who had been sick, not my father.

'I should have known,' shrieked my mother. 'The bloody *drek*. He always does this to you.'

Then she reminded my father again of that business when they were both little boys. When Phil had wet his pants, their mother asked who did it, and Phil blamed my father.

'For pissing in his own pants! And what did he say to her?' my mother bellowed for the millionth time, because this was another of her never-to-be-forgotten stories like the one about my sugar mouse. 'What did Phil say? He said "Pecky done it!" (Pecky being my father's nickname) and she bloody believed him. Your *drek* of a mother. And now you're sticking up for him again. For what? What's he ever done for you, *scream scream*,' as she mopped up the sick remainders in the bathroom.

I had taken to practising the piano again now that I was at art school. I'd more or less given it up over the last few years, through O Levels and the beginning of art school. But it was still handy when I wanted to get away from the rows that went on through the hatch, my mother screeching from the kitchen side, my father grunting back from the living-room side. It was difficult to completely drown out the shrieking, except with some really loud Brahms or Beethoven, but I still got the gist of it, because snatches unavoidably broke through in the diminuendos.

My mother had shouted ferociously about Phil before, and once thrown plates at him as he nipped off down our front garden path after leading my father astray on some other occasion. The plate-throwing had accompanied her wildest outburst of screaming, which ended up with her being unable even to utter proper words, but just terrible wails, so that by the time Phil had disappeared down the street, she was hysterical, breathing with difficulty and almost fainting with fury at his misdeeds.

But my father loved Phil, his big brother, with all of his heart. Being a doctor, Phil had gone into Bergen/Belsen at the end of the war, when the British liberated it, and when he came home he told my father there was no God. My father knew that already, but he always listened to Phil, and he sobbed and sobbed when Phil died, because he'd lost his favourite brother and their big dream, which they were so close to realizing.

Now, in Cornwall, there were boats everywhere, almost in his back garden. He only had to walk down some steps, then a few yards to the beach, where he would go in the mornings and chum up with the fishermen, then if he got there early enough, or if he went out there late at night, he could go out in their boats, dressed as a fisherman with the appropriate hat, and bring back the dinner.

Which was why he was quite happy to buy a small cottage in Porthallow. If he couldn't go all that often, then my mother could drive down herself, with a friend, sometimes Gracie, sometimes Jean Riley, her old midwife who she'd brought to the New Forest, sometimes me and one of my girlfriends, and if she absolutely couldn't get out of it, sometimes even Celia.

My father and his brother Phil (on right), circa 1915.

37: FORCED FEEDING

Auntie Celia only seemed to have one friend. Isabel Salvona. Isabel Salvona, the stuff of my nightmares. She seemed to me to be the most horrible woman on earth. A bitch, an evil influence. A staggeringly rich, pampered, spoilt, snooty, spiteful woman with a pointy face and her dyed black hair scraped harshly up into a tight, knotted bun, flamenco-dancer style. She looked like a witch version of Blanche Walmesley. Why was I so furious with Isabel Salvona? Because she crouched behind Celia like the devil, pouring poison into her ear. I know because Celia told me what she had said. But she took care to tell me when I visited her one day without my mother.

I had dropped in with Ann, because my mother had told me to. We were up in town shopping for Christmas presents, and also we were desperate for a lavatory and a cup of tea, so we called on Celia, thinking that we'd only be there for about 15 minutes. A huge mistake.

'Mischl. My little niece,' said Celia, opening the flat door. 'And who's this? Is this your friend?'

I answered Auntie's questions while she smiled with her head on one side in the usual simpering way, pretending that she was just a gracious hostess and wasn't looking us up and down very carefully and doing a scrupulous inspection.

'Come in, girls. Have you both been shopping? What've you bought? Are you going to show your auntie? I bet you're hungry, aren't you? What would you like to eat?'

Auntie drifted ahead of us towards the kitchen, questioning non-stop, wearing a dark green silky kimono with a brightly coloured embroidered dragon on the back. And matching slippers. She had been forewarned of our visit by my mother.

'Go on. You'd better have a snack. Your mother said you'd be hungry.'

'No thank you,' we said. 'Honestly, we're not.'

We just wanted a cup of tea, we told Auntie. She mustn't bother. We didn't want anything. We could eat when we got home.

But Celia wasn't having any of that. We had to eat something. She insisted. She opened her fridge and it was stuffed full of snacks: smoked salmon, schmaltz herring, cheeses, ham, salami, yogurts. Or what about some nice cake? Look. She had cheesecake and Danish pastries. Didn't we want one with our cup of tea? We must have something. What about an egg? Just a plain boiled egg? Nag, nag, nag.

'What's wrong with an egg? An egg can't hurt you. Have an egg.'

Then she climbed up on to a little stool which had two steps up its side, and opened a high cupboard. A packet of Cornish wafers tumbled out because the cupboard was so full. Celia had barely managed to stuff her supplies into it.

'Look. I've got biscuits.'

Ann and I picked them up.

'Do you like those?' asked Auntie, climbing slowly down, holding on to the cupboard door in an elegant way, as if she were a precious object and must take care not to break.

'You don't have to have those. Look,' she pointed upwards to the stuffed cupboard. 'I've got matzos, I've got digestives.' Auntie wheedled as if *we* had some sort of hold over *her*. 'You get them for me. Go on. Go on the stool. You can do it easier than me. Look. What do you want? Pass the digestives. Put these back. That's right. What a clever girl.'

And then to Ann, 'Did you know my niece was very clever? Well I'm telling you, she is. She takes after her mother. Pass the matzos. I fancy one. Do you? With your eggs? Eh? Pass them. Shut the cupboard door, now be careful coming down. Watch where you're going. Careful. You don't want to break your neck. Your mother would never forgive me. Do you love your auntie, Mishl? Do you?'

'Yes Auntie.'

'Now what are you going to have? That's not much, is it? A boiled egg. You'd better have something else as well.' But we stuck to the boiled eggs, because we thought that might be the easiest. And quickest, and then we could escape. And we didn't want to be any trouble.

'Trouble? How could it be trouble to feed my favourite niece,' said Auntie, still bending and smiling, and she sat us at the table, with placemats, serviettes, little spoons, egg cups, tea cups, matching plates, biscuit selection, and we knew that escape was a long way away.

'Thank you Auntie.'

Ann didn't mind as much as I did. To her Auntie was a fascinating novelty. She'd never come across anyone like that. In her house people spoke directly and stuck to the point. Sometimes they were horribly rude to each other. No one ever pretended to be pleasant. They certainly did not go on and on, offering various options, ignoring answers, continuing to question and insist on you doing what you didn't really want to do, until you gave in.

Perhaps Auntie felt that my mother might find fault if she knew we had visited and not been fed. Celia had her faults, but she knew this rule. All visitors must be fed, especially your sister's child, and her friend, even if they do look like a couple of waifs and the friend is a *shikse*. So we sat waiting for our tea and toast and boiled egg, while Celia fussed about getting everything just so, and then, while Ann went to the lavatory, she told me what Isabel Salvona had said.

'Isabel said you only come and see me because you want my money,' said Auntie, in a sort of innocent way, as if such an idea would never enter her head had Isabel not put it there, and now that it was there, she could barely believe it, but you could tell that she did believe it and it had probably been in there for some time.

'You wouldn't do that, would you, Mishl?' she went on, still looking rather bendy, with her head on one side.

But what was I meant to say to that? I couldn't win, and I knew that Auntie knew I couldn't. Because I had to say it wasn't true, whether it was or not. Sucking up to someone for money would be a ghastly thing to do, even if it was my own money. So of course I said that wasn't why I visited. Although in a way it was, because I was only visiting because my mother had told me to, and she'd told me to because she wanted to stay close to Celia, because of the money. And she also occasionally had to endure Isabel, because she couldn't very well be rude to Celia's best friend, although I know that in her heart, my mother hated Isabel almost as much as I did.

'How's *Mrs Kennisht-Kakken*?'[77] she would ask Celia, when she felt obliged to enquire about Isabel but absolutely could not contain her disgust.

[77] Mrs Can't-Shit.

Then, if my mother had had the misfortune of seeing the two of them together, she would come home and report to my father, all the horrors of that combination, which was too much for her. Even Celia alone was close to unbearable.

'She takes my *kishkes* out!' my mother would moan, collapsing in a chair the minute she got home, almost weeping with exhaustion, fury and the strain of having to be nice to Celia.

Now Ann and I were having a taste of it. At last we finished our eggs and were ready to go, but first of all we had to get out, and before we could do that, we had to listen to Celia's directions. She wanted to make sure we knew how to get to Hyde Park Corner station, which was just below her flat and visible from it, but she felt that we needed to know all the possible routes to it. There were several options. Celia took my arm and led me to the window to point them out. I could go down this way/that way/the lift or the stairs, or the other set of stairs, then I could come out of this door/that door, approaching the station from the right or left, and if I approached it from one side I would have to go across here or there, once I got inside, and then I could go round this or that, or straight across, to the ticket office, which was on this side if I went in that way, but if I entered from the other side, it would be just opposite me.

Behind me, reflected in the glass of the window, I

could see a sort of tumbling figure, bent double, then straightening up again, backwards and forwards. It was Ann, laughing at the performance. Because Auntie had started rearranging her chairs to illustrate the layout of our journey to the station, pulling this one out to signify Boots, and another one to stand for the ticket office. Could I remember that? She gave my arm a little tug, to make sure I was listening. Yes I was. Yes Auntie, yes.

But I wasn't, because that was the trouble with Celia. She went on and on for so long and with such complications, that by the time she'd finished the listener would be totally *farmisht* and *farblondzhet*[78], as my mother would say. You knew less than you had when she started, you hadn't a clue what she was up to, and so you'd say Yes. Yes to anything, even if you didn't know what it was anymore, just to shut her up. Which was probably what happened to my grandma on her death-bed. Imagine a sick and dying person having a reasoned argument with Celia. Not a chance in hell.

Eventually we escaped, me busting with shame and impatience and wanting to scream, but Ann nearly crying with laughter, because to her it had been a fabulous comedy turn, and when we got home, we of course reported every word to my mother, but guess what? Celia had got in first. She had rung my mother and this is what she had said.

[78] Lost, bewildered, confused.

'They turned up and they were starving, Clarice, and I was just going out, I had nothing in the house, but they said they had to have something to eat, so I made them a boiled egg. It was all I had, and then I was nearly late for *blah blah*.'

My mother believed our version, without question. And she loved it, because it proved, beyond a shadow of a doubt, that Celia was the monstrous fibber that my mother had always said she was.

Left to right: Celia, Bill, my mother, father, me with hair-piece, 1961.

38: PAMELA PLANS HER ESCAPE

Once I got to art school, I saw very little of Kathy. She had made other chums, although I still occasionally ran down the road for a quick visit to Gracie when I felt that conditions in our house were hotting up. Her friendship with my mother was rather up and down, because of the *shickering*, which could easily put a bridge game in jeopardy. You needed people you could rely on for bridge games, and Gracie was getting more and more unreliable. I still went to visit her whatever, but didn't always tell my mother, particularly when Gracie was in her bad books. I suspected that she would see it as treacherous. Why would I prefer to go and sit in a shit-hole with Gracie, when I could spend time with my own mother, who was not a drunkard and kept a lovely clean kitchen? What was wrong with our house? Wasn't it good enough for me anymore?

It wasn't so bad when my mother and Gracie had chummed up again, but in the frosty periods I had to keep it a strict secret, and pray that Gracie wouldn't blab it out. Hopefully she had known my mother long enough to understand the risks, because I did moan at her about my mother, but she never moaned back, and only tried, as hard as she possibly could, to convince me of my mother's virtues. What a saint. If she only knew what my mother sometimes said about her – especially after a wrecked bridge game.

But Pamela and I sometimes still met at the station, walked up the hill together to the roundabout, where we had seen the rude man, hoping that we wouldn't bump into her mother on the way, then we would usually go back to my house, because Pamela was now keeping out of the *kurve*'s way as much as she possibly could and staying out as long as possible. Now that we were older, our mothers seemed all the more intolerable, but my mother was by far the better option.

She was in two minds over Pamela. Being an Irish Catholic lost Pamela a few points, because to my mother the Catholics were a generally poor and tatty lot, with waif-like children, and the only fat Catholics were the priests. She had pointed out the proof of this to me when we both went on a short holiday to Sitges in Spain when I was 11, without my father, who was too busy at the bloody factory, as usual. And as usual my mother was right. I saw the Catholics with my own eyes. Crowds of beggar children would follow us about the little town, in grubby, raggedy clothes, their hair shaved very short with little bald patches all over their skulls. What was that?

Some sort of horrid flea-bitten or lousy area, or mange, from being poor and dirty. But who was strutting about in black robes, shiny shoes and with healthy complexions and big, round stomachs? The priests.

My mother was triumphant, but in a despairing and bitter way. It was no fun to be proved right when one is in a heavenly little Mediterranean resort trying to enjoy oneself, and there are half-starved children all over the place, and greedy fat priests. My mother scorned the Catholic Church, but how could she not? They were visibly failing at the one thing in the world which she thought most important. Feeding your children. She was always outraged by fat grown-ups in charge of thin children, and there they were, all over Sitges. Same in Ruislip. Pamela was thin and pasty-looking, but her mother wasn't thin at all, so my mother assumed that Pamela was rather neglected. And having a *kurve* for a mother gained Pamela even more sympathy. A terrible thing for a child, my mother thought, *nebekh*, to have to live with such a cow of a mother.

My mother and I still didn't know the half of it, because Pamela never gave us any proper clues about what was going on, but we both suspected that there was something seriously wrong with Mrs Saunders, as well as her *kurve* behaviour. Because she had never been hospitable. She never seemed to cook anything. To my mother this was deeply suspicious. At least the Bateses and the Andrews had cooked for their own families, even if they had failed to feed me, but Pamela's mother never seemed to feed even her own child. Pamela always had to look after herself.

I hadn't actually told my mother the exact details, but had given her just enough information to make her sympathetic rather than cross, and not enough to enflame her into stamping off down the road to give the *kurve* a mouthful about child neglect or otherwise causing ructions. It was a difficult balance to strike, but possible, because although my mother was always on the look-out for advantage-takers, she was, at heart, kind and generous, and once persuaded that Pamela was a deserving cause rather than a useless *shnorer*, she naturally wanted to feed her up a bit. So Pamela was always fed at our house, where she had begun to meet my new friends from art school. She never brought any of her own new friends. She said she'd met a boy who was a motorbike mechanic and had his own motorbike, but she never brought him to Ruislip, and she didn't say much else about him, except that he took her for rides on his bike up and down the Western Avenue.

Sometimes Pamela and I would see Blanche's daughter out and about. We had never played with her as children, and only knew her by sight, but ever since her mother had made up such terrible stories about my father and proved to be a nutcase, we took more notice of the daughter's comings and goings. She was by now a more voluptuous version of her mother – the same dark hair and Mediterranean complexion, but fatter. And we had noticed one day as she passed by that the back of her cream skirt was marked with green grass stains. We now both knew what that meant. Blanche's daughter had been doing it with a boy in a field somewhere. Probably on Ruislip Common. We both disapproved and laughed together at the poor daughter. Erk. Here was another sex-mad person, just like her mother. But perhaps that was rather mean of us. What must it be like to have a mother like that, who disgraced herself in front of the neighbours by telling fibs? So we talked about her instead of Pamela's mother.

Perhaps Pamela didn't know that my mother and loads of other people all thought her mother a *kurve*. It's not the sort of thing anyone would tell a child. And no wonder Pamela never even told Kathy and me, her best friends, what her mother was up to. Although I was at art school and thought I knew about life, I would never have even imagined all that. I knew a little about prostitutes, not much about lesbians and nothing at all about child abuse. Fifty years later, I would find out that Pamela's mother did all of them. But at the time I would never have guessed that anyone could be a hundred times worse than Blanche.

After a while Pamela and I realized that we hadn't seen Blanche or her daughter about for some time. I asked my mother about them.

'They've buggered off,' said she, 'and a bloody good job too.'

'Where to?'

'How should I know where the *drek*'s gone? She can go to hell for all I care.'

My mother still hadn't quite got over Blanche. She wasn't absolutely 100 per cent sure that my father was entirely innocent. How could she be? All her life she'd watched him being charming to other women, and she'd watched the women simpering round him and remarking upon how handsome he was and how lucky she was to have a husband like that. But what did they know? They didn't know that two cleaning ladies and my auntie's au pair had all left in a bit of flap, and it was something to do with my father, but no one was ever quite sure what he'd done. And it always happened when my mother was away – perhaps in Barrow for a week with me, or in Cornwall with a friend, or perhaps she'd gone to Cannes ahead of him in the long school summer holidays.

Then one day she came back to find that Elsie, the lovely cleaning lady, had left.

'What's happened to Elsie?' she asked my father.

'How should I know?' said he.

Then Elsie's husband came to collect her last week's wages.

'What's happened to Elsie?' my mother asked the husband. 'Why's she left? Has something upset her? Is she ill?'

'Ask your husband,' said Elsie's husband, in a terrible fury, and he turned round and walked away very fast, as if he were controlling himself with difficulty and wanted to get away quick.

My mother never found out what had happened. If she questioned my father she got nowhere.

'Do me a favour,' my father would say. 'Don't *hak mir in kop* about Elsie.' And then he would sulk. Which all made my mother a little doubtful about Blanche. Had my father ever given her cause to think she might be in with a chance? My mother would never know.

Pamela's mother stayed put in Ruislip, but Pamela was spending less and less time there. Sometimes she stayed with her new friends at art school, and soon the new motorbike boyfriend had taken her all the way to Birmingham, where his family lived, and she stayed for the weekend. He drove ever so fast, Pamela told us. Wasn't she frightened? No. It was very exciting and nearly as good as riding. But the more she stayed away, the more horrible and bad-tempered her mother became, which only made Pamela want to stay away more and more, and try harder to get a job, which wasn't that difficult, because who wouldn't want someone as lovely as Pamela in their restaurant or whatever?

She soon got some evening work in a pub, and once she had her own money, she wouldn't need to come home at all, if she could only find a room somewhere. Or perhaps the motorbike boyfriend would get serious, and if he didn't, then she'd find somebody else, which probably wouldn't take her long. But even if she stayed the night at my house and we were together for hours, she never said very much. She never gave details. Everything was a bit vague and floaty, and although she outlined her plans and admitted she was fed up with her mother and couldn't wait to get out of there, that was all she said.

It was always Kathy and me who made the plans and decisions, and Pamela who went along with them. Kathy was the most bossy, I was middling bossy, and Pamela was never bossy at all. She never seemed to mind what we did, she smiled, she joined in, was never bitchy and seemed happy enough. How did she manage it? Because by now her mother seemed to hate her, and her father didn't love her either.

39: ANOTHER MAD FAMILY

It is late spring and my second term at art school. I have got the hang of the clothes now, and am feeling more confident. Not enormously confident, but more than I was at the beginning, so I decide to try a blouse and skirt, and eye make-up. A daring move. I have a straight, just-above-the-knee-length skirt in a subtle dark blue and brown check, and have dyed an old, round-necked school blouse dark brown, and sewn a frill round the neck, to match the skirt, because no shops have a suitable blouse. The eye make-up is particularly difficult. It is Cleopatra style, and it takes me forever to get the eyeliner into the right shape in the corners, but I manage it. This is a tremendous break-through for me, because I am not wearing a big, loose jumper, but am trying to make myself look like an attractive girl. At last, despite the nose, I feel that this is possible. I get to school, I climb the few front steps to the entrance, but just as I reach the revolving doors, I bump into Mr Drew, Headmaster, and Bill Brooker coming out together.

'Hallo Michele,' says Brooker cheerily. 'Someone given you a black eye? Ha, ha.'

They both have a laugh. Why did I bother? I now feel an idiot with my silly eye make-up plastered on. And I can't get it off, because I haven't brought cotton-wool and cleaner lotion, because how was I to know this would happen? That horrid Brooker would be so rude, even before I got through the door, so that I hardly dare go into the classroom. What will everyone else say if my make-up is so wrong? How silly do I look? How will I ever have a boyfriend? Does Brooker know how crushing he is? Yes. Does he care? No. Of course not. I can, at least, tell Ann.

But where is she? Some days she just doesn't turn up. She doesn't even know why. She sets off for our art school in the normal way from her home in Acton, heading towards Ealing Broadway, and then, a few hours later, she finds she's walked all the way to somewhere like High Street Kensington. Why? She doesn't plan to do it. She doesn't think why until she gets there, then she wonders what she's doing. But when she is at school we have a laugh. Aren't people mad? You only have to hang about in the girls' lavatories and listen to the girls from fashion, and you're bound to hear some little gem or other. Ann has been ear-wigging in there and she comes to lunch with some amusing news. Two fashion girls – how inferior they are to real artists like us – have been chatting about boyfriends. One of them has a new one. Why does she like him so much? asks the other.

'Because he's manly without being brutal.' Ann's impression is spot on. She pulls her chin in, just as Lesley did when reading Daisy's letter out loud. But we feel justified because these fashion girls are not innocents like Daisy. They are just silly fluffies. What a laugh we have.

Ann needs a laugh. Life in her house is much madder than in mine. On the scale of mad it is much higher than either mine or Kathy's, and nearer to Pamela's. Ann's father is the maniac. He will not speak to her mother at all. Neither does she want to talk to him, and who can blame her? Ann and her sister Susan are on their mother's side. The father won't even speak at table, preferring instead to pass notes asking his wife to pass the butter, or whatever, or if he has no pen and paper handy, he addresses her via Ann and Susan.

'Ask your mother to pass the potatoes.'

And he has recently taken to pouring salt into the mother's orange juice and other drinks. What a pig. She gets a terrible shock when she drinks them. And he puts hairbrushes in the fridge.

'Your mother's going funny, Ann,' he says. 'She's at that age.'

But he's a chief police inspector at Scotland Yard, so what else could you expect? Driving Ann along in the car he likes to point quickly at something he finds interesting as they pass, keeping his hands on the driving wheel, just sticking one finger out rapidly in the direction of whatever it is.

'See that?' he snaps, but Ann hasn't, because it's gone by in a flash and she hardly had time to see the finger or which way it was pointing.

'No.'

'You're not very observant for an artist, are you?' says he, with a little smirk.

No wonder Ann is wandering about a bit.

Me dressed as a girl, 1960.

40: CELIA THE MATCHMAKER

Olga is now also in London. She's come down here to study languages at the Lycée Français and is living in student accommodation near the Albert Hall. This is only a few stops on the bus from Auntie Celia's flat in Park Lane. Auntie's days in this flat are numbered. A Hilton Hotel is to be built there, but why should Auntie move? She likes it there. And her upstairs neighbour won't move, because he has built a fabulous mosaic in his ceiling worth an arm and a leg. The Hilton people are going to have to pay a fortune to get rid of him, and so long as he's staying they can't pull the flats down, so Auntie might as well stay too. Then perhaps she too will be paid a fortune to get out. Upstairs aren't the only people to have spent thousands on their flat. Look at the time and money she's spent on hers, so she's hanging on, and invites Olga to dinner.

But what an odd dinner. Olga reports back to me – not to her mother, because Betty doesn't really like her to see Celia. Betty would never tell Olga what to do, but Celia makes her absolutely sick, especially since she wrung so much money out of Cyril for her share of the shop. But Olga still goes. Why not? Auntie is a relative who lives minutes away and Olga fancies a look at her flat and some dinner. She's very impressed by the coat cupboard in the hall which lights up and fills with warm air when you open the door and hang up your coat. Auntie gives her beans on toast with some very posh white wine. Typical.

But that doesn't mean that Celia doesn't care about her niece. Uncle Bill cares equally for us both. He has given Olga free tickets to shows in his theatres in the north while she was still in Barrow, and me free tickets to shows in the south. And Celia seems to care about both of us, because neither of us has a boyfriend, and she can help us here. A friend of hers has a nephew who is coming over with another friend of his, from New Zealand. Celia spots a potential double *shidekh*.[79] These are bound to be very nice boys. Not only are they Jewish, but also her friend has recommended them and it's about time, she thinks, that we both had nice boyfriends. And they have decent jobs. One is a chemist, one is a car dealer. What could be more useful? Your car will always be mended, free, and a chemist is only a step away from being a doctor. You need never worry about your health.

This is the last thing I want to do. Go out with two boring boys chosen by Auntie Celia. Quite clearly they

[79] Match, marriage, betrothal.

are not going to be the sort of boy I like. I bet they will be wearing horrid suits and ties. But Olga doesn't mind. She herself is comparatively square. To her there is nothing wrong with a car dealer and a chemist, and she would like a day out. It is normal for her to wear an ordinary dress and cardigan, and high heels. Ridiculous. And that means I shall also have to wear a dress. Luckily I have an Indian striped bedspread-material one that I made myself. I cannot compromise any further, and I certainly cannot wear high heels as I don't have any. If I must wear shoes, then it will have to be sandals. There is no chance that I could possibly fall in love with a boy who had been chosen by Auntie Celia.

But even my mother wants me to go. Why suddenly trust Celia when she knows from a lifetime's experience that Celia always has an ulterior motive? There must be something in it for her. And I bet I know what it is. I bet she's hoping that if I marry a rich chemist/car dealer, my mother won't have to worry about money anymore, and Celia will be off the hook. Free to fritter everything away at the Curzon Club. I point this out to my mother but it makes no difference. What she hasn't grasped is that I would never, ever marry anyone for money. How immoral. And nor do I care about my bloody inheritance. I have told my mother this, but she takes no notice. She still goes on and on, driving herself mad sucking up to Celia, just so that I get my money. Pointless.

The plan is that Olga will come to our house, then

these boys will drive to Ruislip, collect us and then drive us to Beaulieu to see more cars. What a waste of a Sunday, but I can't get out of it.

'You haven't even seen them yet,' says my mother crabbily. 'They may be very nice. How do you know you won't like them?'

Sometimes I do not understand my mother. Is she completely raving mad? She ran away from an arranged marriage to an epileptic butcher who had fits and wet his pants in the cinema, then came to London, worked in a baker's shop in Petticoat Lane, then met my father, who she married for love. How can she even contemplate an arrangement for me, organized by, of all people in the world – Celia? How desperate is she for me to marry someone Jewish? All right, I will go to shut her up, and because Olga fancies an outing.

Celia, glamour-puss, 1934.

These boys turn up in a Jaguar, because the car boy specialises in Jaguars. The chemist boy is better than the Jaguar boy, who has red hair and big ears. Olga agrees with me. She much prefers the chemist, but because she likes him, she deliberately sits next to the car-dealer boy, who she doesn't like so much. How peculiar. So I'm stuck with the chemist, who isn't too bad. But that's going to be the end of that. For me.

But not for Olga. She goes out with the Jaguar boy again. Only because her car breaks down a few days later, which gives him the excuse to come over, drive it away as it's still just about working, and mend it. Free. And then she goes out with him again, and again.

41: THE BOYFRIEND AND THE BOMB

Two years above me at art school is a girl who used to go to my girls' grammar school. What a coincidence. I don't know her very well, because she's older than me, but now we are both here together, we make friends. And one of her friends is a boy called Lawrence. She introduces us. He visits me in Ruislip with his guitar. He forgets it. Which means he has to come back the next day and collect it. Hoorah. The romance is on and I have a boyfriend. My first proper boyfriend, and a dream boyfriend – so perfect, that even my mother likes him. He is tall, handsome, plays the guitar and is charming and funny. He is a commercial artist, because he has to earn a living, but really he is a proper artist. His paintings are excellent. This is a huge relief for my mother. She was beginning to think there was something wrong with me, especially after the disappointment of the chemist and Jaguar boys produced by Celia. But now, even though Lawrence is not Jewish, she is rather excited. My father is not.

One evening, a few weeks into this romance, my parents went off to the cinema and left Lawrence and me alone together in the house. We were in the piano room, lying on the carpet in opposite directions, not together, and listening to one of the records that Uncle Phil had given me before he died. For hours on end, we listened to the violin concertos. That's all we did. My mother noticed on her way out, because the curtains were not drawn, the lights were on, and she could see us as she walked all the way down the path and along the pavement, parallel to the windows, that we were positioned in opposite directions, listening.

She also noticed upon her return that nothing had changed. We hadn't moved an inch. She was disappointed. Serves her right for spying, and then telling me, and having a laugh. Erk. Yet again I was disappointed by my mother's vulgarity.

What did she expect us to be doing in her house? It would be perilous to even think of such things with my mother and father hovering about. Who knows when they might appear? What if the film was disappointing and they returned early from the cinema? But these thoughts didn't run through my mind. They were instinctive, because my mother's proximity put a freeze on them. There were things that I just did not even contemplate doing within a mile of my mother. It would have been a terrible risk, like the rude and forbidden Doctors and Nurses games of my childhood, but far worse. I absolutely did not want Mummy to be thinking about, seeing or, worst of all, laughing at, my personal life. And a boyfriend was the most personal of all. She mustn't have the slightest clue about what was going on or not going on, which was why I would never have even dreamed of holding a boy's hand in my mother's presence. There was nothing much physical going on between me and Lawrence anyway, and never would be, but my mother would be bound to jump to the most horrible of conclusions.

Much better to just listen to records. Or to go to Lawrence's place. He rented a room in the house of a woman called Biddy Youngday, and shared her kitchen. Biddy was the complete opposite of my mother. She was also an artist. My mother painted still lives and flowers, Biddy painted serious portraits. My mother painted at evening classes, but Biddy painted at any time in her front room, which was her studio, packed with mainly portraits in rather sombre colours. She also cooked jugged hare, and gave us some for dinner which was very rich and rather thrilling for me, because I'd never tried it before.

I did not mention the jugged hare to my mother. Not just because hare was not kosher. Neither was pork, but my parents were mad on bacon and ham. The dietary rules in our house were not the normal Jewish rules, but an adaptation of them to suit our taste and standards. They were fairly lax, but there was a line beyond which my mother would not go, and I knew that hare was on the other side of that line. She would never eat an animal that had been hanging about for a week, then cooked in blood and port wine. 'Yech!' she would have said, sickened by the thought of stinking, mouldering game and the thick, bloody gravy. On top of that, it was always risky to praise another woman's cooking or behaviour. I still knew my mother's cooking was superior, but I thought Biddy's behaviour far more admirable. She was not interested in what I might or might not be doing on the lounge floor or anywhere else with my boyfriend, or in *shidekhs* or babies and everything that went with it. She had more important subjects to concentrate on: the painting, politics, a possible Third World War, and so did we.

Biddy was in the Committee of 100, a sort of hardcore, direct action part of CND, the Campaign for Nuclear Disarmament. I'd never heard of it before. But I knew that along with the jugged hare, it would not go down well with my mother. All sorts of things were piling up that would not please her, which I felt I had to keep quiet about – jugged hare, the bomb, my romance, and what would be the point of telling her that Biddy was a Communist? My mother sometimes voted Liberal, but sometimes voted Conservative, which I now realized was a terrible thing to do. Nearly all my new friends were left-wing, and I could tell that they were right and my mother was wrong. Obviously. It was just common sense, but what was the point of mentioning CND and politics to my parents? They were not the slightest bit interested.

Why tell them that I had been plunged into a world of serious Labour Party people and frightening information? As soon as I heard the details, I was terrified. It wasn't long before I knew all about fall-out, nuclear holocaust, people staggering around with their skin hanging off, Hiroshima and Nagasaki, and what London would look like should a bomb drop on it, and that included Ruislip. Particularly Ruislip, because of the hateful American air-base. To think that my parents and I had once thought it a good thing – a source of jolly, bridge-playing friends and bourbon, or boys in jeans and bobby-socks. Now I knew what it was really doing for us – making Ruislip a target. What would the Soviet Union missiles head for? Ruislip US air force base, which harboured US missiles. Everything would be flattened. What terrible doom and suffering lay ahead. The world was clearly run by madmen. It was quite likely that these idiots would even set off the bombs by mistake.

Lawrence and his friends John and Dicky were very keen on CND. Who wouldn't be, knowing all that? They all admired Biddy tremendously, and so did I. After the end of the war she had managed to get out of Germany, where her husband had been hanged by the Nazis, and was flown with her two little girls to England by the British. Who says the Russian soldiers went mad and raped all the women when entering Berlin? Rubbish. Biddy had been there, with her daughters, and the Russians behaved perfectly. Now here she was living in Acton, taking part in direct action: marches, sit-downs, demonstrations, for which she had been sent to Holloway Prison. How could I not join CND? Just as I was about to escape from dreary old Ruislip and our lives were getting exciting, the world was about to be blown to hell.

'Ban the bomb,' my parents called out merrily, as I went off to the demonstration in Whitehall, I marched all the way from Aldermaston to London, and I went to the sit-down at Ruislip base, with my chums in our duffle-coats and CND badges.

'Fat lot of good you'll do,' said my father in a mocking way. 'Ban the bomb? You'll be lucky.'

But we were serious. We had our instructions from the Committee of 100. 'We ask you not to shout slogans and to avoid provocation of any sort. The demonstrations must be carried out in a quiet, orderly way ... remain limp if arrested and refuse to co-operate in any way until inside the police station.'

We also had Bill Otani, from my class, advising us. Bill had a black belt in judo, and knew how to deal with the police. Should they attempt to pick us up, we must roll into a special judo-style ball, and they wouldn't be able to.

Bill tried this himself at the Ruislip demonstration. It worked. Then he leaned, in a particular judo way, against a row of policemen, and the whole row almost toppled over. They were not pleased. They couldn't pick Bill up, because he was in a ball, but his glasses fell off and the police trampled them. On purpose, we were sure of it. Then a milk-cart driver lost his patience trying to get through the crowd of demonstrators, and drove over somebody's ankle. Uproar. The crowd was furious, but luckily for him, because we were non-violent, we did not drag him from the cart and beat him up. Any other crowd would have done so.

With Lawrence, the boyfriend, 1960.

42: RUISLIP LIBRARY

It was difficult not to think about nuclear war, once you knew all the facts, and I found myself considering it a lot of the time, especially in textiles, which I was bored with and could no longer concentrate on. Before I knew it, I was sitting there thinking of mass death and a burnt and blasted landscape, with a few of us still cowering in cellars, about to emerge into what? Devastation. A new stone age, with a few maddened and mutant survivors? These were my thoughts as I sat on my tall stool in front of my more or less blank drawing board looking down at Sid's Café. Which would soon, like everything else, be burnt to a crisp.

This was a horrible state of mind to be in. Sometimes, if I thought about it too much, I would start grizzling quietly with fright. I didn't want anyone to see, because it was a bit wet of me, and what good would it do, crying? And going home didn't help. The last people to understand the horrors of nuclear war would be my parents. So I started going to the library more often.

Ruislip Library was about twenty minutes' walk from our house, down to Eastcote Road, and along to the bottom of Ruislip High Street. On the corner of the High Street was the George pub, where Laraine lived. From her bedroom window at the front of the pub, she could see the row of little houses and shops across the road: the sweet shop, the very old toy shop, the pond to the left of the shops, and behind them the library, in what used to be a sixteenth-century barn, surrounded by gardens, a duck pond and a bit of original moat. It was a lovely old building, built of bricks at the base and the rest in timber. In front of it, what used to be the old farmyard had been turned into a park and grassed over, with some trees and bushes planted, and benches that you could sit on and picnic or read your library books. Ruislip High Street may have been dull and more modern, but the library was in a little world of its own, and inside you could see the original old wooden beams, which made my thoughts of a nuclear wasteland all the more heartbreaking, because wouldn't it be terrible to have the lovely library flattened?

Once I got inside I was all right, because I had discovered some sets of very old books which went on for volumes and volumes, so that you could sink into them for weeks at a time and forget CND altogether. Four volumes of *Tom Jones*, four of *Amelia*, two of *Joseph Andrews*, three of *Roderick Random*, three of *Peregrine Pickle*, but only one sadly of *Humphry Clinker*, my favourite, which I particularly liked because it was so robust. It described filth, squalor, good and bad food, illness and health, sensible and stupid people – my everyday life, my mother's concerns – but all in such wonderful language, with such excellent jokes, and written hundreds of years ago, so you could escape into the eighteenth century, which I have loved ever since. And I could take the books home with me, where we had mainly *Readers Digest* condensed volumes of everything.

Or I could call at Laraine's on my way home and have a snack in her pub kitchen, at the great big wooden table. The snacks here were high quality. Even my mother would have approved: chunks of fresh bread, butter, great big lumps of cheese, pickled onions, chutneys, salad and slabs of hand-carved, home-roasted prime beef sirloin, left over from the Sunday joint every week, and sent down to the bar as a cold cut. We could help ourselves to anything, perhaps because Laraine's family were not straightforward English Christians. Her father was part Dutch and there was some complicated history about her grandma, so that somewhere in her background, she told me, but she didn't know where, was a tinted person, which accounted for Laraine's big arse, frizzy hair and good sense of rhythm, she thought. And her father was just as rude and forthright as my mother, perhaps even more so. He had been frightfully rude about Laraine's bare feet and eye make-up.

'Black eyes to match your bloody black feet?' he shouted coarsely and often roared out 'fuck' this and 'fuck' that, but Laraine's family didn't care. That was how pub landlords were meant to behave.

43: LIFE AFTER BILL

Bill has dropped dead. Suddenly, in the Park Lane flat. Celia went out shopping and when she came back he was dead in the armchair. Just like that. Heart attack. Bill, who we all liked but couldn't understand because he had adored Celia. How did he manage that? How did she not drive him mad, with her fiddling about, taking all morning to *kak*, her lateness, her repeated questions and instructions, her greed, her love of money, her terrible fibs and her shameful behaviour in restaurants, hotels and shops, always on the look-out for a bargain even though she was rolling in money? Still he loved her, and she loved him too, and missed him terribly when he'd gone.

What would she do without her Bill? Who was she to cook for, and shop for? Who was she to go on cruises and holidays with? What could she do on her own? She needed company. And what company did she have except for horrid Isabel? She had us which was bad luck for my mother, because Celia needed even more attention than ever before. She needed lifts everywhere: down to her other flat on the sea-front in Hove, to Cannes, to our house in Ruislip. Why not if my father was in town for the day? He could bring her back with him. But how was she to get home at night? She'd have to stay. Or she needed a lift. She couldn't possibly go home on the tube. And she needed visitors, and someone to go everywhere with her: to the Carvery, to Selfridge's food hall, to lunch in her favourite restaurants. She couldn't stand cooking anymore. How should she cook just for herself? She had no appetite. If my mother was making fish cakes, perhaps she could save her a couple? Or four? She could always freeze them. And she desperately needed someone to accompany her to the Curzon Club, where she could not only have a decent meal, but also gamble, which took her mind off her troubles. It was an even better bargain if you took a friend, because you then got two meals for the price of one, and a bargain always cheered Celia up.

The Curzon Club was just round the corner from Celia's flat. She had spent time there with Bill, or sometimes without him, when he was working in the evenings, which he often had to do, being the manager of so many grand theatres and cinemas. There was nothing wrong with going there alone when you had a husband alive in the background, because you were not really alone, and the staff were tremendously respectful: Mrs Hockman this, Mrs Hockman that, special table for Mrs Hockman? How was Mrs Hockman tonight? Also, the dinners were fabulously high quality, and at a reduced price for persons about to gamble. But it wasn't so great if you were really on your own – a widow. A pitiful, lonely figure, even if the staff were all extra-kind to her and still did their Mrs Hockman routine as if nothing had changed. But Celia knew she wasn't really a proper Mrs Hockman anymore. She went to the Curzon even more than before, because what else was she to do? She would eat, and then go upstairs to the roulette tables and throw money away. But how long would it be before she got through Bill's money and her own, and started on mine? My mother asked my father these questions and felt desperately anxious, but as usual his replies were inadequate.

'I should know?' he would ask, and then his usual 'Do me a favour', because my father's method, when anxious, was to say next to nothing, and the more worried he was, the less he said, whereas my mother did the opposite and talked more and more, going over her worries out loud, and then louder and louder as things got worse. They were getting worse because she was pretty sure that Celia had become even more reckless since Bill's death. Nothing mattered so much to her anymore, which probably meant that she was more easily able to throw money down the drain. She was unrestrained. There was no Bill to comfort her or advise her or notice their joint bank account.

So who could accompany Celia to the Curzon, and keep an eye on her? Not that anyone could stop her gambling, but perhaps she might be a little less daring with someone watching. My mother couldn't bear the place, and my father certainly wouldn't go. Although he was mad keen on gambling, nothing on earth would persuade him to spend a whole evening with Cissy, which left me. Because I was now 18 and allowed in, and old enough to share a bit of my mother's burden.

Not only did Celia drive me mad, but I had very strong views on gambling. I disapproved, and had done for some time. My parents had already taken me once to the Palm Beach casino in Cannes, and even offered me some chips, but I refused them. On principle. Bad enough that I had to be there, never mind join in. Then I had wandered around the tables, watching the very rich waste their money while half the rest of the world starved. What a disgrace. But while I was wandering about, I passed a roulette table, and something told me that number 2 would come up. Having no chips, I couldn't bet anyway, but did I want to? No. Of course not. The 2 came up. I would have won 36 times the 10 franc piece my father had offered me, had I placed my bet. Three hundred and sixty francs. Was I disappointed? No. It would have been ill-gotten gains, but I was rather thrilled at my own potential gambling skill. Perhaps it ran in the family. I did not tell my father.

Now here I was at the horrid, immoral, decadent Curzon with Auntie Celia, feeling even more left-wing, now that I had my CND socialist chums, but having to be polite and grateful through a whole sit-down dinner, being served by waiters and waitresses, which was painful for me as a beginner socialist, and having to over-eat luxury food among the greedy, and then enter that capitalist cess-pit, the actual casino, and I mustn't say anything rude about it. Did my parents really understand what a hell this was to me?

After dinner I would follow Auntie up the thickly carpeted staircase, but on the threshold of the gambling area she ordered me to stop and say '*Merde*', twice, which would bring her luck. Then I must hang back and after a few minutes I could enter, but must keep my distance from Auntie, and on no account was I to speak to her again until she'd finished. Otherwise it might break the spell, and her luck would be buggered. Auntie held up her finger to her lips, to reinforce the no-speaking rule, and with a little wish-me-luck smile, she glided away, to presumably squander what was left of her money and mine.

While I waited for Auntie, I would drift aimlessly around the brightly coloured tables, with their green baize, the red and black checks of the roulette layouts, and the blurred colours of the wheel, keeping a good distance from Celia and trying not to notice the huge amounts that some people were frittering. But I couldn't help notice one fellow breezily losing £100 chips as if they were pennies. Again and again the croupier's giant rake slid out across the chequered table, dragging away mountains of chips. Hundreds and thousands of pounds gone in one sweep. There was my father slaving away to earn money, my mother tormenting herself over my inheritance for years and years, and all the starving millions everywhere, and here were these *dreks*, playing with money and throwing it down the drain. Unbearable to watch.

So I left the gambling area and went outside, where I leaned on the reception desk, behind which two men in maroon and gold uniforms sat, taking coats and handbags from the idiot gamblers. I felt that I could speak to these men, as they were staff. They just looked on, rather like the chef at the Carvery had done, watching the greed and madness in front of them, unable to intervene. But they seemed to be having a jolly time. They were not embittered. How did they do it?

I asked them whether they thought this was the most dreadful waste of money and mentioned the £100 chips, but they only laughed cheerily and said, 'Only a hundred? Ha ha. Peanuts.'

But despite my help with the gambling outings, my mother's burden increased considerably after Bill's death. It just grew and grew, as Celia mourned, wasted more money, looked increasingly helpless and then got cancer. How could one not look after such a person, especially if she was your own sister? We drove to town one day with the usual supply of *gefilte*[80] fish, some boiled, some fried, and next to my mother Celia looked rather pale,

[80] Minced fish cakes.

despite all the months and years of cruising and lying about on the Côte d'Azur. For a moment in her kitchen, my mother's and Celia's shoulders were right next to each other – Celia's papery, pale and freckled, my mother's smooth, shiny and brown. There was no way in which my mother could possibly ask Celia about money now. How can you go on nagging and questioning a sick and bereaved woman? So it was still weedy Celia who held all the cards, and it was my mother who was the slave, working away to save my inheritance, and even if there had been no such thing, she now had Bill's death and the cancer to make sure that she looked after Celia until the very end.

Bill, Celia, my mother and father, circa 1956.

44: LESBIANS

Ann's wandering off to Hampstead and other odd places had got so bad that she was sent to Roffey Park, a sort of semi-nuthouse, for people who weren't properly barmy. It was just down the road from the real loony-bin, where you were sent if you got worse. Dicky and I went to visit Ann and sat on her bed in the ward chatting. She still seemed perfectly normal to me, but a few beds away sat Mrs Hall, another patient, counting out the matches from one of those big boxes.

'52, 53, 54 . . .' went Mrs Hall, on and on.

'She does that all the time,' said Ann, not particularly bothered.

Then bang! Something hit Dicky on the head. Mrs Hall had thrown a spectacle case at him. Ann returned it, and as Mrs Hall seemed to be getting a little agitated and we couldn't really relax and have a laugh in the ward, we went off to the canteen for tea, which wasn't up to much. The only sandwiches were filled with sandwich paste. Yuk. I opened one out and had a look inside.

'It looks like sick,' I said, and upset the lady sitting next to us.

'Stop her!' she cried out to Ann in an anguished way, picking fiercely at the palm of her left hand. 'Make her stop!'

I stopped at once, and Ann managed to soothe the woman.

'Have you got your teeth in, dear?' she asked in a sympathetic way, which calmed the woman down. How did Ann manage that? She had instantly reassured a very agitated nutter in an almost professional way. What a genius. There was clearly nothing wrong with Ann at all. Why was she even here?

Ann was in there for a few months, and when she came back to school, a few months later, everyone seemed to know that she was a lesbian, and so was Laraine, and that Ken was a pouf. Who cared? Not us. At art school most people didn't seem bothered about that sort of thing. In theory. We liked to think ourselves too sophisticated to care, but there were still quite a few snidey comments, and poufs were still a bit of a joke.

Wherever Quentin Crisp was modelling, loads of people who weren't really in that class suddenly found a reason to come and have a stare at Quentin's bouffant purple hair, purple nails, eye make-up, and rather worryingly loose jock-strap. He sometimes posed in an odd way, leaning over a chair with his head down, until his face went more and more purple, nearly matching his hair, which rather worried Ann. But he was used to the staring, which is why he always walked along the corridors in his rather floaty way, looking neither to the right nor left, only straight ahead, so that he never caught the eye of a gawper.

But on the whole, Ann, Laraine and Ken didn't need to be so secretive, which was a relief for them all, because Laraine had had to pretend for years that Ken was her boyfriend, when quite clearly he was a pouf. Everybody could tell. If you asked him the time, he would bring his wrist up in a very pouffy way, so that we kept asking him.

'What's the time, Ken?' Up came the wrist.

Now they could all stop pretending to be normal. What was wrong with being a lesbian or homosexual anyway? Nothing. The only sad thing about it was that Bill Otani had fallen in love with Ann. What a pity, because we all liked him. He was one of the best of the boys. If you wanted a boyfriend, you couldn't have done better than Bill Otani, but there was no hope for him. Ann only really cared about her work when she was at school. She liked Bill very much, as a friend, but she had already met a woman while in the bin – Dorothy, who was very thin, wore suits and looked rather like Chopin.

We had stopped calling lesbians 'lesbians' anymore. Ann didn't really like the word, so we called them 'lady pouves' instead, or 'bristles', because of the short bristly hairstyle that some of them tended to go for, and which Ann had first noticed in Roffey Park. Very unusual.

The bristles had their own club just off the King's Road in Chelsea, called the Gateways. Ann and Laraine took me along there. You went into an ordinary-looking door in an ordinary house, and once inside, you went downstairs into a basement with a red light, which felt a bit secretive, as if entering a criminal underworld. At the door were two fierce-looking lesbians in blue denim jeans and jackets, and Brylcreemed hair. It was packed out, hot, smoky, noisy, exciting and choc-a-bloc with women dancing, but I found it strangely relaxing, perhaps because there were no boys to worry about, until someone pinched my bottom. Who was it? Help. I was not a lesbian and didn't want women pinching my bottom. Was a lesbian after me? No. It was only Laraine having a laugh, so I could relax again, and this was Ann's new world. She moved out of home and in with Dorothy.

Perhaps I needed a new world too. I was growing sick of art school. I sat in textiles staring at my rubbish designs. I had one large leaf pattern that I was rather proud of, but couldn't think of much else. All I did were variations on the leaf pattern. Perhaps this was not the career for me.

Mr Brooker cast the final stone. I was trying to arrange my mounted sheet for the intermediate exam, and Brooker was strolling around the class looking at our efforts. Foolishly I asked his advice, but in the wrong way. I had selected what I thought were my best pieces from museum study, but how should I place them on the sheet? I was holding the absolute best one up, wondering whether I should put it bang in the middle.

'What shall I do with this, Sir?' I asked, meaning how should I position it on the page. Silly me. I should have known better.

'If I were you Michele,' said Brooker, 'I'd tear it up into little pieces and make a mosaic out of it.'

He walked off smirking. Hateful man. And that was the end for me, really. Because that piece was the best I could do, so why bother anymore? Mine wasn't the only career in art Brooker crushed. Joe Spibey, in my class, was thinking of becoming a teacher. He was patient, kind, good at art and played the trumpet. Perfect for a teacher. And then Brooker asked him what he was thinking of doing when he left.

'I'd like to be a teacher,' said Joe.

'What?' said Brooker, as if he'd just heard a rather pathetic joke. 'With a voice like that? You haven't got a chance.'

Because Joe sounded a bit cockney. So he gave up that dream. He never even tried it, or asked anyone else.

At least Mr Platt, the painting teacher, was more encouraging. His classes were a sanctuary, where you knew you were safe from sneering and criticism or accusations of phallic symbolism. I had been doing a series of paint-ings of tormented-looking crucified figures. An odd thing to paint, and if Brooker had seen them I'd have been done for, but I was safe in Mr Platt's class. He only encouraged us, and he seemed not to mix with the trendier teachers. He had his lunch down in the basement with the technical staff, and in any other spare time he had, he copied out music from a set of large books. I saw him doing it in the lunch hours. What was he up to? He explained that he was copying out all Scarlatti's harpsichord sonatas, because he couldn't afford the music. Scarlatti wrote about 500 sonatas. They must have been pretty good if Platty was copying them all out. What a mammoth task. So I tried some. He was right. They were worth it.

Perhaps that's what I ought to be doing. Music instead of art. At least music moved along. Art only stayed still. What were you meant to do with art? Only stand about staring at it, which I couldn't do for long. Twenty minutes in a gallery staring was about my lot. Then I got a sort of collywobbles with boredom, and needed to move about quickly – hurry to the snack bar or museum restaurant for a tea and cake to keep me awake, or find someone to talk to, because just looking was so dull, dull, dull. And after Brooker's damning verdict on my work, I felt I might as well give up. I applied to music school. After all, what had I been practising so hard for all these years? True, my piano playing had lapsed a bit through the GCEs, but since I'd been at art school, the practising had hotted up. I was at it for hours. My parents were mad keen on Liszt's *Consolation*, but they would ruin it, of course, with their usual vulgarity.

'Play the Constipation,' they would call out. 'Ha, ha, ha!'

45: IMPROVED NEW WORLD

The trouble about my piano playing was that it was only classical. That was all I could do, or wanted to do. I couldn't play jazz, which is what my friends were doing. They were all particularly keen on Charlie Parker, and would sing it together – King Pleasure singing Parker's tunes. Secretly, I didn't like it at all. To me there was something sleazy-sounding about that sort of jazz, like downstairs in the Heaven and Hell, but ruder. As I listened to it I imagined a world of American gangsters and rather voluptuous women sprawling on sofas in black satin dresses, smoking and drinking heavily. I was still a bit of a square, but my friends weren't snooty about it. They tried to help me along, assuming that eventually the more hip music would click. And they were broad-minded. They could appreciate whatever I was playing, so I tried with their jazz, but I preferred the trad jazz at the 100 Club in Oxford Street, or Jazz on a Summer's Day, Alexis Korner at the Ealing Club, just up the road from school, and Georgie Fame at the school dances.

My parents never heard any of this music. It wasn't like Elvis or Buddy Holly or the Everly Brothers, which I used to play downstairs in the lounge in front of them. But to them even Elvis didn't sing proper tunes.

'What a bloody cacophony!' my mother would call from the other side of the hatch, so I knew that the new stuff would have been quite beyond her. She was miles behind it, and we were now miles ahead, our music so exciting and new, that it left our parents behind in the dark ages. Bill Haley was about as trendy as they got. That was rock and roll for beginners, and if they thought that was wild, whatever would they have thought of Count Suckle and his ska parties, which even frightened me. Jimmy Harris had taken us to one in a big house somewhere in Ladbroke Grove.

Jimmy had a lot of West Indian friends, so he knew where the party was and was allowed to go. The only white people in the whole club were us: Jimmy, Lawrence, Johnny, me and Jill. And everyone else was black, all crowded in, with hardly an inch to move. It was smoky, boiling hot and much more scary than the Gateways because the black people didn't seem at all pleased to see us in there. Did we really have to shove our way through them to the other side of the room? Couldn't we stay by the door? No, because Jimmy was already pushing his way across to his friends, chatting and laughing as if he were somewhere normal. But we were in a foreign country light years away from Ruislip, which

I wouldn't have dared describe to my mother. What if she had seen this? Me squashed in a club full of strange *schwartzers*, jigging about to ska in the All Saints Road?

What would have been the point of describing my new life to my parents? They would only gang up and take the piss.

'She's very unusual,' they would say again and again, pulling Auntie Annie's face.

I realized why. They had rather simple taste, I thought, now that I was entering a thrilling new world of music I didn't always like and films I often couldn't understand. But at least I could tell that something exciting was going on, and one day, if I kept at it, I would probably get the hang of things and turn out groovy. But my parents would not. It wasn't my father or mother's fault that they'd left school at 12 and 14 respectively. I'd have felt sorry for them if they hadn't been so rude.

'Load of shit,' my father would say, laughing crudely, if he ever heard a snatch of anything later than Mario Lanza. 'Music? Do me a favour.'

My father did not appreciate my attempts at self-improvement.

'It's the Genius,' he would say as I appeared. 'Our daughter, the Genius,' laughing as usual.

Trust them to like any film with Burt Lancaster, Kirk Douglas or Tony Curtis in it, especially Kirk and Tony, because as well as their looks, muscles and acting ability, they were also Jewish.

'*Unsere*,' my parents would say proudly, '*kenenehora*.'

They were hopeless and tasteless. They would never ever get it. At least I was making an effort with the weird new films. I couldn't understand the half of them, especially *Last Year in Marienbad*, but at least I knew it was a brilliant film. It had to be, if everyone else said so.

Friends, 1960. Lynne and John in front.

46: EZE-SUR-MER

Cornwall was all very well, but the weather is often a bit of a let-down. It is unreliable. You can *schlep* all the way there and it will piss down for a week, so what's the point? And the beach is stony. You can't lie on it without a li-lo. My mother missed the lovely, baking heat, endless blue skies, azure sea, and soft, golden, sandy beaches of the Mediterranean. But why not try somewhere else instead of Cannes? We've seen Cannes. This year Cissy is in bloody Cannes for the summer, so my mother picks Eze-sur-Mer, along the Côte d'Azur towards Italy. It is just near enough for a day trip to see Cissy, which is all my mother can stand.

There are two bits of Eze: the sur-Mer bit down by the beach, and the old village of Eze, up the mountain. You can either climb up, or drive up a zig-zaggy road. Our villa is sur-Mer. It is painted a creamy yellow and is just a few minutes' walk from the coast road and beach, past the hotel and up a slight hill. I have brought my old school friend, Lynne Harrison – from whom my mother expects a small contribution towards food – and Lawrence and his friend John are coming down on the train to join us for two weeks' holiday. Perfect. There's room for them to stay in the villa. They can sleep in the living room in their sleeping bags. And John is going out with Lynne.

Well he thinks he is, until he gets there a week later, by which time Lynne has found herself another boyfriend, Robert, an English boy who's working in the hotel for the holidays. Bloody hell. What will John do when he arrives and finds out? Lynne doesn't care. I think she is rather heartless.

Lawrence and John arrive at our villa. Luckily my mother is out with her friend Sophie when Lynne tells John the news in the living room, just minutes after he has arrived. Naturally he is furious and tells Lynne she can fuck off. The atmosphere is horribly tense, with Lawrence and I embarrassed, Lynne defiant and John glaring.

Then, bad luck, in comes my mother, with her friend. She can instantly tell that something unpleasant is happening.

'What's going on here?' says she, loudly and rather insensitively, I feel.

'It's none of your business,' says John crossly, and leaves the room.

Explosion. My mother goes mad at once, screaming after him.

'How dare you! In my house!'

To Sophie, 'Did you hear how he bloody spoke to me? The little *schtunk*! Did you hear that? Did you? I should mind my own business? IN MY OWN HOUSE!!! *scream, scream*.' And then the words went haywire and turned into wails and Mummy could hardly breathe, just as she'd wailed and nearly fainted when Uncle Phil had upset her so badly.

'He's upset,' I explained to my mother, but it only made things worse.

'UPSET?' she howled wildly. 'HE's upset? What about me? He comes here, to my house, and he tells me to mind my own business? In my house ...' All this was dotted with terrible howls and sobbing, which even her friend could not stop.

'It's all right, Clarice.' Sophie put her arm round my mother's shoulder, trying to soothe her. 'Don't upset yourself. It isn't worth it.'

I am not keen on Sophie. She is tanned to a deep, orangey brown and has on a tightly fitting shiny cream sun-dress, with very pointy bosoms and her hair set in big, stiff blonde curls. Whatever does she look like?

'I invite him here, her *ferckuckteh* bloody friend, I offer him hospitality, and the little *drek* tells me to mind my own business ...'

On and on goes the screaming, and Lawrence and I go out. There's nothing we can do. I know from experience it will go on until my mother collapses exhausted and weeping, and will turn into a simmering rage, which will never go away. She will hate John forever because he is the one and only person who has ever told my mother to mind her own business.

But John doesn't know that. On our way down the road, Lawrence and I bump into him looking fairly chirpy. He is on his way back to apologise to my mother. Help! He must be stopped. We take him the little beach café and describe the state of my mother, the hysterics which followed his departure, and the danger, should he reappear now, while she is still in an agitated state. Perhaps he might try and apologise later, when things have settled down. I knew that this would also be pointless, but I didn't tell John, because he wouldn't have understood. Although his mother was Jewish, he had no experience of the *broyges*, and he hardly knew my mother. He was busy reading the works of Alfred Adler, and assumed that, with an apology and discussion and explanation, this type of thing could be sorted out. But it couldn't. Reason had nothing to do with it, because my mother's reasoning and his reasoning did not match. They never would.

Here is my mother's side. She is keen to get me to the South of France. I am looking a bit pasty and need sunshine. She has kindly let me invite three of my *drek* friends to stay, even though they are all *goyim*, just to get me here. She will let John and Lawrence sleep in the living room in their sleeping bags, and she only wants a couple of quid a week towards food from Lynne, and even that's like getting blood out of a stone, even though it's *khai kak*[81]. How much more generous and kind could she be? What more can she do to make me happy? Will I ever be satisfied? Nothing seems to please me since I went to that bloody art school. I have turned into an argumentative, *farpisht* little *drek*. I look like God knows what, but she's still doing her best to make me happy. And do I appreciate it? No I do not.

Here is John's side. He's come all this way from England to the South of France to see his girlfriend, and she immediately tells him that she has found another boyfriend and wants nothing to do with him. He's very upset, my mother barges in shouting, and his reaction is perfectly natural. And he's prepared to apologise.

And here's my side. I didn't want to come to France in the first place. I do not wish to spend six whole weeks with my mother. Whatever will I do when my friends all leave in a fortnight and I'll have three weeks left with her? I can't stand it. She never, ever stops shouting, and I absolutely do not want to lie on the beach with my face in the sun. I am not a child. As I have taken the inter-mediate examination in arts and crafts, probably not done very well, have left art school, and am now planning to go to music school, I obviously need to be practising all the time. But here I am stuck in France without a piano.

*

---

[81] Next to nothing.

Deadlock. My poor mother cannot understand me. John cannot stay in the villa, so he goes and finds somewhere to sleep up the mountainside in his sleeping bag. Lawrence may still sleep in the living room, but he thinks that's rather unfair on John, so he goes to live up the mountain with John for the fortnight. Why not? It's boiling hot, it never rains and the mountainside is utterly beautiful and fascinating. They are both happy up there. I visit them daily. Lawrence sketches the scenery – new leaf shapes, tall grasses and reeds, twisty little trees and shrubs; he can draw it all for hours, and John observes nature. For example, he spots three ferocious French ants fighting on a rock as we pass. Two hours later we come back and they're still fighting. Fantastic. A three-way fight.

While they're doing all that, I also spend some time with Lynne, because she is an old friend after all, and she can't help who she does and doesn't love or fancy, but she is usually off with Robert, so I spend most of my time up the mountain, or on the beach away from my mother, who I think is completely unreasonable.

This is a difficult time for my mother and me. We are sick to death of each other. We both think we are doing our best to behave properly, but it isn't working, even if we are in the lovely South of France. What good is the beach and the sun and the wonderful cool, spacious villa, if my mother and my friends are at loggerheads? And where is my father? He has stayed in Ruislip and is no help to us at all. My mother is battling me and John all by herself because, as usual, the Business Comes First.

I stick it out for week after my friends leave, and it is bearable only because I have cleverly found a grand piano to play nearby. On my way to the dreary, boiling, lonely beach one day, I hear, as I pass a large villa only yards from our own, the sound of piano playing. Just coming out of the villa is a woman. I ask her who's playing the piano so beautifully, and what luck, she is not French, she's English and it's her half-French daughter who's playing. The daughter has liver problems and must stay in. But I can come in and meet her.

Inside the house is dark, cool and shady, with the shutters nearly all closed. The furniture is old-fashioned, with crocheted doilies all over the place, and the girl is my age, but a pale, creamy yellow colour, and her hair is black, making her look rather dramatic and poorly, but she's very kind and friendly. She doesn't see many people and would like to practice her English with someone other than her mother. If I want, say the woman and her daughter, I can come here and practice, so I do, every day for an hour or so. It's an ideal swap, English practice for piano practice.

My mother is not pleased. She brings me here for fresh air and sunshine and I lock myself away in a dark bloody room and *kak* about on the sodding piano. And then I go a step too far. I practice one day for six solid hours. I go into the gloomy house at 10 a.m. and I don't come out until 4 o'clock in the afternoon. The mother and daughter have let me in and left me there, because they have to go to the hospital for the day. Perfect.

When I come out my mother has just about had it. She has a bit of a scream. Where the bloody hell have I been? But after a while she gives up, goes quiet and looks rather blank. Her mouth is clamped shut and her eyes are slightly watery. I have defeated her. She is sick of me moping and dripping around sulking. If I want to go home, I can bloody go home, and stay at Lynne Harrison's house. She buys me a train ticket for the day after next. Goodbye.

Our apartment (ground floor) at Eze. Scene of the crime, 1961.

47: THE BIG BETRAYAL

Back in England, my father is having his own problems with the Business. Something odd has happened. My father was in the habit of saving up little wodges of money, from small cash deals with friends – perhaps a belt or a bag or a waistcoat for someone or other's birthday. He would store this money in his desk in his office, and give some of it to me for spending money. While I was away, the stash had mounted up, to £400. He planned to give it to me in bits, weekly. But now he looks in his drawer and the money has gone. He's sure he put it there, but who can have taken it? Dave Martins has left, there are no crooks in the factory, God forbid, so how can it have disappeared? Perhaps he didn't put it there. Perhaps he is getting *farmisht* and has put it somewhere else. But where?

Only one person goes into my father's office – Joe Posner. He wouldn't take it. Surely not. He is a friend. And he is *unsere*. It is unheard of for a Jew to steal from a Jew. At least my father has never heard of it. It would be a terrible betrayal. My father assumed that Jews were meant to help each other. Nobody else would, so we had to. My father couldn't believe that Joe was a *ganuf.* Well he could, but he was trying not to. Because he had noticed that some stock had been going missing. He and John had been trying to put an order together and there had been only a dozen one-inch black patent with gilt buckles left, when they'd both been sure they had plenty more than that, and also they seemed oddly low on the red cummerbunds and the two-inch suede sash belts, in all colours, so something funny was going on. What else was missing? My father began to feel a bit sick.

So did John, because he'd noticed that Joe had been showing his brother-in-law round a few times recently, and making up a few orders, and nobody else did that except him and my father. Bad enough that John had to tell my father about Dave Martins. He couldn't bear to have to do such a thing again. And because my father trusted Joe, he sometimes left him to lock up. He was the last to leave the factory at night. The bastard.

My father had a horrible feeling in his guts that he was being taken for a sucker all over again, and by a so-called friend. Terrible. He knew, once he faced up to it, that Joe and Eva had been behaving rather peculiarly lately. My parents hadn't been seeing so much of them socially, and since my mother and I had been away in France, my father hadn't seen them at all, and you'd have thought that as they knew he was on his own, they might have asked him round for a meal once or twice. But they hadn't, and Joe had not been very talkative lately. My father could hardly bear it. He kept waking in the night with palpitations. He didn't fancy eating. Good job my mother wasn't around, because she'd have guessed. And then she'd have gone bloody raving mad, so he decided to sort it out before she came back. He would deal with this crap by himself. He and John decided to check the stock properly, and found that quite a bit of it was missing.

My father felt very bad indeed. To be made a *shmuk* of once was bad enough, but twice was unbearable. He wanted to get it over and done with, so he just called Joe into his office the next day and asked him straight out. Had he taken the money and stock? Joe tried to deny it but my father could tell by his face that he had. My father could hardly bear to look at him. He just told Joe to get out. GET OUT! And Joe went. Straightaway. My parents never saw them again. This time my father did not go to the police, because he was so ashamed.

48: NURSE ISABEL

Celia is in the Royal Marsden. She has had a lump removed. She went in just before my mother returned from Eze, and ever since then Mummy has visited almost daily. She is sick and tired of it and my father won't go, so I go to see Auntie. Isabel Ghastly Salvona is just leaving. To keep out of her way until she's gone I pretend I want to go to the lavatory. But to get to the lavatory I have to go through the ward and past lots of patients. One is sitting up in bed. He is large but skeletal, bare-chested and very yellow. It's a horrible shock to come round a corner and see this person, like someone from a concentration camp.

Thank goodness Celia doesn't look that bad. In fact she looks fairly normal to me, but when I get back from my nightmare trip to the lavatory, bad luck, Isabel is still there on the look-out for nurses while Celia has a last sip of champagne before Isabel goes. She can't drink it without an accomplice and always keeps a stash of it in the little cupboard beside her bed. She can't be that ill, if she's still glugging champagne. Then Isabel whips the glasses away and goes off to wash them. She is back in a trice before Auntie and I have really said much.

'Now will you be all right my darling?' Isabel asks Celia, as if I'm not there at all. I am a wraith, unfit to take over her caring duties.

'Yes Isabel,' says Celia meekly. 'Mishl's here. My little niece.' She smiles up at me sideways. 'You'll look after me, won't you Mishl?'

Auntie clutches one of my hands with her thin, freckly fingers and Isabel can't get out of it any longer. She has to admit that she knows I'm there.

'Now you see that you do.' Isabel gives me a pointy look down her nose. It says that I am a good-for-nothing scrounger. I have no genuine love for my auntie, as she has, but am only in it for the money. And furthermore, says Isabel's look, I am a grubby beatnik and have no right to be visiting a delicate, sick person in a lovely clean hospital and am probably carrying germs.

'Goodbye, Celia darling. Now you take care. Promise me?' with another quick, fierce little glance at me, because Celia is now surrounded by danger and needs to take care of herself, because I am incompetent. 'You'll call me when you're ready to leave and David and I will collect you. Don't you worry. You just call us at any time. Promise? *Mwah, mwah.*'

Then off she goes. Whoosh. Without saying goodbye to me.

My art school style of dressing has probably put the wind up Isabel. I no longer wear the school uniform or frocks and skirts she remembers, but instead have on my usual tight, dark stripy jeans and giant jumper from M&S. I'm still wearing the art school style because I like it, and I assume it will be suitable for music school. Musicians are bound to be more or less the same as artists, aren't they? Anyway, it has now become my own personal style. I'm also carrying my lovely cane gondola basket which perfects my outfit, and in it I'm carrying my soft toilet roll, handy for hay-fever and my never-ending nose-blowing, and much cheaper than paper hankies. What do I care if Isabel thinks me weird? What is wrong with a visible toilet roll in my basket? Whose opinion is more important, old witch Isabel, or my own friends?

Auntie Celia isn't keen on my style either, even though, unlike Isabel, she's seen it plenty of times before, but she just can't get used to it. Good job she never saw the dress I wore on the double date with the chemist and Jaguar boys. She was bound not to have liked it. Now that Isabel has left, Auntie can have a proper look at me.

'Isn't that jumper a bit big?' she asks, as usual, grabbing at the back of the neck with her thin fingers, and look-ing for the label and size. 'Come nearer.'

I'm sitting on her bed and I have to bend backwards so she can reach.

'Ooh look! It's a 44! That's not your size. Does your

mother like it? I bet she doesn't. It's a bit *shmatedik*[82], isn't it? She'd like something a bit brighter, wouldn't she? Your mother likes bright colours. You're not making the best of yourself. And you used to look so pretty.' Auntie lies back on her pillows and scrutinises my whole outfit.

'She doesn't mind.'

'I'll bet she does. Your mother's a very smart woman. She loves nice clothes. Has she seen this jumper? Has she? You're not doing yourself any favours. And what's that for?' she points at the toilet roll. 'Your *tokhes*?' Vulgar as usual. What else could I expect? 'Still, you're a good girl to come and see me, aren't you? You don't mind coming to see your auntie, do you? I might not be here for much longer.'

'Course you will.'

'Don't kid yourself. D'you want a chocolate? Look. Look in the cupboard. I've got some lovely chocolates. Have some. Go on. You eat them. I can't. I've got no appetite. Do you love your auntie? Do you?'

'Yes Auntie.'

I ate two chocolates while Celia watched me fondly.

'My artistic little niece,' she said in a soppy way, as if she really liked me.

Did she? I don't know how she could. We could hardly talk to each other properly. What can you say to someone like that? I completely disapproved of Auntie, not

[82] Raggedy, rubbishy.

just because I had been kept informed of her misdeeds all my life, and had witnessed some of them myself, but look at her now. Wasting money on champagne and luxuries when the world is on the edge of catastrophe and I am in the CND and busy marching to Aldermaston and Trafalgar Square with revolutionaries. How can I honestly care about a rich, spoilt auntie, even if she is poorly? And look what her money had done. Had it made her into a lovely person? No it had not. We both disapproved of each other. We did worse than that – we despaired of each other. What did I need money for? I didn't even know how to buy clothes. That's what she must have thought.

So I came home even more convinced that money was not worth fighting for.

'Don't bother,' I told my mother yet again. 'I don't want her money. I don't need it. Don't drive yourself mad. You don't have to be nice to her. She's never been nice to you.'

In my opinion my mother should not have wasted all her time and energy, tormenting herself, worrying about money and crawling around Celia for years on end. For as long as I can remember, from the minute my grandma decided that I was her only official grandchild and beneficiary, my mother had had no peace. And if it wasn't that, there was always something else to terrify my mother: my eczema, my asthma, the dangerous Christians who treated me badly, the Germans and anti-Semites who still lurked around, the non-stop stream of crooks waiting to cheat my father, the women always simpering around him, and Blanche, the most dangerous one. Surely all that was enough for anyone to bear, without worrying about Celia's money as well? But however many times I told my mother to stop bothering, it made no difference. She just went on and on doing it. For me.

Soon Celia was out of hospital and needed more looking after. My poor mother was up and down to Park Lane with supplies of *gefilte* fish, mainly boiled, and chopped liver, and anything else that Celia could eat without bothering to cook, or even heat up, and other bits of shopping

My mother and Isabel Salvona, circa 1961.

that Celia hadn't the strength to get herself. Sometimes Celia had to be collected from town and driven to Ruislip, fed, and driven back. And in a couple of months, when Celia was feeling more like her old self again, she would probably be well enough to be driven all the way to Cornwall. Because luckily her lump had been successfully removed and the cancer had gone, for the time being. It might come back soon, it might not come back for years. Or ever. Celia had a reprieve, but my mother did not.

49: THE PARTY

Fortunately for my mother, Isabel Ghastly Salvona was fond of fussing around Celia. 'She thinks I care?' my mother asked nobody in particular. 'She can get on with it. Celia likes her, she can have her!'

Although my mother was thrilled that someone else was sharing the burden of Celia, she seemed to resent Isabel's unspoken claim to be the best and most caring nurse. 'Mrs *Kennisht-Kakken*!' she muttered in the usual way with her nose wrinkled up whenever Isabel had to be mentioned, but at least while Isabel was on duty, my parents could have a break.

It was the very end of the summer and my father had had no holiday at all, only terrible aggravation, so they nipped down to Cornwall for a long weekend, leaving me in charge of the house and Lusty, who was too old for such a long drive. And why try to take me on holiday? They were never going to bother again. Eze-sur-Mer had finished them off.

Olga was to stay with me in Ruislip, because for some

reason my mother thought that she was more sensible. Good. We could have a party. Not a huge one, but at last all of my friends could visit at once. Normally, with my parents around, two or three at a time would be the limit, more than that was a bit much for my mother. She could cope with a couple of arty-farty-looking visitors, but if there was a whole crowd of us, it got her rather agitated. How could she feed all that lot? But how could she not? She had to give them something, so she felt torn. She liked to be hospitable, but the house wasn't a bloody hotel was it? And she couldn't help being a bit disappointed that none of them were Jewish, most of them looked like *dreks* to her, except for Lawrence. He was at least a commercial artist, a respectable job. Two of the others were plumbers, one was a sound technician, and not one of them wore decent clothes. So far, she'd only expressed her opinions to me, but who knows? If a whole crowd turned up something might upset her, and she might easily make some terrible comment, and of course John couldn't come anywhere near my house when my mother was around, or there was bound to be another Eze-type eruption, so this was my chance to have my friends visit, risk-free.

My parents seemed not to worry about leaving me in charge. I was now the least of their worries. The business with Joe Posner had upset both of them, because it wasn't just my father who'd been taken for a ride. For the first time ever, my mother had been tricked and betrayed as well. This time she had not been right. Her own friend Eva, who she had played bridge with, stood next to at *shul* and had known and trusted for ten years, had ripped my father off. That a Jewish woman should be a crook shocked my mother to the core. A Jewish man, shocking enough, but a Jewish woman? Unthinkable. A woman should prevent her husband from going to the bad. She should be on the look-out, as my mother always was, to see that he wasn't making some terrible mistake, not join in and help him to be a criminal. Who would ever imagine that a woman could do that sort of thing? My parents had both been taken for suckers. No wonder they needed a little holiday.

They could at least trust me, especially with Olga there. I might be annoying, ungrateful and think I was so bloody clever, but perhaps they sensed that I did nothing dangerous or forbidden. Oddly, despite being an art student, I did not drink, I did not smoke and I had little to do with sex, even though all around me most of my friends were doing some of it. None of us really smoked, except Pamela, and who could blame her?

Our parties, of which this was the first, were still relatively innocent events. Perhaps not quite as innocent as I thought, but nearly. At this first one we had no alcohol at all, and if there was any sex, I didn't know about it at the time, and somehow everything was screamingly funny: the stuffy Andrews next door, our own jokes, the ordinary Ruislip people passing by who thought us peculiar. Ha ha, they were the peculiar ones, but they couldn't see it. They thought our clothes odd, but what about their clothes? Ridiculous. And we had found a new use for the hatch, as a stage for puppet shows or comedy turns, one or two of us on one side performing, the rest of us the audience in the lounge. We had our own band: Lawrence on guitar, Alan on bass, Dickie on drums, Johnny on sax, and there wasn't too much Charlie Parker, thank goodness. They could play and sing anything. When we tired of the hatch we drew cartoons, or added joke captions to newspaper photos, or walked about the garden in an odd way, or threw a lemon over the fence and on to the Andrews' lawn. Hilarious. We weren't drunk, but we felt drunk. What a sophisticated and witty lot we were. Even funnier than the Goons.

My new friends came from new places – from art school, from CND, from outside Ruislip. John came from Yiewsley, which to my mother was like the Wild West – a perilous, slum area. A murder had been committed there, some child had been beaten to death in a club by a gang and any mention of Yiewsley made her shudder. It was not a place that she wanted me to visit. Luckily she didn't know about my visits to the hundred-times more dangerous Ladbroke Grove.

Yiewsley was beyond Uxbridge, which was right at the end of the Piccadilly and Metropolitan lines, and Uxbridge was bad enough. Teddy boys met there in gangs, and fought the young Americans from the base with bicycle chains that they hid inside their shirts. Military police from the base had to be called out to stop the fights and take the young Americans back there. John had seen it all. To my mother, Yiewsley was still even worse than Uxbridge, but it no longer mattered what she thought. She wasn't here supervising anymore. We were too old to be supervised and didn't really need to be.

We made surprisingly little mess. We slept in all the four bedrooms and on sofas. Olga did however find condoms under my mother's bed. Sacrilege! We never worked out who was responsible, but the condoms certainly weren't anything to do with Olga, even though she had stayed there with Jaguar Boy, who was now her fiancé. All sorts of romances must have been going on that I hadn't spotted, and perhaps a little drinking.

Kathy wasn't there. She had new friends somewhere else, but Pamela came. She seemed cheery, but a bit quiet, but then she always was fairly quiet, and later in the evening she was sick on the wall, half-way up the stairs. It could have been our takeaway curry. What an odd place to do it. But I had a large selection of poster paints, so we carefully painted the pattern back on. Brilliant. You absolutely could not see the difference, and it hadn't been an easy pattern to reproduce — a sort of criss-cross webbing pattern in creams and beiges. Lucky we were artists. From the front our forgery was faultless. But then we spotted it from the side, disaster. The original paper was slightly glossy, but our painting had a matt finish, and so a large, dull patch was clearly visible.

What would my parents say when they came back? I could never tell them it was Pamela. I knew that she was slightly nervous of my mother and would not have weathered a telling-off, but she would rather be in our house than her house, whether my mother was here or not. Pamela stayed the night, because she felt a bit weedy after being sick, and anyway she couldn't just go back to her parents anymore. She had a flat, which was over in Harrow, and the last bus had gone. Pamela was the first one of us to move out, but Mrs Saunders didn't seem to care anyway. When had she ever cared much? Our parents were losing their grip, but some of them didn't seem to want to grip anymore. My parents didn't even care about the hall wallpaper. They hardly said anything about it and kept on nipping down to Cornwall, so the parties continued.

But Pamela only came to one more. She married the motorcycle boy. Why not? She was nearly 18, and look at Shirley Butterworth who got married when she was just 17, so there was nothing odd about Pamela doing it. When she'd finished at art school, she told us, they were going to live in Birmingham. That sounded a bit dreary, and we hadn't even met this boy. She could at least have brought him along to show us, but she didn't. Why? Was there something wrong with him?

50: GOODBYE, BLOW-WAVES

Over in the George pub, Laraine was also having parties with Ann and her other lesbian and pouf friends. Her father never remarked on the visiting lesbians, but he couldn't help giving Laraine a little nudge when Ken arrived, in a long, white fur coat, with his boyfriends, who were mainly ice-skaters and dancers.

'They're a load of bloody shirt-lifters,' Mr Smits would say benignly to Laraine, as Ken, having parked his Reliant Robin in the pub car park, would walk in with his chums, through the public bar, where all the rough Ruislip fellows drank.

'Wahay!' they would all shout to Mr Smits. 'Look at them, Guvnor!'

But Ken and his friends were quite safe. The pub's rough clients (and there were lots of them in Ruislip) respected Laraine's dad. They knew that if they did not, they'd find his hands on the back of their collar and his knee up their arse, and they'd be out. And if Mr Smits accepted the pouves, then so did they. Ken just swanned through boldly, and went up to Laraine's room above the big kitchen, to dance and party. Mrs Smits longed to join in, being a lively woman, but she couldn't really think how to, so she would just pop upstairs now and again, put her head round the door and ask, 'Does anyone want a banana?' She didn't mean anything by it, but they already had savoury bar-snacks, and that was just something else she could offer them, by way of pudding.

Things were looking up for the poufs and bristles. True, people did sometimes spit at Ann and her girlfriend Dorothy when they were out and call out 'lezzers' and other more horrid names, because Dorothy did look rather chappish, but it didn't have to be such a big secret anymore. And here were obvious poufs even going in and out of an ordinary Ruislip pub. In Laraine's house and my house, there was little restraint. We could do, and wear, more or less what we wanted.

My parents had more or less given up on my clothes. My mother nagged on, still occasionally begging, after all these years, for me to have a blow-wave and wear a nice frock, even though in her heart she realized she had lost the fight. But my father, being in the fashion business, realized that even if I looked like a bloody idiot, I probably knew what was trendy. He knew things were changing, but he didn't know what they were changing into. So he took me on a two-day trip to Paris to a buckle wholesaler, to help him choose some buckles for his new range of belts. I'd already thought up the decorated suede belts, and the school belts, which were still selling like mad, and he thought I might know what The Young would like.

Yes I did. Easy. His stuff was so old-fashioned, all bright nickel and gilt with twirly bits. So Ruislippy. So I advised some big, plain, chunky, dull iron buckles, mainly square, to go on two-inch belts. And in suede, webbing and leather, not his usual corny old vinyl.

My father pulled a bit of a face, like a shrug, as if the world had gone mad, but why should he worry?

'If you say so,' said he, almost proud of me, because he realized that I knew things that he didn't know, even if they were *meshugene* things. 'You're the Genius.'

He couldn't understand for the life of him why people would want to buy such *drek,* but he knew they would. He'd checked. He'd been into my art school and come looking round the textile room – very embarrassing. No one else's parents ever did that – and he'd seen what was going on and what the girls were wearing, so he ordered what I chose. Again, they sold like hot cakes.

'Any more clever ideas?' he asked.

Yes, actually. Vinyl carrier bags just the right size to carry LPs. We could screen-print the panels – matt vinyl on gloss, patterns designed by Ann and me, and we could print them in Ruislip in the garage with the doors open, or even out in the back garden, if it wasn't raining, then the fumes would just float away, and my father could sell them. And he did. Even to John Lewis.

'Two Geniuses,' said my father, at last daring to think that he might really have a successor to his business, even if I was only a girl. I was his only hope. Who else could take over his lifetime's work? But he was going to be out of luck. I had more exciting plans. Working in a ladies' belt factory in Ruislip was not part of them.

Only Jacqueline, who had been the wildest of us all, became a bit of a square. She was about to get married and was allowed, by her fiancé, to come to our parties, but only briefly. At 10 p.m. he would come and collect her, and if she wasn't ready, he would sit reading the *Watchtower* in his suit, disapproving. What a bore. Why was she marrying him? Why have someone else bossing her about, now that her parents couldn't? Mad. But the rest of us were free.

Our parents were not. For them nothing seemed to change. Gracie went on drinking more and more, Mrs Saunders went on doing all sorts of awful things and breaking Albert's heart, my parents went on sulking and shouting, dancing at the Orchard, playing bridge and worrying about The Business, Celia and The Money. They had their holidays and trips to Cornwall, but they always came back to Ruislip. They seemed stuck there for life. That wouldn't happen to us. We did not intend to stay.

My plans to be a brilliant artist may have crumbled, but now there was music school, and so perhaps I could be a brilliant musician instead, but whatever happened, I would never end up like my mother. None of us wanted to. We need never be housewives with blow-waves, who stayed at home waiting for sulky or dreary or deceitful husbands. We felt as if we could go anywhere and do more or less anything, even if we were girls. And perhaps, with a bit of luck, there might never even be a nuclear holocaust.

The last blow-wave, 1962.

ACKNOWLEDGEMENTS

I would like to thank my old friends and members of my family, particularly my cousin Olga Sedgwick, for helping with my research and for remembering all the bits I forgot. While this book endeavors to give a faithful account of my experiences, some names and dates have been changed to protect the privacy of the individuals involved and in order to best represent the story. Thanks to my daughter Amy and all my current friends, for cheering me on, and I am especially grateful to Jennifer Woolfenden and Ian Whitwham, who have listened to me reading endless chunks of this book to them over and over again, day after day, desperate for reassurance and praise, which they supplied without a murmur of complaint. Thanks also to David Rosenberg, for his patience and help with the Yiddish; to Fred Kogos, whose book *From Schmear to Eternity* helped me to understand all the Yiddish I snootily ignored in my youth and which

I now love; to Jeremy Lewis, for insisting from the very beginning that I keep going, to my agent Laura Longrigg, for never giving up on me, to Kerri Sharp at S&S for her tremendous enthusiasm and thinking these memories worthy of a book, to Angela Herlihy, for her meticulous, but never bossy, editing, to all the grown-ups in my book whose lives were such a struggle, and to the friends I have written about who have died much too early.